Shaping Our Struggles

SHAPING OUR STRUGGLES

NIGERIAN WOMEN IN HISTORY, CULTURE AND SOCIAL CHANGE

edited by

Obioma Nnaemeka and Chima J. Korieh

Africa World Press, Inc.

P.O. Box 1892
Trenton, NJ 08607

P.O. Box 48
Asmara, ERITREA

Africa World Press, Inc.

P.O. Box 1892
Trenton, NJ 08607

P.O. Box 48
Asmara, ERITREA

Book and cover design: Saverance Publishing Services

Library of Congress Cataloging-in-Publication Data

Shaping our Struggles: Nigerian women in history, culture and social change / edited by Obioma Nnaemeka and Chima J. Korieh.
   p. cm.
Includes bibliographical references and index.
   ISBN 1-59221-745-1 (hard cover) -- ISBN 1-59221-746-X (pbk.)
1. Women--Nigeria--History. 2. Women--Nigeria--Social conditions.
3. Women in development--Nigeria. I. Nnaemeka, Obioma, 1948- II. Korieh, Chima J. (Chima Jacob), 1962-
   HQ1815.5.N55 2010
   305.48'89669--dc22

                                        2009050051

Table of Contents

Introduction

LONG JOURNEYS OF IMPEDIMENTS AND TRIUMPHS

Chima J. Korieh and Obioma Nnaemeka

Recent years have witnessed an upsurge in the number of scholars and commentators studying women from historical and contemporary perspectives. Africanists and African women scholars in particular increased their efforts to assert African women's identity and lay bare their contributions to the knowledge and understanding of their societies. Despite considerable efforts in this direction, writing about Nigerian women, as is the case with women elsewhere in Africa, is fraught with difficulties.

The task of writing about past and present roles of Nigerian women is challenging on many levels. Moreover, the cultural and historical diversity of the country makes any generalizations on Nigerian women problematic. This problem is further compounded by the pre-supposition that women have historically been a marginalized group whose circumstances did not merit a systematic study. Nonetheless, long before the feminist movement brought women's issues to the forefront, the place of women in some Nigerian societies had received considerable attention. As early as 1868, for example, J. A. Horton described Yoruba women as "very litigious . . . very good looking, nicely shaped and formed although marked."[1] The Reverend Bishop Johnson described the Igbo women early in the twentieth century as "very industrious and hardworking... far superior to the men in this, and are said to have few more character in them than men."[2] While there are few accounts that will help in an overall assessment of the status of women relative to men,[3] Nigerian case studies reveal a highly mobile and independent group of women. With the establishment of effective colonial administration in the early years of the twentieth century, this profile resurfaced as women's issues increasingly became prominent in political, social and economic discourses. Efforts made by the colonial government to create policies and establish an environment conducive to the economic exploitation and political domination of the colony resulted in women's resistance throughout most of southern Nigeria. Thus, from the mid-1920s, women's issues became part of the discourse associated with the ills of colonialism.

Colonialism, with its mechanism of systematic exploitation of wealth from the colonies and the imposition of Western culture, had a tremendous impact on local population. The indirect rule system in particular altered existing political structures and affected indigenous gender ideologies, undermining women's participation in the process. In northern Nigeria, colonial authorities experienced less resistance because Islam provided well-defined gender ideologies that both suited the British colonial policy of indirect rule and maintained the status quo. Contrarily, the new political structure undermined pre-colonial gender ideologies in most of southern Nigeria, which was amalgamated with the north in 1914.[4]

In the economic sphere, the incorporation of Nigerian societies into the world economic system, first through the Atlantic slave trade and later through commodity production in the colonial period, created opportunities for increased capitalist accumulation at certain periods, and in some places, and was a source of frustration and insecurity for others. As a result, new gender ideologies and contestations for resource control developed. In some areas, the new cash economy was dominated by men and was sustained by three factors: First, men were persuaded by the need to meet their taxation obligation; second, a new consumer culture based on imported European goods suited for marketing by men was introduced and third, the European demand for export (cash) crops grown primarily by men grew. In all of these changes, the household, especially women, bore the brunt of the uncertainties of the economic sector and a world market whose conditions went beyond the control of local population. Women, as a result of their continued role in the production of subsistence crops, bore the task associated with food security, and were affected by the class inequality that resulted from the political and economic restructuring of their societies.

In Nigeria, initial research on these changes focused on women's responses to political changes. This resulted in the publication of important articles, monographs and anthropological reports dealing with women in certain parts of the country. The publication of Sylvia Leith-Ross' book *African Woman* deserves a special mention here.[5] Other anthropological monographs also focused on women and some contain substantial information on women.[6] Nina Mba opened the discussion of women and political resistance in Southern Nigeria with *Nigerian Women Mobilized*.[7] Bolanle Awe has done substantial work exploring the history and contributions of Yoruba women to Nigerian history.[8] In Northern Nigeria, Rene Pittin and other scholars remind us of the dynamism and visibility of women often seen as constrained under Islamic rule. These studies indicate the mobility of women and their contribution to society.

These studies, however, make it clear that colonialism deeply undermined women's autonomy throughout the country as much as Islam undermined women's mobility in northern Nigeria. Colonial gender ideologies were at odds with what existed in pre-colonial societies. In Eastern Nigeria for example, Igbo and Ibibio societies clearly reveal societies where women's mobility and individual capital accumulation were not totally constrained by patriarchy. In western Nigeria, women were important in the economic, political and social affairs. Women performed important ritual and religious functions which empowered them and made their contribution to maintaining social harmony and cosmological balance important. Because colonial administration was established and maintained by a male dominated bureaucracy, it is no surprise that women were effectively excluded from the new dispensation. In the northern parts of Nigeria, where there was an already established male dominated theocratic system, the colonial officials were unwilling to disrupt the social, religious, political and economic order. Radical changes would require more personnel and funds. Furthermore, resources that were in short supply for the colonial state had to be produced by men. The policy worked in northern Nigeria but faced increasing opposition from women in the east and some parts of western Nigeria.[9]

Despite these scholarly advancements, recent works on Nigerian women are bedeviled by generalizations, regional isolationism and thematic concentration. Indeed, a critical assessment of women's roles in Nigeria needs to be based on a considerable regional analysis and framework. On a more general level, studies on women of the three major linguistic groups in Nigeria, Hausa, Igbo and Yoruba, abound. While there are many works dealing with Igbo and Yoruba women, we have little information on specific cultural groups within each of these linguistic enclaves, and of women from many other ethno-linguistic groups in the country. In a multi-ethnic society such as Nigeria, what we have is the silenced voices of many women, their stories and experiences.

In order to encourage more comprehensive and comparative research and information in all aspects of lives of women of African descent, Women in African and the African Diaspora (WAAD) organized conferences in Nigeria in 1992, the United States in 1998, and Madagascar in 2001. The aim of these conferences was to foster understanding and exchange of ideas among researchers working on issues related to women of African descent, and to particularly call attention to new research agenda by asking new questions about women. The panels focused on the history of women, women's health, women's rights, women in development, the impact of globalization and structural adjustment programs on women, as well as cross-cultural studies that highlight women's circumstances in the continent and the African Diaspora.

Some of the chapters in this volume are revised versions of papers originally presented at the First International Conference on Women in African and the African Diaspora held at Nsukka, Nigeria in 1992. The other contributions are recent original essays. The volume covers major issues on Nigerian women in historical and contemporary perspectives and investigates major causal factors related to women in history, society, culture, and development and how they affect women's lives. Most importantly the book surveys women's responses and engages some of the internal and external dynamics of change and how they have affected and continue to affect women's lives. The authors present materials that vary in analytical and theoretical perspective from the pre-colonial period to the present. The chapters not only engage some of the sources of constraints, which women have to overcome, but reveal successes in women's struggles for equality and socioeconomic and political changes.

As some of the contributions to this volume argue, it is difficult to work out the relationship between women's historical experiences and the contemporary realities in Nigeria today based on our current state of knowledge of Nigeria women's history. Our goal is to present the major arguments and perspectives on the role and place of women in Nigerian societies through a multi-disciplinary approach that engages women and their relationship to society. We acknowledge, however, the changing nature of women's experiences over time. Thus, the volume challenges stereotypes about women, and provides rich empirical data that are useful in engaging women in Nigerian societies and the development discourse.

It would be important to address some of the methodological and historiographical issues that have defined the discussion of African women in general. We consider it appropriate in light of their implications for past representations of women to outline the major chronological developments which have guided our own perceptions and interpretations. The analyses of past representations enrich the presentation of women in historical and contemporary perspectives explored in this volume. They also helps to broaden our understanding of a range of factors which determined women's position in Nigeria. While we are not dealing with entirely new issues, our effort to edit this book is stimulated and sustained by the broad geographical coverage of the data from which to analyze Nigerian women's lives and the ways they have been impacted by change. As distinct from the politically oriented literature of the early 1980s, this volume covers a broad range of historical, political, cultural and developmental issues concerning women. We have attempted to articulate and bring together the different aspects of Nigerian women's lives into this volume.

The past thirty years have witnessed a rapid change in the trends and quality of research dealing with African women. Recent analysis and research on African women have affected how women are perceived and the understanding of institutional frameworks within which they operate. The periodization of the literature shows that three central concerns have dominated the general methodological and theoretical framework adopted by scholars.[10] The pre-1960s saw an increasing interest in women by amateur scholars who were influenced by missionary and free lance writings of European travelers and anthropologists. Emphasis was on social processes such as kinship relations, social structures of law and order as well as patriarchy. This trend continued in the 1960s with the production of ethnographic and anthropological monographs.[11] The questions raised in these early analyses were articulated in Western thought while the narratives about the lives, experiences and activities of women were largely based on stereotypes that related little to the lives they represented.

The decolonization of African countries in the 1960s and 1970s was followed by attempts by African leaders to advance social, economic and political progress in African societies. The scholarship that emerged in this era sought to emphasize that women had a history that derived from their complementary role to men and a history that derived from their more specific roles in social life. This approach to studying African women was part of what Imam has described as the concept of "the Golden Age of Merrie Africa"[12] in which pre-colonial Africa was seen as a land of peace and harmony that often distorted African realities. For African researchers, Hafkin and Bay have argued, the impetus is very much that of the anti-colonial feeling generated in nationalistic struggles and the resurgence of interest and pride in African indigenous institutions.[13] For American and European researchers the influence of the Black civil rights movements led to interests in Africa's past glories, while the women's movement heightened interest in women's conditions. However, Hafkin and Bay point out that some of the literature that emerged early in this period presented a romanticized and historically inaccurate view because most writers described great queens, amazons and matriarchy.[14] Research tended to concentrate on the activities of women as leaders, leading personalities and matriarchs but was generally silent on the generality of women.[15] Like histories of African societies after the colonial era, the history of African women tended to focus on the achievements of women leaders.

We challenge some of these ideas and emphasize that gender ideologies have often been constructed, imposed and re-evaluated by both western and non-westerners, based on their particular agendas. These applications are not limited to the realm of academic treatment of African women alone, but are evident in the uncontested adoption of western-oriented approaches. Oftentimes, consideration is not given to the investigation of the politics inherent in the production of knowledge and for whom that knowledge is produced. Similarly, despite the numerous attempts by feminists to make the distinction between sex and gender clear, the glossing over of such distinctions limits our understanding of gender-based functioning in many non-Western societies.

We have attempted to unravel such cultural and theoretical formulations, derived from western experiences and imposed on African societies, through an African-based framework that recognizes African particularities and realities. In actuality, Western-derived frameworks failed to interrogate the systematic privileging of men in traditional society while at the same time inventing women as an analytical category even where such gender categorization did not exist until modern times.

The 1980s witnessed a massive production of literature dealing with African women. The trend in this period was influenced by neo-colonialism, feminism and worsening economic conditions in Africa. This body of literature focused on drawing attention to women and their lot in the face of continued economic decline in Africa, and the impact of state policies, such as structural adjustment programs. Some of the literature criticized the development and modernization agendas. Yet, the approach focused on the ways in which women have been active in establishing their authority and independence, especially as producers, and sought to validate the experiences of African women. Ironically, the process of making women visible was also the vehicle through which women's actual roles and positions were undermined. For instance, Marxist-feminist derived interpretations that emerged in this period, in particular, ignored the variations in women's status within different African societies and presented women as a homogenous group with similar experiences. Indeed, while feminist informed perspectives have contributed in significant ways to the theorizing of gender inequality and understanding the structures of subordination such as class and state mechanisms of control, it has failed to adequately explain, (in the case of the Third World in particular) the role of the world system in generating inequality in society.

The 1990s produced the most complex and far reaching trends in the exploration of the lives of African women in historical writings. The period witnessed the emergence of scholarship that looked at women as separate historical actors—distinguished by race, ethnicity, class, and gender. The focus was on ordinary women rather than those who occupied the upper echelons of society. Such history from below payed attention to women farmers and what Margaret Jean Hay noted as a rather dramatic "shift from queens to prostitutes and from heroines to victims."[16] Feminist political economists in particular found the political economy tradition useful in explaining the realities of the specific political, economic and social matrix of colonialism and post-colonial Africa.[17]

There have been many important publications on Nigeria women, some of which address specific issues. Others have examined women's conditions in specific regions in the country exploring the gender dynamics of Nigerian societies and the specific constraints that women face as a result of these constraints.[18] Nina Mba's *Nigerian Women Mobilized* shows how the colonial process undercut women's political and economic autonomy and how women responded to colonialism. Other authors have focused attention on the social implications of the colonial experience for women. Initial colonial education was gendered to the extent that women's education prepared them for domesticity.

More recent works on Nigerian women have continued to highlight the pre-colonial autonomy of Nigeria women, their increasing subordination under colonial rule and how these tendencies continued into the post-colonial era. The research also recounted how women broke the chains imposed on them by state policies. Gloria Chuku's *Igbo Women and Economic Transformation in Southeastern Nigeria, 1900–1960* demonstrates that some women seized the opportunities offered by the colonial economy in the palm oil trade and commerce, despite the policies that favored male farmers and traders.[19] Nwando Achebe's book, *Farmers, Traders, Warriors, and Kings: Female Power and Authority in Northern Igboland, 1900–1960* challenges the notion of women's invisibility in African societies by documenting women's preeminent roles in both spiritual and temporal matters.[20] The chapters in this book have followed this trend by affirming women's independence in the past, and substantially including research on women from neglected regions of the country. Although some of the pioneering essays in this volume may not be definitive on various aspects of women's lives, they continue to remind us of the assessment of previous studies and issues that need further research. One underlying feature of most writings on Nigerian women, as is evidenced in both colonial and Africanist literature, is the emphasis placed on the degree of female autonomy and independence. Yet, several writers present alternative views by describing how colonialism and British policy of indirect rule undermined women's autonomy.[21]

The chapters in this book draw attention to the pitfalls of the interpretation of women's and gender experiences that ignore the cultural context of Nigerian societies. What we present here is the history and activities of Nigerian women on their own terms and presented from a local perspective. Some of the papers in this volume systematically scrutinizes what Oyewumi calls the building blocks of historical knowledge and in that attempt question the popular image of a male dominated society.[22] In a way, we argue for a new conceptual framework in writing about African women that is fundamental to correcting these misconceptions. It is vital to bring out both the specific social, political, economic and ideological constraints within which women live and the ways they have interacted in relation to them.

Adiele Afigbo's paper in this volume presents an overview of women's position in Nigerian societies. He explains that contrary to the popular notion of women's inferiority, African women "had an honored and recognized place in society which made it possible for the gifted ones amongst them to rise to positions of political, economic, and social eminence from which they led and dominated not only their fellow women, but the common run of men." (5) The indigenous social structure of many African societies which allowed for both "vertical and horizontal mobility" provided both men and women to "contribute significantly to the synthesis of their way of life."(ibid.) He rejects the masculine super-ordination versus feminine-subordination paradigm in favor of the complementarity of the sexes paradigm in which men and women played different but important and complementary roles. He stresses the centrality of class, rather than just sex, as an important element that divides society.

The analysis of the position of women in African societies has often been based on a universal patriarchal hegemony over women. Such analysis often fails to consider the different social contexts and other structures within which women operate. The universalization of women as a single social category therefore poses problems and calls for resistance to such universal notions of women as they offer little guidance to understanding African women. Indeed, Nwando Achebe's paper emphasizes the autonomy of women in traditional Igbo society. Exploring what she terms "Ogidi Palaver," Achebe investigates an episode in the history of Ogidi, during which Igwe Walter Amobi moved his community's main market, Afo Udo, from its spirit-sanctioned location, to the outskirts of a newly built colonial highway for which the women challenged their ruler. While there is wide agreement that colonialism and the incorporation of Nigeria societies into the colonial system undermined women's roles and autonomy, Achebe shows that British policy of indirect rule, which effectively excluded women from the political process, did not altogether eliminate their ability to call upon traditional idioms and sanctions to assert themselves and challenge the new institutions and structures that sought to undermine their socio-political and economic power.

Similarly, Chima Korieh re-examines a well-known protest movement led by Igbo women in 1929. Known as the "Women's War," the protest was directed against British economic and political policies in Eastern Nigeria. He notes that, in framing their resistance, the women drew upon female based cultural traditions and norms which represent a strong moral imperative of their society. Their consciousness was permeated by traditional notions of their position in rural life and the moral claim to certain privileges that derived from their femininity and roles as subsistence producers and providers. Indeed, the transformations that came with colonialism and the commercialization of production transformed existing gender relations in Nigerian societies. In most cases, women suffered disadvantages. Women protested for both economic and political reasons, but reforms were slow to come.

Many of the papers in this volume show that colonialism created new gender divisions and exacerbated existing ones. Violeta Ekpo examines the changing status of Ibibio women in the colonial society revealing that many of the contemporary discriminatory practices emerged in response to the new social, economic and political circumstances of the colonial development in Africa. Her focus on the specific role and status of Ibibio women in the pre-colonial society and the changes affecting them shows that "the female gender in traditional culture connoted sacredness, primordial potency and divine ritual powers for the perpetuation of the human existence and culture." (90) Ekpo shows that colonialism and contemporary social changes have introduced new practices which are at variance with "customary practices." (ibid.) Post-colonial state policies have not been a radical turnaround from colonial policies.

In constructing women's history, Raphael Njoku sees the era of the Atlantic slave trade as important in the historical transformation of many pre-colonial African societies. He provides a broad overview of social change and gender relations in the Igbo area of southeastern Nigeria in the period beginning from about the mid-seventeenth century to the eve of British colonial rule, focusing on the vectors of change that came with expansions in both regional and overseas trade relations (including the slave trade), cross-regional migrations, the rise of Aro oracular power, and the impact of these occurrences on the restructuring of power relations, gender roles, lifestyles, family systems, agricultural production, division of labor, dietary habits, social values and behaviors in the Igbo area. Without any visible and direct European influence, the southeastern Nigerian society was already experiencing far-reaching changes in the precolonial era, even though the later colonial presence radically accelerated and eclipsed the pace of the previous trends. Thus, it is important to underscore African initiatives in the development of historical transformations in order to demonstrate that Africa has agency and that the various indigenous societies were not static before the era of colonialism. An important strength in these essays, however, is the extent to which they reveal the changing relationships and dynamics between men and women over the course of the twentieth century, taking into account specific Nigerian experiences.

There is a diasporic dimension to this volume that deals with both local and international voluntary/involuntary immigrations, all largely associated with the Atlantic slave trade. The essays draw on examples from Africa as well as the Atlantic diaspora to show how the transatlantic slave trade affected women. While this is not the main focus of this volume, the few contributions touching on this issue more than suffice, however, to make the case that the study of Nigerian women can be enhanced by investigating the African Diaspora phenomenon. In this context, Lisa Lindsay explores the experiences of Brazilian immigrant women in Lagos and their attempts to modify their living conditions and improve their economic conditions following the abolition of slavery in Bahia in the nineteenth century. Her essay raises fundamental questions as we contemplate the crimes that were visited upon the enslaved Africans during the more than 400 years of the human trafficking and the attempts to repatriate them when their labor and the plantation complex that it supported became obsolete. When the slave trade ended, the European nations engaged in it devised means to rid themselves of the free black population. Linsay's essay describes how legislations were enacted and state sanctioned deportations pursued to achieve this goal. Working on materials drawn from court cases between 1879 and 1882, Lindsay explores the attempts by these Brazilian immigrants to use their skills and experiences to improve their lot upon return to Lagos. She uses these court records to explore the peculiar situation of women in colonial Lagos, their preoccupation with trading and other economic activities. Largely, immigrant women helped to redefine domestic and economic life and ownership of property in Lagos. Lindsay concludes by proposing a connection between the exploration of women immigrant's position over time and the link between African and African Diaspora histories.

New theoretical formulations are informing how gender relations in Nigerian societies can lead to a better understanding of women's roles in pre-colonial and contemporary society. The historical and culturally determined concepts of female and male roles, including power relations between the genders inform the background of some of the papers in this volume. The role of women in pre-colonial Nigerian societies took different forms. Yet, any discourse on women's participation in traditional society should address the importance of understanding the definitive difference in what is called tradition and what is labeled history in African societies. Oyeronke Oyewumi has called attention to the fact that history either as lived experience, a record of lived experience that is coded in oral tradition or simply written history, is constantly being re-invented to reflect a particular interest. Written history in particular is very much tied to European encounters with Africa and the introduction of "historical writing" as a discipline and an avenue for professional practice.[23] Oyewumi argues, for example, that the Yoruba conception of tradition in particular speaks to the problem of the interplay between the past and the present and the agency of the person who 'recounts' history at any point in time. We want to emphasize that these male-biased versions of history are not rooted in African cultural experiences. Ihuoma Abaronye in this volume has shown the centrality of gender as a patterned normative order around which the Ibibio organize their lives.

Funso Afolayan alludes to the importance of women in the political-economy as well as ritual life of pre-colonial Ìgbomìnà. These roles made women indispensable in economic production and state formation processes before the 1900s. Yoruba women's prominence in local politics, rituals, religion and cosmology faced serious interventions following the nineteenth century Yoruba wars and colonialism.

Biodun Adedirian and Olukoya Ogen draw examples from the Yoruba kingdoms in present day Benin Republic, Oyo and Ondo in present day Nigeria in examining women's ritual function as a powerful factor in traditional Yoruba social and political structure. Ritual and political functions guaranteed women's participation in public affairs and acted as checks and balances to male excesses. They point out that the roles played by women in palace politics linked them inextricably to state policies and politics.

Such dynamics of change at the local level were also examined, especially in relation to regional migration and intercultural change. Joseph O. Charles traces the origin of diaspora and the role played by women in stimulating fundamental social changes. His essay explores the role of marriage in forging new social ties and effecting changes. Indeed, Elizabeth Isichei and Western scholars had observed, for example, that during the slave trade many Igbo women were retained in the coast as concubines or wives. Thus they were the agents of social change and the social mechanisms that ignited such changes under different circumstances. Charles provided new valuable information on women's inter-cultural marriages and the complex set of social dynamics that resulted from such alliances and how they served as catalysts for the processes of state formation in the coastal regions, as a result of the slave trade. The enormity of social change and its consequences presents a trajectory of new relationships, alliances, and social problems that offer opportunities for further examination of the role of women from the Biafra hinterland.

The late 1960s was a time of optimism for many of the newly independent states in Africa. Two decades later, however, many African societies were faced with economic and political crisis. Frustration on the part of African states and international organizations has led to the re-evaluation of the development agenda and the role of women in development. While we are not concerned here with development models and their suitability for African societies, they provide a lens through which to view the development agenda and the place of women in it.[24] There is widespread agreement, however, that women are often largely excluded from access to and control of productive resources because the development agenda has often been defined and articulated to reflect Western development models. Thus, the present situation of women in Nigeria as elsewhere in Africa is partially the consequence of a long history of ineffective state development models that often create unsuitable conditions for women in particular. Indeed, George Dei has argued that any approach to the development issues "must speak to the social, spiritual, cultural, economic, political and cosmological aspects of African peoples."[25] Some of the essays in this book reflect these tendencies. The volume however articulates the role women are playing in subsistence production, culture, and civilization. For example, Donna Flynn's chapter shows that among the Yoruba and eastern Benin, gender ideologies do not fall into the simplistic typology of male domination and female subordination. Rather, a multifaceted gender ideology determined by sex, social network, social relations, and ritual exists and calls for a more complex analysis of gender.

It is impossible to talk about women and their role in society without reference to their health. As part of integrating women into the development agenda and ensuring their optimum contribution to national development, women's health issues have featured prominently in the development agenda. Integrating health and social issues into the development agenda and making women part of the process ensures qualitative outcome. Some of the contributions in this volume reflect the need for the physical well-being of women. In particular, the reproductive health of women are seen as an essential aspect of any attempt to empower women and achieve their optimum health. Issues of fertility, power and authority reflect the role of socio-cultural factors in mediating decision making processes and women's fertility decisions. Elisha P. Renne's contribution, in particular, shows the cultural norms associated with infertility, which is often perceived as a woman's problem. It is our belief that this attitude disavows the male factor in infertility cases and often leads to psychological health problems for the women involved.

Ibrahim Umaru and Theophilus D. Lagi argue that gender ideologies are contested and subjected to constant redefinition within a society. Their analysis of the gender implications of communal conflicts focusing on the Egbirra-Bassa communal conflict and the impacts it has on women in the affected areas shows that gender divisions are often blurred and in constant flux. They argue that the Egbirra-Bassa conflict, like other conflicts of its nature, has its origin in deep-rooted social and economic injustices, identity politics and prolonged periods of targeted deprivation. Yet their implications for the society are gendered. In the heat of hostilities in armed conflicts, women are often compelled to play new roles in the 'family' and 'home' life of soldiers. They reveal that conflicts transform women's roles, gender ideologies, division of labor, and household subsistence strategies. If not drafted as combatants in the war front, women often end up as spies or captives forced to stay in military camps to provide sexual services to their abductors. In fact, Obioma Nnaemeka analysis of women's perceptions of the Biafra-Nigeria civil war reveals the changing nature of group norms, women's role and the processes of household sustainability.[26] Yet these problems are rooted in the history of Nigerian societies and are part of a larger historical experience and women's resilience in particular historical circumstances.

This volume leaves many areas and regions in Nigeria unexplored because responses from some areas were limited or absent. The response from northern Nigeria is limited to two papers.

However, some papers have opened up new grounds for further research. The Atlantic Diaspora, the impact of the Transatlantic Slave Trade on African societies and their gender implications are areas that need further examination. Lindsay provides us with very useful historical information on the Atlantic Diaspora by examining the Brazilian immigrant community in Lagos in the last quarter of the nineteenth century. The social dynamism of the slave trade and its impact on Nigerian societies need such studies.

New theoretical and methodological conceptions of development should reflect not only local conditions but an all encompassing context that caters to different aspect of women's lives. The 'women in development paradigm' should reflect production, reproduction, sustainability, mobilization, and health issues. A new development paradigm should aim at a gender sensitive equitable distribution of socioeconomic and political opportunities. This volume addresses these issues as it focuses on the role of women in culture and development and the avenues through which women's voices could be heard.

Notes

1. J. A. Horton, *West African Countries and Peoples* (New edition with introduction by George Shepperson), (Edinburgh: The University Press, 1969), 148.

2. Bishop Johnson, "Missionary Journey," *Lagos Standard* 29 April 1903.

3. See Martin K. Whyte, *The Status of Women in Preindustrial Societies*, (Princeton, NJ: Princeton University Press, 1978), 170.

4. On indirect rule, see Adiele Afigbo, *The Warrant Chiefs: Indirect Rule in South-Eastern Nigeria, 1891-1929* (London: Longman, 1972).

5. Sylvia Leith-Ross, *African Woman: A Study of the Ibo of Nigeria* (London: Routledge &. Kegan Paul, 1965).

6. M. M. Green, *Ibo Village Affairs: Chiefly with Reference to the Village of Umueke Agbaja* (London: Sidgwick and Jackson, 1947).

7. Nina Mba, *Nigerian Women Mobilized: Women's Political Activity in Southern Nigeria, 1900-1965* (Berkeley: University of California Press, 1982).

8. See for example Bolanle Awe, ed. *Nigerian Women: A Historical Perspective* (Lagos: Bookcraft, 2001); Laray Denzer and Bolanle Awe, *The Iyalode in*

Ibadan Politics and Society, C. 1850-1997 (Ibadan: Sam Bookman Publishers, 1998).

9. See, for example, Afigbo, *Warrant Chiefs*.

10. For an excellent review of these approaches which I have cited in several parts of this work, see, Imam, A. Mei-Tje, "The Presentation of African Women in Historical Writing," in *Retrieving Women's History: Changing Perceptions of the Role of Women in Politics and Society*, ed. Jay S. Kleinberg (New York: Berg, 1988), 30-40.

11. See for example, Evan Pritchard, *The Position of Women in Primitive Societies and other Essays in Social Anthropology* (London: Faber, 1965).

12. Imam, "The Presentation," 34. See also, M. M. Green's anthropological study of an Igbo community, *Ibo Village Affairs*.

13. Nancy J. Hafkin and Edna G. Bay, eds. *Women in Africa: Studies in Social and Economic Change* (Stanford: Stanford University Press, 1976), 4.

14. Ibid.

15. Imam, "The Presentation," 36.

16. Margaret Jean Hay, "Queens, Prostitutes and Peasants: Historical Perspectives on African Women, 1971 – 1986," *Canadian Journal of African Studies* 22 no. 3 (1988): 431-47.

17. Simi Afonja and Bisi Aina, *Nigerian Women in Social Change* (Ile-Ife, Nigeria: Obafemi Awolowo University Press, 1995), 7.

18. See for example, Ifi Amadiume, *Male Daughters, Female Husbands: Gender and Sex in an African Society* (London: Zed Books, 1987); Phoebe V. Ottenberg, "The Changing Economic Position of Women among the Afikpo Ibo," in *Continuity and Change in African Cultures*, ed. Bascon Russell William and Melvin J. Herskovits (Chicago: University of Chicago Press, 1958), 205-23; Caroline Ifeka-Moller, "Female Militancy and Colonial Revolt: The Women's War of 1929, Eastern Nigeria," in Shirley Ardener, ed. *Perceiving Women* (New York: John Wiley & Sons, 1975), 128-132; Judith Van Allen, "Sitting on a Man: Colonialism and the Lost Political Institutions of the Igbo," *Canadian Journal of African Studies* 6, 11 (1972): 165-81.

19. Gloria Chuku, *Igbo Women and Economic Transformation in Southeastern Nigeria, 1900–1960* (New York: Routledge, 2005). See also Chima J. Korieh, "The Invisible Farmer? Women, Gender, and Colonial Agricultural Policy in the Igbo Region of Nigeria, c. 1913–1954," *African Economic History* 29 (2001): 117–62.

20. Nwando Achebe, *Farmers, Traders, Warriors, and Kings: Female Power and Authority in Northern Igboland, 1900–1960* (Portsmouth, NH: Heinemann, 2005).

21. See Van Allen, "Sitting on a Man; Afigbo, *The Warrant Chiefs*.

22. Oyeronke Oyewumi, *Invention of Women: Making An African Sense of Western Gender Discourses* (Minneapolis: University of Minnesota Press, 1997), 84.

23. Ibid., 80.

24. For an analysis of the different development models, see Margaret C Snyder and Mary Tadesse, *African Women and Development: A History* (London: Zed Books, 1995), 1-15.

25. George J. S. Dei, "Sustainable Development in the African Context: Revisiting Some Theoretical and Methodological Issues," *African Development* 15, no. 2 (1993): 97-110.

26. Obioma Nnaemeka, "Fighting on All Fronts: Gendered Spaces, Ethnic Boundaries, and the Nigerian Civil War," *Dialectical Anthropology* 22 nos. 3-4, (1997): 235-263.

PART I

HISTORY, POLITICS AND SOCIETY

Chapter 1

WOMEN IN NIGERIAN HISTORY

Adiele Afigbo

INTRODUCTION

There are many neglected themes in Nigerian history, but probably only few are as neglected as the role of Nigerian women in our history. Yet what bits of information we have on the subject tend to suggest that, contrary to prejudiced fashionable opinion, women were recognized amongst various Nigerian peoples as constituting a very vital factor not only in the making of our indigenous cultures and institutions, but also in determining some of the ways we reacted and adjusted to the challenges of European rule. One can come to such a conclusion on the strength of the evidence uncovered and preserved by indigenous historians like Reverend Samuel Johnson and Jacob Egharevba on the one hand and by colonial anthropologists like M. M. Green and Sylvia Leith-Ross on the other.[1] But for reasons which need not detain us here, the pioneering efforts of these people have not been quickly followed up by later-day scholars. One is, however, happy to observe that some scholars are working on different aspects of the role of women in Nigerian history. K. Okonjo, a sociologist, for example, is concerned with the role of women in social change, while the others like Nina Mba, a historian, has investigated the contribution of women to the political evolution of Nigerian under colonial rule.

Because the subject has so far not been investigated in detail by our own scholars, who are less likely to carry into their study alien ideas and assumptions, the popular books continue to repeat the distorted and fanciful views which characterized the rabidly racist phase of European colonial rule in Africa. During that period the average European visitor to or writer on Africa saw the continent as the last retreat of barbarism and tyranny, a land where rulers oppressed and exploited their subjects, masters maltreated their slaves, and husbands subjugated their wives. With regard to the subject of this paper the popular view was that African women were hewers of wood and drawers of water, a class just a little better than slaves when one considered the amount of human rights they enjoyed. If they did not always do all the work while the men loafed about endlessly and drank wine furiously, they at least did most of the difficult work.

For instance, refuting Sir John Cecil Rhodes's racist belief that Africans were incorrigible loafers, Leonard Barnes wrote as follows:

> African women must be among the most industrious human beings who have ever lived; and even African men, who admittedly cannot hold a candle to their sisters, work as well as any.[2]

Similarly repeating the more generalized idea that Black Africa was a man's world, R. A. Levine said that all or most of the societies of sub-Saharan Africa "had a traditional idea of male domination"[3] as if he could mention one society in Europe or America where the opposite was the case or one that had the idea of parity between the sexes. To reinforce his observation Levine also wrote: "women carry the heaviest burdens, usually on their heads, while men occupy their leisure with a variety of prestigeful and important activities."[4] Here we note how in this tendentious writing what women do during the working period is contrasted with what men do at their leisure in order to sustain the idea of African men barbarously reducing their women to beasts of burden.

The argument of this paper is not that African women enjoyed absolute parity with their men. Even in the Western World, women did not have such good fortune. On the contrary the contention is that African women had an honored and recognized place in society which made it possible for the gifted ones amongst them to rise to positions of political, economic, and social eminence from which they led and dominated not only their fellow women, but the common run of men. It was the opportunity for vertical and horizontal mobility that Africa's indigenous societies provided for women that enabled them to contribute significantly to the synthesis of their way of life. It is further contended that to understand the role which women played in history, we have to jettison the masculine super-ordination/feminine-subordination paradigm in favor of the idea of the complementarity of the sexes. Under this idea men and women were seen as playing different but important and complementary roles. Another point is that in dealing with this topic it is necessary to keep steadily in view the fact that just as there are elite men and non-elite men, there are elite women and non-elite women. At all times and in all societies these two categories of humanity (the elites and the non-elites) play different roles. Just as among the men, so among the women, only very few attain elite status and it is these few whose personalities and life histories form part of national histories.

WOMEN IN PRECOLONIAL NIGERIA

The traditions of many Nigerian groups clearly show that women occupied important positions not only in the economic sphere, the one usually given great prominence in sociological literature, but also in the political and social spheres. Taking the political sphere first, we find that in many of these communities women are said to have occupied leadership roles on many occasions. In the Central Sudan, for instance, two women figure prominently in the early history of the Hausa communities. The first of these was Queen Dauranam, mentioned in the Bayajidda legend as the ruler of the state of Daura at the time of the supposed last series of invasions that led to the emergence of the seven Hausa states (Hausa Bakwai) out of formerly apparently weakly coordinated communities of this region.[5] The point here is not whether the legend contains authentic historical facts or not, but that the assigning of such a central role to a woman suggests that there was nothing inherently anti-feminist in indigenous Hausa culture.

Another woman of note in Hausa political traditions, Queen Amina of Zaria, was a figure whose historicity is perhaps not in doubt. This remarkable woman whose political and military exploits dazzled all Hausaland in the sixteenth century came to the throne of Zaria only a few decades after the foundation of Zaria city by Sarkin Barkwa Turunku. At that time the Jukun of Kwararafa of middle Benue were said to have been the scourge of the Central Sudan. Zaria, being the southernmost of the Hausa states, was invariably the first to come under the onslaught of the Jukun whenever they were on the move against the states of the central Sudan. It therefore fell to her to form the frontline of Hausa defense against Jukun invasions. Sarkin Barkwa Turunku had succeeded in holding the Jukuns at bay while her daughter, Amina, when she came to the throne, is said to have turned the tables on the Jukuns and reduced them to tributary status. But her military exploits apparently did not stop there, for traditions attribute to her the conquest of Nupe (a member of the Banza Bakwai) and of Kano and Kastina whose growing commercial prosperity was beginning to make them the envy of their neighbors.[6] A tradition which scholars tend to regard as doubtful also attributes to Amina the introduction of the art of fortification into Hausaland.

Again the career of Queen Amina of Zaria would seem to suggest that in indigenous Hausa society femininity *per se* was no barrier to political leadership or social mobility. At least amongst them no "Salic law" operated to bar gifted women of royal birth from accession to the throne. It is necessary to bear these two examples in mind because it is in Hausa society that the status of

women is considered to be particularly depressed. This was probably a later development attributable to the impact of Semitic
ideas, especially to the impact of Islam as practiced by its later-
day adherents.

If we turn our attention to the indigenous societies of Southern Nigeria, we are also likely to discover that women were not
excluded from participation in politics. Among the Yoruba, for
instance, women were involved actively in the political process.
Reverend Samuel Johnson's study of the political system and
constitution of the Oyo Empire clearly shows women occupying
important political offices.[7] There was, for instance, the group
of women whom he describes as "the ladies of the palace" or as
"the king's wives." Among these were (i) the *Iya Oba*, the Alafin's
"official mother" who played mother to the king (ii) the *Iya Kere*
who being in charge of the king's treasures and royal insignia was
said to have exercised far-reaching political powers. Since she
had custody of all the paraphernalia used by the king on state
occasion, she could disrupt state occasions and draw attention
to serious breaches of custom or protocol by simply refusing
to surrender these to the king, if she was not satisfied with his
conduct. She also had the duty of placing the crown on the kings
head during the coronation ceremony; (iii) the *Are-Orite* who,
as the king's personal attendant, took charge of his meals and
bed and was constantly by his side on state occasion; (iv) the
Iya Mode who was the priestess in charge of the veneration of
the spirits of departed kings. It is said the king looked upon her
as a "father" and addressed her as such. So important was her
job that the monarch was said to salute her kneeling—the only
mortal to whom he gave such an honor. These were some of the
women who were referred to in European accounts by the term
"harem" to give the impression of hordes of voluptuous women
specially assembled to satisfy the carnal lusts and passions of
fierce male African potentates. We now know that many of them
were important ritual functionaries whose duties required them
to be celibate or at least to have already triumphed over the sins
of the flesh.

But it was not only through these specially celebrated palace
women that Yoruba women participated in the political life of

their states. In addition, according to Fadipe, every Yoruba town, especially among the Oyo Yoruba, had the organization known as *Egbe Iyalode* (the association of the First Lady), which constituted a recognized political pressure group. "Any representations made by this body," says Fadipe, "to the political authorities, are listened to with respect whether they are concerned with their political interests or with some broader political issue."[8] In some of the Yoruba states the association was represented in the state council by its president, the *Iyalode*. In Ibadan, at least, this practice is said to have continued until about 1914.

Our last example for this section is taken from Igboland. For most of Igboland, where political authority was widely dispersed within each autonomous unit, it is difficult to single out any woman or group of women whose political roles could be discussed in terms similar to those used for Hausa or Yoruba society, where authority was for the most part centralized. But the observation made with respect to the role of women in precolonial Nigerian societies is also true for Igboland. In some respects this extremely diffused political situation would appear to have given the women wider scope for organizing and running their own affairs—with the men being called in only on such occasions as the women's groups or organizations failed, either because of incompetence or factionalism or the like. But beyond that women were often represented in the councils of elders by their most distinguished, most mature and most gifted leaders, some of whom, in communities where that was the case, had taken such titles as were open to women. In the elders council the views of such women leaders were listened to with respect and taken seriously into account when decisions were being reached. But one group of women, the *umuada* or *umuokpu* as some Igbo call them, were particularly powerful and important. They were feared and respected alike by the menfolk and the women. The *umuada* of a village were the women born in that village but who had married outside it. They rarely intervened in the affairs of their natal village, but whenever they intervened, they did so with decisive effect. Not only could they settle internal disputes in the village of their birth, but they also could stop wars and settle disputes between that village and the ones into which they married.

But apart from the above example, which existed in most of Igboland, there is another deserving of mention. This existed among the riverine and Western Igbo whose political system was somewhat modified by practices and institutions apparently borrowed from the states of Benin and Igala. There is among many of the communities in this group the institution of *Omu* (Queen) as the female counterpart of the *Obi* (King). In the riverine Igbo city-state of Ossomari, for example, there is the institution of *Omu Igili,*⁹ which was one of the most elevated titles in that city state. The occupant of that title, usually a distinguished woman of wealth, intellect and character, reigned with the *Obi* as co-sovereign with responsibility largely for regulating women's affairs. Apart from being the chairwoman and spokeswoman of Ossomari mother's council, she took responsibility for maintaining law and order in the market and for advising the *Obi* on state matters touching the interests of women. She also played a leading military role. According to tradition her war canoe led the Ossomari fleet into battle as she was believed to be the possessor and keeper of a particularly powerful charm which made her shield impenetrable to enemy arrows and could make Ossomari warriors invisible while in battle.

Thus in pre-colonial Nigeria not only did women of ability rise, as the occasion demanded and permitted, to provide different kinds of leadership to their communities in peace time and in war, but many communities had entrenched constitutional provisions which assured women a continuing interest and participation in the queen of the professions—that is in politics and administration.

That women occupied a very important economic position in pre-colonial Africa is a fact recognized by all, and one that has generally been given more than its fair share of attention by students of African society, especially by European scholars. This issue has been so emphasized that it hardly needs any more emphasis here. However, to fail to mention it at all would cause some imbalance in the argument of this paper. In all the main areas of economic activity—agriculture, trade and manufacture—women played outstanding roles. In agriculture they were a major source of labor. But to concede this, is not to subscribe to the view that women did all or most of the work while the men loafed or discussed politics. Their importance as a source of labor derived largely from their numbers. One of the arguments for polygamy was that many hands make a light work (*aka otutu di mma n'oruru*). The same argument provides some explanation for the value that was placed on the rearing of many children. The average farmer was a polygamist. And many times, especially in societies where the levirate law applied, he also had as part of his household all the wives of his deceased father and brothers whom he maintained and who in turn helped him with his farm work. But it was not only that they helped to provide general labor, but also there were specific aspects of farming that belonged exclusively to women. These included weeding, and for the forest region, the planting of such subsidiary crops as cocoyam, cereals, vegetables and so on, which helped to support the major crops of the community that more often than not were monopolized by men. Furthermore the women were responsible for the processing of farm products into food. By processing here I mean all the different stages of treatment which food crops undergo from the time they are harvested to the time they are offered for eating. This would include plain cooking as well as the winnowing and treatment of grains, the preparation of palm oil, and the manufacture of various categories of spices—*ogiri, dawadawa* and so on.

With regard to trade, they played two main roles. First, they monopolized local and therefore retail trade. Partly because they were burdened with rearing children and partly because of the harassments of land pirates or headhunters or both, they did not figure prominently in long distance and therefore wholesale trade. But through virtually monopolizing local trade, they played a key part in distribution and thus met vital economic needs at the grass roots level. But still it would appear there were some Nigerian communities among whom the women participated to some extent in long distance trade. Professor Nadel found that among the Nupe, sterile women were allowed to engage in long distance trade. This, he thinks, was because the society was prepared to tolerate sexual laxity amongst them.[10] But I suspect this was because being childless they could afford, unlike nursing mother, to be away from home for days. Also, or at least according to indigenous belief in the matter, they enjoyed more robust health than child-bearing women, while their hip joints, undisturbed by child-birth, could take the strain of long treks.

The other important exclusive role of women in trade had to do with the fact that, through marrying outside their villages and clans (or even linguistic and ethnic groups), they helped to create and establish vital links and contacts between communities which benefited trade. This was particularly important among those peoples like the Igbo, Ibibio, Ogoja and many peoples of the Middle Belt who did not evolve large centralized states that could maintain law and order along trade routes over wide areas. In such decentralized communities, long distance traders and other travelers commonly protected themselves against demands for toll or attacks by land pirates by taking wives from prominent families along their trade route. The homes of their fathers-in-law also provided them with warehousing and hostel facilities, which also served as points in which their clients repaid according to agreed schedules to receive old and place new orders. Without such marriage links, it is difficult to conceive how long distance trading on the scale we now know existed could have been possible in many decentralized Nigerian communities.

In the area of manufacture, women also occupied commanding positions, especially when we think of the manufacture of cloth, pots and other earthen vessels, various categories of plaited household articles and so on. In many Nigerian communities, they monopolized the growing and harvesting of cotton, the spinning of it into yarn, as well as the dyeing and weaving of it. Similarly they tended to monopolize the manufacture of various household items requiring the use of clay.

Women thus played a very important part in the economic life of pre-colonial Nigeria. And it is doubtful whether they would have exhibited as much initiative, enterprise and dynamism as they did if they were the unregarded beasts of burden which colonial literature tended to make them. The fact is that their special status and individuality were officially recognized by society and protected. The necessary encouragement they needed was supplied by the fact that, in most if not all the communities, the women had recognized property rights. What they acquired they could hold and make use of in the interest of their families and of their individual selves. It is true that among many Nigerian peoples, a woman and her property were said to belong to her husband to deal with as he pleased. This theory was so modified by practice that it largely became non-existent. In the normal course of events, for as long as a woman identified herself with her husband's people, hardly anybody questioned her right to hold and use the fruits of her labor. But if a serious quarrel arose and divorce became likely, then of course her right to property came into jeopardy. The fact is that most of these communities saw land as the ultimate source of wealth, and since most wives were "strangers" in their husband's villages, they had no title to land and by extension to the fruits of the exploitation of the land. Here a wife was in the position of a slave who also came into the community of his master empty-handed. Looked at sociologically, the regulation which "denied" women ultimate right to property helped to make for the stability of married life, for only in extreme cases of brutality would a woman decide to lose all her life's earnings as well as the right to her children by choosing the course of divorce.

Social roles are more difficult to pinpoint than political or economic roles, but a study of social life in pre-colonial Nigeria also shows the women fulfilling very vital functions. Probably the most important in this respect was their almost exclusive responsibility for the early education of the children. In many of these societies, children, at least until they were up to six or seven years of age in the case of boys, were in the exclusive care of their mothers. This meant that for the most part the very fundamental job of inducting them into the group through teaching them the language and norms of the group were done by women assisted by slightly older children. They achieved this through the singing of lullabies, the telling of folktales and the recounting of the great epics of the group.

Apart from the above the women acted as a stabilizing force not only for society as a whole but even for individual men. The stability and harmony within each socio-political group was often believed to derive from the strict observance of native laws and customs handed down by the ancestors of the group. Refusal to observe these rules was believed to cause harvest failure and premature deaths. The women were particularly concerned with staving off these two disasters. If the harvests failed they would be the first to feel the pinch of it, as famishing children were more likely to harass their mothers than their fathers. Also, women believe that they feel the death of children more than the male folk because, they would argue, it is women who bear the burden of pregnancy and of nursing the baby to adulthood. For these reasons, women were inclined to insist on rigorous observance of any rules and regulations whose observance society saw as the *sine qua non* for a peaceful, ordered and prosperous existence. In this sense, women were a very important source of social stability. They also tended to stabilize individual men. This too was widely recognized. Hence the general cure for rascality or irresponsibility in young men was considered to be marriage. This was so much the case that, in many Nigerian communities, an unmarried man, no matter his age, was not taken seriously by his married compeers and elders or even by his juniors, which was even more humiliating and sobering.

But to say that women promoted social stability through a tendency towards conservatism is not to say that they were not also a source of social change and progress. In certain spheres of life, they helped to bring about healthy innovations. No two communities, no matter how closely situated, had precisely the same techniques for doing the same things, for instance for weaving, making pots or preparing dishes. Since, in many of these Nigerian communities women tended to marry outside their villages, at times outside their clans, they were a very important means of diffusing new techniques especially in crafts, music, entertainment and cookery. The diffusion of such new techniques at times led to changes in craft organization, in the market prices of the finished goods, and in their distribution along the trade route and so on.

WOMEN IN COLONIAL NIGERIA

Colonial rule created a new political, economic and social situation in Nigeria demanding of men and women far-reaching adjustments and new roles. By and large Nigerian women were successful in responding to the challenges posed to them by this new situation. In this period, the roles of the outstanding women whose life histories now form part of our national history fell into two categories. In the first category were a number of women who sought to play prominent roles in political and economic matters more or less in the time honored tradition of their pre-colonial predecessors. These were not pre-occupied with the need to liquidate or reform the colonial regime. In the second category were those whose social, political and economic resentment of the colonial system led them into varying degrees and kinds of anti-colonial activity. These later could be said to belong to the celebrated group whose life and achievements were ultimately responsible for the achievement of independence by Nigeria. We shall now take each of these categories in turn for fuller discussion.

Madam Tinubu of Lagos and Abeokuta is the first person we shall deal with in the group of women who successfully manipulated the economic and political opportunities available to them in the new era without getting quite involved in the early anti-colonial movement. Madam Tinubu's achievements have been made known to us by the researches of Saburi Biobaku.[11] She was born in Egbaland where she had her first training in trade and commerce before moving to the costal community of Badagry where she built up a lucrative and powerful position with the Brazilian slave dealers there as middlemen. It would appear she traded mainly in slaves and tobacco. By 1864 she had become a prominent member of the commercial elite of the town.

A political dimension came to be added to her career when she attached herself to Akitoye, the exiled king of Lagos. Using her powerful economic position, she built up a faction devoted to securing the restoration of Akitoye to the throne of Lagos. It is therefore not surprising that when Akitoye returned to Lagos in 1851, Madam Tinubu followed him, at the same time transferring her business from Badagry to Lagos. In the latter place, she became the power behind the throne, a position which she augmented substantially when the weak character, Dosumu, succeeded his father Akitoye as king in 1853. As would be expected, she soon aroused opposition amongst people jealous of her success. Commercially she was in competition with the Sierra Leone and Brazillian emancipadoes who were interested in building up a dominant position in the trade between Lagos and the interior. In this conflict, Consul Campbell took the side of the emancipadoes. At the same time, her political influence on the throne of Lagos was resented by a number of prominent Lagos chiefs. Some of these had in fact risen in rebellion in 1853 because of her influence on Akitoye. But eventually it was Campbell who got her exiled from Lagos to Abeokuta in 1856 through calling in the gunboats as a means of exerting pressure on the vacillating Dosumu.

But for Tinubu, exile only meant a change of platform rather than political or economic eclipse. In Abeokuta, she quickly re-established herself as a leading middleman trader, this time dealing in munitions of war. This was a highly strategic occupation at that time, when a state of war existed between the kingdoms of Egba and Dahomey. Her manipulation of this business soon brought her to the forefront of Egba political and national life, for when the Dahomeans attacked in 1864, she played a key role in organizing the defense of Egba land and securing the defeat of the aggressors. According to Biobaku:

> Her compound was converted into a veritable arsenal from which arms and ammunitions were issued to the Egba forces on their way to the front. Then she took up a position at Aro Gate, nearer the front at which the wounded were nursed by her and her female associates, where soldiers whose powder had exhausted in battle replenished their store and from which any would-be deserters were sent back with a renewed determination to fight the Dahomey and save the Egba metropolis from destruction.[12]

It is understandable, therefore, that at the end of the war and with the Dahomeans defeated, the Egba recognized her services by conferring on her the title of *Iyalode*—First Lady. To such an extent had her fame and standing been augmented that she now sought to become one of the kingmakers of the Egba state. In 1869 she was a leading member of the faction that wanted to install Oyekan instead of Ademola as Alake. Her faction lost but succeeded in 1877 when Ademola I died. With her candidate on the throne, she once again became the power behind the throne.

Equally illustrative of the point we are making, but probably less dramatic than the example just given, was the career of another remarkable woman, Okwei (1872-1943) of Ossomari of the riverine Igbo.[13] Born of the royal line of Ossomari, she learned to trade in the Igala country, where she also learned the Igala language, which, along with Igbo, was an important commercial language on the lower Niger. After three years there, she went to Atani and established on her own. There she soon made the acquaintance of Chief Joseph Allagoa of Brass, a trader of longstanding and some means. She married him and had a son Francis, before the marriage broke up after one year or so. But the fleeting union had enabled her to expand her business as she now came to be known to the leading merchants of the lower Niger—both African and European alike—and so came to have access to more credit. A second marriage, this time to one Opene of Aboh, made her transfer her business to Onitsha which in the 1880s was becoming the most important trading station on the lower Niger. She traded mainly in produce which her agents collected from the primary producers and sold to the European companies who paid her largely in trade goods for distribution at Onitsha and beyond.

Recognizing her dependence on the agents of these companies and on the long-established delta merchants, Okwei strained every nerve to win and retain their goodwill. To this end, she raised young girls, mainly slaves and pawns, and gave them to the agents and traders as mistresses. In time too her son by Opene grew up to become a clerk in the Niger Company, which gave her added advantages as she could now get inside information on the state of trade. Her son Francis Allagoa was also well placed. He joined the colonial service and in time held such powerful and greatly envied positions as District interpreter and Court Registrar. Meanwhile, Okwei was expanding her businesses to include land speculation by which process she came to own about a third of the land on the Onitsha bank of the Niger. She was also a moneylender and gave loans at rates of interest varying from 60 to 90 percent. She was a transporter, and her lorries and canoes were said to have plied as far afield as Calabar, Port Harcourt and Degema.

Okwei was thus a highly successful businesswoman but not merely a commercial wizard, for she used her wealth to acquire political power. She helped to get her husband, Opene, appointed member of the Onitsha Native Court. She herself got crowned the Omu of Ossomari in 1935, a position which, as we have already seen, was a very powerful one in Ossomari society. But she would not leave her business at Onitsha to go and live at Ossomari. This meant she was by and large an absentee Omu. But regardless of this, Ossomari tradition speaks of her as the most powerful person to have held that position in Ossomari history. Because she lived away from the local factions in the city-state, she could intervene decisively in the affairs of the community when she chose to. Located at Onitsha and with contacts reaching out to the commercial and political elite of that growing city, she was admirably placed to act as Ossomari's "foreign minister" and "ambassador" whether it was before the people of Onitsha or the powerful Divisional Officer or the agents of the European commercial firms.

Our third example under this category is Ahebi Ugbabe of Ogrute in Enugu-Ezike, Nsukka. According to the traditions of her people she was a woman of average height, well built, light-complexioned and beautiful.[14] Ahebi had been kidnapped from her home and sold into slavery in Igala about the time British rule was being imposed on the Nsukka people in the first decade of this century. At Igala her purchaser decided to convert her into a wife and she had two daughters for him. There at Igala, Ahebi learnt to speak not only Igala and Nupe languages but, even more important, pidgin English. These added to her natural intelligence made her a fearless and forceful woman. Thus when her master-husband started to oppress her, she brought the matter before the Attah of Igala and the Divisional Officer. The Attah and the Divisional Officer decided in her favor and declared her free to return to her people, an opportunity that she happily seized.

When she got back to her native village, she was received with much warmth and enthusiasm. Her linguistic skill gave her access not only to the leading Igala and Nupe people who dominated much of northern Nsukka this time but also to the Divisional Officer and his officials (the interpreter, court clerk, policemen etc). It also brought her much respect from her people. The latter therefore came to transfer their loyalty from Ame Nwa Iyida, their government-recognized headman, who spoke neither Igala nor English and thus had limited political reach, to Ahebi whose social and political reach was very extensive. Naturally this led to a fierce struggle for power in Ogrute in which most of the people stood behind Ahebi. Impressed by the following that she had, the administration decided to recognize her and so made her a warrant chief. With this, she rose further in esteem and importance, took many titles, and came to occupy the traditional position of the Eze of Ogrute. This was a case of a woman first winning recognition from the new colonial authority and then returning to traditional status and legitimacy. Reporting on Ogrute in 1931 Charles Kingsley Meek, the government anthropologist said:

> The present Eze, being a woman, is arbiter in all disputes between women, and takes prominent part in settling matrimonial differences recovering runaway wives and remonstrating with husbands who ill-treat their wives. She makes arrangement for the public sacrifice which the women offer periodically in the market place...The Eze, who is a member of the Native Court, is unmarried.[15]

And now we come to the other documented response of the women to British rule. There were two sides to their role here. On the one hand the majority of them continued with their conservative role which we delineated above. They saw most of the changes introduced by colonial rule as changes for the worse and thus blamed the British for what they considered the increased incidence of pre-mature death, growing sexual immorality and rising prices. In Igboland, the tension which this created in the women led to repeated demonstrations against the colonial authorities.

The first of these took place in 1925 and was known as Nwao-biara Dance or the Dancing Women Movement.[16] The message, which the women spread in relay fashion through a large part of Igboland, was that their god had appeared to some of them at Okigwe or so and had ordered that everybody should return to the customs and traditions of their fathers. To achieve this, people should no longer patronize European ways. They should boycott the native courts, reject European currency, deny the hands of their daughters to Christians, reopen the old footpaths and use them in place of the new main roads. Brides and foods were to revert to pre-colonial prices and girls were to go about nude until they had their first babies. One of these frenzied groups saw girls returning from school and stripped them naked to enforce what they preached.

The second incidence of this attempt by the women to play their old role as stabilizers of society, prices and manners took the form of the more widely known Women's Riot of 1929/30. Shallow scholarship and colonial propaganda have presented this movement as aimed primary at the warrant chiefs. But closer analysis reveals that it was aimed at the entire colonial structure, and that it was an instance of cultural nationalism. The women were opposed to the introduction of taxation not only because they were reluctant to part with hard-earned cash, but also because it was associated with practices which the women believed undermined the moral foundations of society. Their desire to expel the British in order to return to the tried and tested ways of their fathers came out clearly in one of their demands. The Ohuhu women, for instance, insisted "that all white men should return to their country so that the land in this area might remain as it was many years ago before the advent of the white men."[17] One woman talking to the Commission of inquiry which subsequently investigated the riot said: "Our grievances are that the land is changed—we are all dying."[18]

But the role of Nigerian women in the nationalist movement was not just limited to participation in nativistic agitation—that is in movements whose idea was the restoration of what was believed to be the people's golden age. The women also participated in the modern nationalist movement whose ideal is the building of a modern nation-state based on living and dynamic ideas borrowed from European experience and African experiences. To this end, they participated actively in the campaigns of the leading nationalist political parties of the day. Here two names come immediately to the mind—Mrs. Fumilayo Ransome-Kuti and Mrs. Margaret Ekpo, both of whom distinguished themselves as leaders of N.C.N.C. women's wing. Mrs. Ransome-Kuti, President-General of the Nigerian Women's Union and treasurer of the N.C.N.C Western Working Committee, was not only active in national politics where, *inter alia,* she campaigned for the enfranchisement of women in Northern Nigeria, but like Tinubu, her great predecessor in Abeokuta, she also took an active part in the affairs of the Egba Kingdom. Mrs. Ransome-Kuti was a leading figure in the conflict that began in 1948 and later led to the resignation of the *Alake*. Here she stood against the taxation of women and for the reduction of the powers of the monarchy.[19]

CONCLUSION

The foregoing would seem to suggest that we require more research and more critical thinking to come to a full and balanced appreciation of the role of women in Nigerian history, especially during the pre-colonial period. What little evidence we have on their role would appear to suggest that whatever women's limitations were in traditional society, Nigerian women still had the scope and the ability to play vital social, political and economic roles like women in any other society—African or European. When therefore we talk of Christianity and European rule improving the lot of Nigerian or African women, we should know precisely what we are saying. We should at least be clear in our minds that we are not saying that before the coming of European rule our women were the hapless and helpless slaves of their men folk.

If non-African influences have helped to improve the lot of African women, we must also remember that non-African influences have helped to depress the lot of women in Africa. This is particularly true of Semitic influences. There is reason to believe that traditional Islam, with its low view of women, helped to circumscribe the role of women in those parts of Africa where it took root. A comparison of the status of women in Islamized Africa with their counterparts in non-Islamized Africa is highly suggestive in this regard. Even Christianity, which again is a Semitic social ideology, is not completely free of this. The idea that Eve (the first woman) was created out of the rib of Adam (man) is basically an assertion of the primacy of man over woman. First and foremost, it means that man is prior in time to woman (he was created first), and second, that woman is a dependent part of man. A Northern Igbo creation legend,[20] on the other hand, says man and woman came down from heaven at the same time—an idea, which if it does not logically mean equality for both sexes, at least does not suggest sub-ordination for either sex. On the contrary, it suggests the complimentarity of both.

Notes

1. Samuel Johnson, *The History of the Yorubas* (Lagos: CSS Ltd, 1921); Jacob Egharebva, *A Short History of Benin* (Ibadan: Ibadan University Press, 1968); Sylvia Leith-Ross, *African Women: A Study of the Ibo of Nigeria* (London: Routledge and Kegan Paul, 1939); M. M. Green, *Ibo Village Affairs: Chiefly with Reference to the village of Umueke Agbaja*. (London:Sidgwick and Jackson, 1947).

2. Leonard Barnes, *African Renaissance* (London: Victor Gollancz, 1969), 59.

3. R. A. LeVine, "Sex Roles and Economic Change in Africa," in *Black Africa: Its Peoples and their Cultures Today,* ed. J. Middleton (London: Macmillan, 1970), 175.

4. Ibid.

5. M. G. Smith, "The Beginnings of Hausa Society, A.D. 100-1500," in *The Historian in Tropical Africa,* eds. Jan Vansina, R. Mauny, and L. V. Thomas (London: Oxford University Press: 1964), 339-57.

6. Ibid.

7. Johnson, *The History of the Yorubas,* 63-66.

8. N.A. Fadipe, *The Sociology of the Yoruba* (Ibadan: Ibadan University Press, 1970), 253.

9. F. I. Ekejiuba, "Omu Okwei: The Merchant Queen of Ossomari," *Nigeria Magazine* 90 (1966): 213-20.

10. Cited in LeVine, "Sex Roles," 177– 8.

11. S. Biobaku, "Madame Tinubu," in *Eminent Nigerians of the Nineteenth Century*, ed. K. O. Dike (Cambridge: Cambridge University Press, 1960), 3– 41.

12. Ibid.

13. Ekejiuba, "Omu Okwei."

14. Oral tradition collected from Enugu-Ezike.

15. C. K. Meek, *Ethnographical Report on the Peoples of Nsukka Division Onitsha Province* (Lagos:Government Printer, 1930) paragraphs 138-0.

16. A. E. Afigbo, "Revolution and Reaction in Research Nigeria: 1900—1929," *Journal of the Historical Society of Nigeria* 3, no. 3 (1966): 539-57.

17. Quoted in Afigbo, "Revolution and Reaction."

18. Ibid.

19. R. L. Sklar, *Nigerian Political Parties* (Princeton: Princeton University Press, 1963), 62, 25ln, 402, 419, 467.

20. This refers to the Nri creation legend in which the first man, Eri, and the first woman, Adanma, came down from heaven together.

Chapter 2

"OGIDI PALAVER*": THE 1914 WOMEN'S MARKET PROTEST

Nwando Achebe

On July 9, 1904, Igwe[1] Amobi I of Ogidi was consecrated. His name Walter was not all that had changed in the years preceding his enthronement. His transformation from Okafo to the formidable Walter—the first monarch of all of Ogidi was one that was years in the making and would usher in a new era of absolute rule into Ogidi and its environs.

Okafo Amobi came from privileged beginnings. He was born to Akatosi and Jideofo Amobi of Ajilija, Uru Ogidi, *oge Anam-agu-agu*,[2] i.e. during the time of the *Anam-agu-agu* age grade—a period that fell roughly between 1860-1864.[3] Okafo was the first of five male siblings—Chidebelu, Okoludo, Udegbunam and Ofonyili.[4] He later grew up in the palace of the Obi Ogene, later Ezeoba of Onitsha[5] and was educated there—becoming one of the first Ogidi boys to attend missionary school.[6]

The circumstances that propelled Okafo to Onitsha are clouded. Some sources suggest that Okafo was handed over to Ezeoba, the Ogene of Onitsha, by his father Jideofo, as security on a loan. As the story goes, Jideofo invited one of his in-laws from Abatete to attend the Uta feast and festival[7] according to custom. On his way home, his in-law was kidnapped. A humiliated Jideofo swore to avenge his in-law's capture. He subsequently handed over one of his sons, Okafo, to the Ezeoba as collateral because the latter had loaned him some money with which to conduct the search. Okafo, according to this account, thus lived with Ezeoba as a pawn.[8] Another rendering simply maintains that Okafo was sent to Onitsha, not as a pawn, but in order to "be trained in the ways of the whiteman."[9] Whether pawn or freeman, we do know that his master/guardian Ezeoba sent Okafo Amobi to the Crowther and Taylor,[10] later called the Bishop Crowther Memorial School, which had been founded in 1857.[11] He would graduate from there and subsequently enter the service of the Royal Niger Company, where he was attached to one of the Company's steam boats, as an interpreter. From there Okafo joined the Company's Constabulary Force.[12] Amobi would later serve the Church Missionary Society (C.M.S.) as interpreter and evangelist and a few years later in 1892, would become instrumental in the founding of the first church in Amago, Ogidi.[13]

Okafo Amobi would later return to Ogidi, stopping first at Iyi Enu Ogidi where he was given land to build a school.[14] He returned home, accompanied by Europeans and the soldiers of the Niger Company, during a time collectively remembered as *aro ntiji egbe*—the year the guns were destroyed. It was thus remembered because Ogidi and neighboring Nkpor were engaged in a furious warfare—a dispute of which Amobi, serving as interpreter of the Royal Niger Company (agents of the soon-to-be colonial masters) was said to have helped settle. It was this dispute that ultimately culminated in the subjugation of the area by the British.[15] In the aftermath of the war, all Ogidi and Nkpor people were forced to bring out their guns and they were destroyed by the invading Europeans.[16] This *aro ntiji egbe* happened around 1900.[17]

"Ogidi Palaver" investigates an episode in the history of Ogidi, during which Igwe Walter Amobi moved his community's

main market, Afo[...]
outskirts of a new[...]
tions may have b[...]
influx of people o[...]
new highway—ho[...]
the market, Ogidi[...]
women, working w[...]
unleashed their sco[...]
demonstrations, wh[...]
efficient and devas[...]
sitting on man—to [...]

"WE NEV[...] WALTER AM[...] TRANSFORMATION INTO WARRANT CHIEF AND "KING"

The town of Okafo Amobi's birth, *Ogidi Ebo Teghete*, so named after the nine original sons of Inwelle—five of whom were said to have migrated out of their present abode—was under the rulership of the four remaining progenitors, leaders or Ezes[19] of the Ogidi quarters: Akananso,[20] Uru,[21] Ezinkwo[22] and Ikenga.[23] Okafo, now, Walter Amobi, like many Igbo warrant chiefs of the time was the only person in his town that understood English and therefore would come to serve as a link between the colonial masters and the traditional leadership of his town.[24] In time the Ezes would witness their power and authority usurped by Walter Amobi, who had become the colonial government's pick to secede and govern all four quarters of Ogidi—this, in recognition of his invaluable services as a government interpreter. Walter readily assumed the political function that he was charged and would first take the Ozo title[25] and name Kwochaka,[26] then the honorific and in essence, invented, title of Eze of all of Ogidi, i.e. King of all of Ogidi, as the British claimed, to extend his power and privilege.[27] This move was contested by at least one traditional ruler of Ogidi.[28] Following his coronation, Eze Walter Amobi would take on the added title of Igwe[29]—another invention that allowed him to subject his monarchical reign on the people of Ogidi until the 18th day of the last

25

month of the year 1925 when he died.[30] Walter Amobi had posited that the people of Ogidi made him Igwe, but many contested this, insisting instead that he coronated himself through "trickery"[31] and Ogidi people were at a loss to do anything about it.[32]

Igwe Amobi's seat of office was Ikenga; however, his influence extended as far south as Oji River, which represented the boundary between his area of jurisdiction and that of the notorious Chief Oyeama of Eke.[33] He oversaw this area with the aid of the *Ndi Ichie* (Red Cap Chiefs) and the warrant chiefs of Abatete, Eziowelle and Abacha.[34]

As Igwe, Amobi's first course of action was to build a court at Ikenga that would serve all of Ogidi and by so doing severe what had been Ogidi people's compulsory sojourn to the Onitsha Native Court. What was more, building a court at Ikenga elevated Amobi's status because warrant chiefs from all over Ogidi had to come to Amobi's seat of office to try their cases. And each time they did, they had to pay homage to him. Igwe Amobi accomplished this in 1911 when the Ogidi Native Court was opened.[35]

A few years earlier, Igwe Amobi had brought the Church Missionary Society's Dispensary which had been situated at Ozalla, Onitsha, to Iyi Enu, Ogidi, where it was established as a full-fledged hospital in 1907.[36] This hospital would come to serve all of Igboland as far north as Nsukka Division.[37] Iyi Enu hospital also produced the first set of midwives in the country. It had a Nursing School which was one of the earliest in the country to produce trained nurses.[38] It was also during Igwe Amobi's reign that the Enugu-Onitsha Trunk A road was constructed—a detail that ties together the histories of Walter Amobi with that of the Ogidi women who spearheaded a palaver of unforeseen proportions for the Igwe in 1914. But more about that later.

OGIDI NA-OLU-IGWE—OGIDI PEOPLE ARE ALWAYS WORKING FOR THE IGWE

Walter Amobi was extremely high handed during his reign. He subjected his people to a most gruesome form of forced labor which encouraged the people to call his reign: *Ogidi na-*

otest

olu-Igwe and ... is a
complaint, a... ays
working for ... the
forced tasks, ... nd
the fact that ... e a
metaphor for ... ats
and excesses. ... vy
loads of ceme... nd
which the pec... ial
government o... n-
ment employe... :h
heavy loads an... of
the Igbo week, ... d
connecting On...

that Igwe Amobi provide Ogidi labor to build the first few miles of the road connecting the lands between Idemili River and River Niger before they would step in to complete the job. Igwe Amobi did so, to the share frustration of the Ogidi men and women who were forced to work for him for little or no pay.[42] These same Ogidi individuals were forced in 1912 to labor without payment or reward in the construction of Igwe Amobi's palace.[43] What was more, Amobi was said to have wrongfully arrested countless numbers of people who grieved against him.[44]

Other excesses of Igwe Amobi included forcibly taking men's wives and daughters for himself. The husbands of these women where then obliged to come to Igwe Amobi's palace and take back the bride price paid on their wives, hence representing a forced dissolution of the marriage.[45] Many other Ogidi women were encouraged with the reward of food, to scrub Igwe Amobi's palace with mud and decorate the walls with *nzu* and *uli* powder.[46]

Walter Amobi did not stop there. As Igwe he was entitled to and given the fattest yams of his subjects' harvest. He also bestowed on himself the title, *Ogbu Okoto Koto* or "Master Huntsman" and ruled that he was to be presented with the head and other ritual parts of any significant hunt killed in his community. What was more, in the extraordinary event that a hunter happened to kill a leopard, *agu*, he could not claim to have killed it. The hunter was instead bound to take his kill to Igwe Amobi, who would touch a knife to the throat of the dead leopard consequently symbolizing a transfer of the "killing" from the actual hunter to himself. Moreover, Igwe Amobi positioned himself as the only person in Ogidi who could be saluted *Ogbu Agu*— Killer of Leopards![47] Departure from Igwe Amobi's decrees was severely punished by fines in cash or kind, or worse still, forced exile, for those unfortunate souls who attempted to thwart Igwe's commands.[48]

Additionally, Igwe Amobi took pleasure in forcibly squashing his competition—real or imagined. During his reign, there was a man called Ofoka who claimed to be the Eze of Ikenga. Musicians used to play *ufe*—a musical instrument which only a king could have played for him—whenever he went. Amobi, unlike the rest of his people, refused to see the humor in this man's stance and summarily stopped him from performing *ufe*.[49]

Igwe Amobi also introduced a ceremony called *ite omatu*. During this ceremony women representing the four Ogidi quarters were obliged to make contributions of corn meal and rich stew to the Igwe, which he would in turn use to entertain his guests. He also introduced a rather degrading practice called *ise nni* in which the Igwe would dip a ball of pounded yam into soup and place it on a shrine, then instruct each Ozo titled man, to pick up the food and eat it. More than a few titled men felt belittled and consequently complained about this mistreatment.[50] Igwe Amobi's treatment of the Ozo titleholders was particularly appalling since, Ozo titled holders were regarded as the *nzes*[51] of the community. They were believed to be pure, above blackmail, slander, telling lies or receiving bribes. Ogidi people thus had a saying: *ikpe adi ama Nze*—the *Nze* is never guilty. The judgment of the Ozo titleholders was unquestionable.[52]

So many were his abuses that after Igwe Amobi died in 1925, a request by his son Benjamin to be allowed to ascend to the throne of his father was summarily denied. Igwe Amobi's example consequently gave rise to a 1944 "Igweship Constitution" which stipulated that Igweship in Ogidi would not be hereditary, but rather, open to all eligible sons of Ogidi.[53]

POLITICAL ORGANIZATION IN
PRE-COLONIAL OGIDI

In order to appreciate the gravity of Igwe Amobi's *oke ochichi*—his excesses, abuses and over-governing—a nodding acquaintance with the pre-colonial political governance structure in Ogidi is essential. Pre-colonial governance in Ogidi was a community based democratic model. It consisted of two political constituencies—spiritual and human.[54] In Ogidi, much like the Igbo communities that surrounded her, political and religious life were closely bound together, giving rise to governmental structures that centered on the worship of deities and the veneration of ancestors. This spiritual political constituency was composed of all unseen forces that inhabited the spiritual world. The highest governing body in this constituency was the *egwugwu* council.[55] The *egwugwu* were masquerades representing the spirits of the ancestors of Ogidi. As a spiritual body, they were the supreme political entity, or put differently, the spiritual supreme court of Ogidi and had veto over all human governance.[56] The *egwugwu* council usually met at the *ilo* Akanano, the Akanano village square, or at either one of the major market squares— *Oye Udo, Afor Udo,* or *Nkwo Udo.* The pronouncements of the *egwugwu* council were clothed in an aura of mystery, fear and respect. There were four members of the council, representing the four quarters of Ogidi. *Ububa-Agu,* was "The Leopard" from Akanano quarter; *Okwu Azi,* "Talk of the Youth" was from Uru; *Ajo Ofia* or "Evil Forest" represented the Ikenga quarter and *Onyeka Ozulu,* "The Dreadful" was from Ezinkwo.[57] *Ububa-Agu* was considered the most senior *egwugwu* spirit, and therefore the president of the council. This honor was accorded him because he represented the oldest of the four quarters or sections of Ogidi. The other three *egwugwu* spirits were members of the council. In keeping with the tenets of a democracy, every citizen of Ogidi was free to witness the judicial or legislative proceedings of the *egwugwu* council.[58]

Ogidi also had an *ndieze mmoo* council. The *ndieze mmoo* were the priests and priestesses of the deities. *Eze Ani* was the priest of *Ani*, the most supreme deity in all of Ogidi. *Ani's* legislative power extended over all pronouncements connected with the earth and her festivities. *Eze Udo* was the priest of *Udo*, who embraced all matters relating to the markets;[59] while *Eze Ogwugwu*, the priest of *Ogwugwu* was responsible for all matters connected to general and community sacrifices. Last but not least, there was *Eze Idemili*, the priest of *Idemili*, and his deity covered all issues connected with *eke*, the sacred python as well as all sources of water. There was no central council of the *ndieze mmoo*, rather the respective priests played their roles according to the wishes of their divinities. There were also specific families entrusted with the ministering to these divinities—thus, there were Udo families in Akanano, Uru, Ikenga and Ezinkwo quarters, for instance.[60]

Secret societies also functioned centrally in the governance of Ogidi. Exceptional, post menopausal women were invited to share in the secrets of masquerades, *ima mmoo*, consequently acquiring the privilege of interacting directly with these Ogidi ancestral spirits. The women were bestowed the prestigious title of *Nne Mmoo*—"the mother of the masquerade"—a title which guaranteed them full membership in the male ordered masquerade society of the dead who had returned to life—the spirits of the departed ancestors. Masquerades in Igboland performed many religious, political and social functions in society, such as festivals and burials and it was a mark of extreme honor for a masquerade to appear at a person's burial ceremony. Masquerades also helped guard the town against criminals, pronounced people guilty of offences and collected fines from them. As the spirits of the departed ancestors their judgment was final.[61]

The Ogidi human political constituency was divided into two distinct constituencies—one male and one female. The male section of government was made up of the *ndiichie* council— associations of titled elders who took the Ozo title as well as various other titles. Their role in the political life of Ogidi was primarily executive and judicial, but they also played a major role in the legislature of the town.[62] The absence of a centralized political system in Ogidi gave the *ndiichie* the unique status as the people's representatives. Each of the four quarters of Ogidi had an Eze which represented the highest title in Ogidi—conferred only on those who had taken all of Ogidi's collective titles. What was more, the Eze title was restricted to a few families in the respective quarters. As previously articulated, before Igwe Amobi cemented himself as Eze Ogidi, there was no common Eze for all of Ogidi.[63] The people were in essence the government and their system was extremely decentralized.

There were also various *ogbo* or age gr____ ocieties for men. Composed pri___ily of skilled and able bodied m__ within a four-year age spread, they provided th_____ __ or the running of the _____ *isisekpunti* and _____ __hant grass were _____ __ance of law and _____ __inity law enforce_____ __iblic works like b_____ __n of community _____ __ster community.

The fem__ _____ of the *umuokpu* _____ __pu or council of _____ __er. Made up of al__ _____ __he lineage and le_____ __y functioned pri_____ __y. Their legislatio_____ __d women in Og_____ ___ ___ keeping or violation of _____ _____ation. Ogidi women had no age grade system, they instead used the *umuokpu* as a medium through which they could voice their feelings about things that affected their interests as women in the community. The *Umuokpu Ogidi* served as the human supreme court of society, representing the entire community according to *omenani*—the laws of the land. Similarly, the *umuokpu* councils of each quarter represented the concerns of women in those quarters.[67]

Then there was the *ndinyom* or council of married women. Their council functioned to keep the markets clean on market days. They also served as a lower court in which cases between members could be tried.[68] Their rules and regulations governed the conduct of all married women in Ogidi. They had a central council, Inyom Ogidi, which represented all of Ogidi; and like the *umuokpu* they also had sectional councils which represented all of the quarters namely, Inyom Akanano, Inyom Uru, Inyom Ikenga and Inyom Ezinkwo.[69]

Ogidi women took a title that was similar to the Ozo title held by men. Called the *Ekwe* title, it was exclusively taken by exceptionally accomplished post menopausal married women. *Ekwe* titleholders had to be financially sound—enough so that they could afford to meet all of the expenses associated with the procurement of the title. Like the Ozo title, the prestige and privilege of the *Ekwe* office was enormous. *Ekwe* titleholders were selected to be the leaders and spokeswomen of any women's organization that they belonged to. They also performed legislative and executive functions in the community. They regularly assembled themselves to deliberate over punishments for erring women in their community.[70] *Odu* title was another title available to Ogidi women. *Odu* titleholders were said to *igba odu*, i.e. wear heavy and thick ankle and wrist ivory, and were charged with making laws for womenfolk.[71]

WAS THE PALAVER WITH THE WOMEN AMOBI'S FAULT?[72]

Let us now return to Igwe Amobi's story and his palaver with Ogidi women. As previously discussed, the first decade of the twentieth century ushered in the building and subsequent completion of many colonial Trunk A roads in British colonial Nigeria. During this time a new road connecting Onitsha to Awka was completed. In Igwe Amobi's attempt to attract more attention and customers to Ogidi's major market, Afo Udo, he ordered that the market, which was situated at the interior of Ogidi, be moved closer to the new road.[73] Once the market was moved, the market stalls were upgraded into small huts.

Afo Udo market was owned and protected by the oracle[74] Udo. Every year, as was the custom, Ogidi women held an annual consultation with the oracle's Chief priest, Eze Udo, to find out whether the year would be a good one.[75] During their March 23, 1914 consultation,[76] Eze Udo related Udo's stance to the women. Apparently Udo was angry because his market was moved from its original home.[77] Udo through his chief priest Eze Udo challenged the *Umuokpu Ogidi* saying: "How will the year be good when you were all there and the Afo Udo market was relocated? The year will not be good."[78] The *Umuokpu Ogidi* therefore decided to stop marketing at the new location and immediately send a delegation to see Igwe Amobi about this. Four women from the four quarters of Ogidi were selected to go meet with Amobi. One of the women chosen was Emeghaa from Ezinkwo quarter. Emeghaa was the daughter of Nwodika of Uru-Orji, and her own daughter Ajero was married to Igwe Amobi's cousin Ibaku. Emeghaa, as a result of this relationship went to her in-law and told him about the women's intended mission.[79] Armed with the information of the women's impending visit, Igwe Amobi was able to thwart their mission. He was said to have perched himself on the balcony of his palace, yelling in a loud voice to the approaching women not to dare step foot in his palace! The cowed women representatives consequently retreated to the venue where all the *Umuokpu Ogidi* had gathered for a pre-scheduled discussion of the result of their representatives meeting with the Igwe. When the three women told *Umuokpu Ogidi* that their mission failed because Emeghaa had leaked their intent to the Igwe, the *Umuokpu* decided to go over Igwe Amobi's head and have their case heard in Onitsha by the District Officer.[80] Early the next morning, a delegation of *Umuokpu Ogidi* set off to Onitsha on foot.

Igwe Amobi spoiling for a fight, ordered his servants to bring out his wagon and push him all the way to Onitsha. He consequently arrived Onitsha before the women and was able to deliver the following message to the District Officer: the *Umuokpu Ogidi* were disturbing the peace in Ogidi![81] When the women arrived the court and heard about the Igwe's false allegations, their frustration built and they were said to have taken out their anger on the policemen and *kotmas* (i.e. court messengers) present by fighting with them. The offenders, fourteen in number, were arrested and sentenced to jail. They had to be taken across the River Niger to the Asaba prison by canoe.[82]

Once they got there, their heads were shaven[83]—an unfortunate and grave mistake, because only women who had lost their husbands in death ever shaved their hair in Ogidi. Once news of the arrest got back to the *Umuokpu Ogidi*, they organized and marched six miles, some with their children on their backs, to Onitsha where they staged a massive "sit in" at the District Officer's court.[84] Only women recuperating from childbirth, *omugwo*, were excused. *Umuokpu Ogidi* gathered at the court compound, singing in loud voices that Igwe Amobi had no right to move their market.

Every morning, for several days,[85] the women would return singing and dancing until nightfall. At night, they were put up by their Onitsha women friends who provided them with food and a place to sleep. When the women's food supplies were low, a group of them were sent back to Ogidi to replenish them. Even Ogidi men were involved. Each man contributed yams, vegetables and money—and all these were brought back to Onitsha.[86] In all the time the women were at Onitsha, the market was deserted, and their husbands and homes were uncared for. In other words, Ogidi was brought to a stand still.

Undeterred by the hand fate had supposedly dealt them, fourteen days after their leaders had been jailed, some *Umuokpu Ogidi* attempted a daring rescue of their imprisoned comrades. Their actions were documented in an April 30, 1914 hand written note from the Assistant District Officer of Onitsha, H. Rayner Eaton, to the District Officer of Onitsha. In the letter, Mr. Eaton detailed the women's overt action:

> As you are aware a disturbance took place on 9 April over an attempt to rescue certain convicted prisoners, a previous disturbance was made in Onitsha Court by the Market women of Ogidi on 25 March. I am satisfied that but for the presence of a strong police guard at Ogidi on 29[87] [sic] April a rescue would have been attempted of certain prisoners convicted of conduct likely to cause a breach of the peace by attending a meeting at ABOCHA[88] for

the purpose of subverting the authority of the Hd. Chief
AMOBI."[89]

Their rescue attempt having failed, *Umuokpu Ogidi* consequently
stayed in Onitsha until their leaders were released.

On the day of their scheduled release, *Umuokpu Ogidi*
went to Otu Onitsha market[90] and bought an Ijele masquerade.
Singing and dancing in the company of the masquerade, they
chanted insults to Igwe Amobi and Emeghaa, exclaiming for all
to hear: *"Okwo maka ofu ego na sisi Igba ogo ka Emeghaa ji we lia
uno enu Igba ogo."* — "Is it because of 1 shilling and 6 pence; and
because Emeghaa is trying to be a good in-law, that she was able
to climb the palace stairs and betray us."[91] In order to understand
the magnitude of the women's daring, one has to look to Igbo
culture to ascribe meaning to their actions. Two important truths
can be gleaned from the foregoing. First, the fact that the women
"bought" an Ijele masquerade is quite telling. It represents a
very extreme act because women in Igboland are not allowed to
"buy" or more appropriately put, "create" masked spirits. Their
action, called *itiputa mmoo,* symbolized a dissolution of social
discourse—they were in essence saying that things had gotten
out of hand. What was more, the Ijele masquerade was the most
expensive masked spirit in Igboland and Ijele masquerades were
not known to "come out" frivolously. On the contrary, they
only "came out" during important functions. The women were
therefore saying that extraordinary events call for extraordinary
action; and this palaver with the women was an extraordinary
event! Second, the song that *Umuokpu Ogidi* were singing was in
essence an insult. It evokes the remarkable imagery of Emeghaa
climbing what perhaps would have been the only stairway in
all of Ogidi, a stairway which she could only have had access to
climb because of her relationship with the Igwe! The women proclaimed in song for everyone to hear that Emeghaa had betrayed
the women because she was given such a small bribe by her in-law
the Igwe; and it was because of this bribe that he had granted
her access to his palace—palace grounds that her comrades were
not even allowed to step foot onto! Much of Igwe Amobi's mag-
nificent "upstairs" palace was in fact pre-fabricated and imported

from England! Suspicions loomed far and wide that Amobi had misappropriated the funds raised by the community for the building of St. Philip's Church to build this home.[92]

When the women reached Ogidi, they marched to Igwe Amobi's palace, each wearing a replica of his red chieftaincy cap.[93] Their actions represented a mockery of his office.[94] They then sent young Ogidi boys to clear the original location of their Afo Udo market and on Afo day, the women congregated with food at the rightful marketplace. They also took fighting implements with them, suspecting that Igwe Amobi might send the colonial police after them. Igwe Amobi did not disappoint, as suspected he sent word to the police to go to Afo Udo market. In their company however was the District Officer who just so happened to be visiting with Igwe Amobi. The Igwe cunningly instructed the police escorts to take the D. O. the long route to the market—through the Agbaja to Afo Igwe road—so that the he would be deceived into thinking that the original market location was in fact farther and more remote than it actually was.[95]

When the District Officer arrived Afo Udo market, to his surprise it was full of people. He thus sent for Eze Udo, the chief priest of Udo and through an interpreter asked to find out exactly what the market palaver was about. Eze Udo told the District Officer that his god, Udo, had threatened to kill any person who tampered with his market. He further admonished that his god spared no one, not even the whiteman! He ended his oration with a final promise—that Udo's wrath would be visited upon the family of the guilty party for generations to come, unless that person confessed his crime and appeased him.[96] The D.O. listened anxiously, but intently, and in the end instructed Ogidi people to visit his court later that day so that the case would finally be resolved. One Nwasike took the District Officer on his bicycle to the court, but this time, he took him through the fastest route, so that the D.O. could see how close Afo Udo market was to the court and thus expose Igwe Amobi's craftiness.

At the stipulated time, all Ogidi indigenes gathered at the colonial court, including all the *Umuokpu Ogidi*. The Igwe in preparation for this meeting had offered bribes to Ogbunike and Nkpor people so that they could support him, if it ever came to a vote. An *Umuokpu Ogidi* woman by the name of Anyafulu Kuja Okpegbulu Mmoo[97] however foiled Amobi's cunning by boldly standing up and declaring to the D.O. that men did not know what the palaver with the Igwe was about; that only women were affected, because it was they who earned monies from their marketing at Afo Udo—monies with which they fed their children. She further stated that men busied themselves all day going to the farm and therefore could not know about their palaver with the Igwe. Then, in a loud and persuasive voice, pointing to where Igwe Amobi was seated, she accused him of moving *Umuokpu Ogidi's* market so that their children would die of hunger. She ended by maintaining that all of Ogidi was gathered at the D.O.'s court, because the women refused to take it.[98]

When Anyafulu was done, the D. O. asked the people present to indicate by a show of hands those who wanted Afo Udo to remain in its original location. All Ogidi women and men, including the Nkpor and Ogbunike people whom the Igwe had bribed to support his cause, raised their hands in support of keeping the market in its original location. The Nkpor and Ogbunike people did this because they too had marketed there and had enjoyed it. When the D. O. asked for a show of hands of the people who would like to see the market kept at the disputed location, only members of the Igwe's family raised their hands. The District Officer thus ordered that the market be returned to its original location.[99]

The behavior of the women in the 1914 Ogidi women's market protest can be viewed as an extension of the ways in which Igbo women took care of their interests in pre-colonial society. *Umuokpu Ogidi* employed the group tactics of negotiation, striking, boycotting, sitting in and when all else failed, "making war" on offenders.[100] The first action the women took against Igwe Amobi's decision to move their market was to request that the market be moved back to its original location. This request was in essence a negotiation—the first step that women used to right wrongs done them in pre-colonial society. However a crafty Igwe Amobi thwarted the would-be meeting and as a result the women were forced not only to boycott the moved market, but to stage a "sit in" at the D.O.'s court. All last

This teaches used if your separated from your culture you lose your identity [whereboz7] are.

Umuokpu Ogidi marched 6 miles to Onitsha to call attention to their dilemma. Moreover, had Igwe Amobi not once again thwarted their purpose, the women would have staged a peaceful "sit in"—the next punishment in their traditional progression of sanctions. However, Amobi having not only beat them to the Onitsha Court, but also craftily misrepresented their cause to the District Officer, some very frustrated women broke out in physical protest—we are told beating up the policemen and messengers present. The women's action—of roughing up and beating the offending policemen and messengers—was definitely in keeping with Igbo women's most extreme sanction of "making war on a man." The move however resulted in the colonial government coming down gravely on the women—the conviction, several days in an Asaba prison! Refusing to be deterred, fourteen days later a good number of feisty *Umuokpu* women charged the Asaba prison, attempting to release their leaders. Sadly, this was not to be. It could however be argued that this particular action was also in keeping with "making war" on a man—a sanction that allowed Igbo women in pre-colonial society the prerogative to not only destroy an identified offenders' property, but cause all of his animals—or as in the attempted prison break, people—to be released in just punishment for their crimes.

Since the women's brazen attempt to break their comrades out of prison failed, *Umuokpu Ogidi* settled for staging several "sit ins" at the Onitsha court to protest the relocation of their market. It would appear that the women had indeed learned from the bitter experience of their comrades' arrest and as a result, resorted to non-violent modes of redress. This time, their action involved singing songs that outlined their grievances and proclaiming loud and clear that they refused to market at the new location! Still there are other ways in which the women's "sit in" at Onitsha can be interpreted. We are told that the women dressed in traditional war gear and took over the District Officer's court for several days, singing songs that outlined their grievances. The women's continued and unsettling presence at the District Officer's court, dressed in war gear nonetheless, in more ways than one mimicked their traditional "making war on a man" sanction, which called for women to dress in war gear, smear their bodies with charcoal and then march in warlike precision to an offender's home. *Umuokpu Ogidi's* unsettling daily presence at the D.O.'s court undoubtedly contributed to the release of their leaders.

All the days that *Umuokpu Ogidi* were at Onitsha, they were effectively on strike from their household and community responsibilities. Striking as I mentioned earlier was one of the sanctions that pre-colonial Igbo women employed to punish wrongdoing. Moreover, the fact that the women each wore replicas of their Igwe's chieftaincy cap on their return home could be interpreted as calling into question or mocking the Igwe office and in extension autocratic and absolute masculinities. This behavior was also in keeping with the traditional patterns of employing derisive means to outline women's grievances.

In the final analysis, it is obvious that in contrast to Igwe Amobi's claim that the Ogidi Women's Palaver of 1914 could not have been his fault, because as he so adamantly stated: "woman [sic] does not control a Town";[101] Chief Nwanunu's response was more in keeping with the feelings of *Umuokpu Ogidi* and all of Ogidi: "[The Ogidi Women's Palaver] was Amobi's fault because we said we do not want to alter the Market. . . . The market belongs to the women."[102]

Notes

1. The institution of Igwe is a modern construct. In a non-centralized community, the Igwe represents the traditional ruler, a copy of a "king," but without the overreaching power of a king.

2. *Anam-Agu-Agu* or *Anam-Agu-Nma* is a title that the men born during this time period took and it became the pet name for their age grade. It refers to the "I do not need to count" mentality. In other words the men of this age grade believed that they were so prosperous that they did not need to count their yams (which translates into not needing to count money). The *Anam-Agu-Mma* title celebrated the fact that the members of this age group viewed themselves as very handsome and consequently they did not need to count the number of good looking people in their age grade. Many thanks to Professor Chinua Achebe, Charles P. Stevenson Professor of Literature, Bard College for clarifying

this for me. Chinua Achebe, phone conversation with author, 3 March 2007.

3. Ogidi age grades were organizations of men who are about the same age, give or take four years.

4. Ifeoma Catherine Onwugbufor, "The Evolution of Igwe Chieftaincy in Ogidi" (B.A. Thesis, History Department, University of Nigeria Nsukka, June 1992), 54-55; Dike Ibemesi, *Ogidi: Historical Perspective of a People* (Ogidi, Nigeria: A. C. Ekpechi & Sons, Ltd.), 31.

5. See Chukwuma C.C. Osakwe, "Kingship in Ogidi: The Era of Igwe Amobi I and II, 1904-1973," (B.A. Thesis, Department of History, University of Nigeria, Nsukka, June 1984), 18; Chief Louis Okoye, interview by Chukwuma C. C. Osakwe, Akanano Ogidi, 13 September 1983, in Osakwe, "Kingship in Ogidi," 77; Chief Nwosu Okudo, a.k.a Nwawulu, interview by Edward Dike Ogugua Ibemesi, Ikenga Ogidi, 6 August 1981, in Edward Dike Ogugua Ibemesi, "Iyi-Enu Hospital: Origins and Development, 1907-1982," (B.A. Thesis, History Department, University of Nigeria Nsukka, June 1982), 51

6. Chief Nwosu Nwawulu Enwude, interview by Chukwuma C. C. Osakwe, Ikenga Ogidi, 16 September 1983, in "Kingship in Ogidi," 92.

7. Uta is a feast of great magnitude which happens once a year. In every given Igbo community there is usually that one big festival that is staged to celebrate relationships and friendships. Ogidi people were known to invite their friends and relatives from surrounding villages and towns. It is this invitation that is called uta. The feast is very lavish and a way of keeping friendships and creates unifying influences between neighbors. The people whom you invite are expected to reciprocate at some later time. Many thanks to Professor Chinua Achebe, Charles P. Stevenson Professor of Literature, Bard College, Annandale on Hudson and Professor Christie Achebe, for clarifying this for me. Chinua Achebe, telephone conversation with author, 3 March 2007; Christie Achebe, telephone conversation with author, 3 March 2007.

8. Onwugbufor, "The Evolution of Igwe Chieftaincy in Ogidi," 42; Chief Nwosu Nwawulu, interview by Ifeoma Catherine Onwugbufor, Ikenga Ogidi, 19 February 1992 in Onwugbufor, "Evolution of Chieftaincy in Ogidi," 100; Chinua Achebe, telephone conversation with author, 2 February 2007.

A pawn was an individual who mortgaged her/himself as a security on a loan. Such a person would work for the creditor until the debt was paid. A pawn was however only expected to work for her/his master once in the Igbo week *(izu)*, and thus could use the remaining three days to work towards repaying her/his debt. As such the pawn's freedom was not difficult to obtain, so far as s/he was energetic and hardworking. For more on this, see Nwando Achebe, *Farmers, Traders, Warriors and*

Kings: Female Power and Authority in Northern Igboland, 1900-1960, (Portsmouth, N.H.: Heinemann, 2005), 72-73.

9. See Osakwe, "Kingship in Ogidi," 18; Chief Uzowulu Udo, interview by Chukwuma C.C. Osakwe, Ikenga Ogidi, 28 September 1983, in Osakwe, "Kingship in Ogidi" 109.

10. This school was named after Samuel Ajayi Crowther and Reverend J. C. Taylor who were both Yoruba and Igbo ex-slaves, now missionaries, were instrumental in spreading the word of God throughout Yoruba and Igbolands.

11. Osakwe, "Kingship in Ogidi," 19; Clement Chibuzo Amobi, interview by Chukwuma C. C. Osakwe, Uru Ogidi, 12 December 1983, in Osakwe, "Kingship in Ogidi," 120.

12. See Osakwe, "Kingship in Ogidi," 19; Mr. Haford C. Amerobi, interview by Chukwuma C. C. Osakwe, Uru Ogidi, 21 September 1983, in Osakwe, "Kingship in Ogidi," 107; Clement Chibuzo Amobi, interview by Chukwuma C. C. Osakwe, Uru Ogidi, 12 December 1983, in Osakwe, "Kingship in Ogidi," 120.

13. Ibemesi, *Ogidi: Historical Perspective of a People,* 66-67; Onwugbufor, "The Evolution of Igwe Chieftaincy in Ogidi," 56.

14. Chief Louis Okoye, interview by Chukwuma C. C. Osakwe, Akanano Ogidi, 13 September 1983, in Osakwe, "Kingship in Ogidi," 78; Chief Nwosu Nwawulu, interview by Ifeoma Catherine Onwugbufor, Ikenga Ogidi, 19 February 1992 in Onwugbufor, "Evolution of Chieftaincy in Ogidi," 102; Chief Uzowulu Udo, interview by Chukwuma C. C. Osakwe, Ikenga Ogidi, 28 September 1983, in Osakwe, "Kingship in Ogidi," 109; Mr. M. O. Onwugbufor, interview by Chukwuma C. C. Osakwe, Ezinkwo Ogidi, 3 October 1983, in Osakwe, "Kingship in Ogidi," 114.

15. Chief Lawrence Agulefo, interview by Chukwuma C. C. Osakwe, Ikenga Ogidi, 14 September 1983, in Osakwe, "Kingship in Ogidi," 84; Obiamaka Amaifeobu, "Socio-Religious Importance of Ofala Festival in my Town Ogidi," (Diploma Certificate, Department of Religion, University of Nigeria, Nsukka, June 1986) 10; Mr. M. O. Onwugbufor, interview by Chukwuma C. C. Osakwe, Ezinkwo Ogidi, 3 October 1983, in Osakwe, "Kingship in Ogidi," 115.

16. Chief Lawrence Agulefo interview by Chukwuma C. C. Osakwe, Ikenga Ogidi, 14 September 1983, in Osakwe, "Kingship in Ogidi," 84; Chief Louis Okoye, interview by Chukwuma C. C. Osakwe, Akanano Ogidi, 13 September 1983, in Osakwe, "Kingship in Ogidi," 77.

17. Chief Lawrence Agulefo interview by Chukwuma C. C. Osakwe, Ikenga Ogidi, 14 September 1983, in Osakwe, "Kingship in Ogidi," 84; Amaifeobu, "Socio-Religious Importance of Ofala Festival," 10; Chief

Nwosu Nwawulu Enwude, interview by Chukwuma C. C. Osakwe, Ikenga Ogidi, 16 September 1983, in Osakwe, "Kingship in Ogidi," 92; Chief Uzowulu Udo, interview by Chukwuma C. C. Osakwe, Ikenga Ogidi, 28 September 1983, in Osakwe, "Kingship in Ogidi," 110.

18. Testimony by Warrant Chief Nwanunu of Ikenga Ogidi recorded in colonial document, NAE, O.P. 174/1914 ONPROF 7/1/13, "Complaint By Certain Villages of Ogidi Against Chief Amobi," 4.

19. While the word Eze literally means king, the title was more honorific than real, breathing life into the ancient wisdom of the famous Igbo adage; *Igbo enwero eze*—the Igbo have no kings.

20. Akananso quarter is made up of the following four villages: Ire, Ezi-Ogidi, Abo, Umuru

21. Uru quarter is made up of the following eight villages: Ntukwulu, Ajilija, Adazi, Umu Udoma, Uru Ezealo, Uru Oji, Umu Anugwo, Ogwugwuagu

22. Ezinkwo is made up of two main villages: Ogidi Ani and Nkwelle-Ogidi

23. There are 4 villages in Ikenga, namely, Obodokwe, Anugwu, Nanri and Odida.

24. The same was true of the famous Warrant Chief in Nsukka Division, King Ahebi Ugbabe, who was in fact the only female Warrant Chief in all of colonial Nigeria. See Nwando Achebe, "And She Became a Man: King Ahebi Ugbabe in the History of Enugu-Ezike, Northern Igboland, 1880-1948" in Stephan F. Miescher and Lisa A. Lindsay, eds. *Men and Masculinities in Modern African* History (Portsmouth, NH: Heinemann, 2003), 52-68; and Achebe, *Farmers, Traders, Warriors and Kings*, 197-224; for more on this famous Warrant Chief.

25. The Ozo title was the highest, but one title available to Igbo men in Ogidi at the time.

26. Amobi's Ozo title, Kwochaka, which literally means— "someone who washed his hands" perhaps alluding to that Igbo proverb which holds that a child has to wash his hands before he can eat with elders—had to be taken before he was crowned "king" in accordance with Ogidi custom. Chief Nwosu Nwawulu Enwude, interview by Chukwuma C. C. Osakwe, Ikenga Ogidi, 16 September 1983, in Osakwe, "Kingship in Ogidi," 91; Chief Louis Okoye, interview by Chukwuma C. C. Osakwe, Akanano Ogidi, 13 September 1983, in Osakwe, "Kingship in Ogidi," 78; Chief Nwosu Nwawulu, interview by Ifeoma Catherine Onwugbufor, Ikenga Ogidi, 19 February 1992 in Onwugbufor, "Evolution of Chieftaincy in Ogidi," 102 and 108; Ezennia Okolonkwo Mbelu, interview by Ifeoma Catherine Onwugbufor, Ikenga Ogidi, 20 February 1992 in Onwugbufor, "Evolution of Chieftaincy in Ogidi," 109.

27. NAE, OP 81 Vol II, ONDIST 7/1/7, B. G. Stone, "Report on the Villages of OGIDI and ABACHA at Present Included in the Ogidi Native Court Area of the Onitsha Division," 7-8. See also Chief Louis Okoye, interview by Chukwuma C. C. Osakwe, Akanano Ogidi, 13 September 1983, in Osakwe, "Kingship in Ogidi," 78; Chief Lawrence Agulefo, interview by Chukwuma C. C. Osakwe, Ikenga Ogidi, 14 September 1983, in Osakwe, "Kingship in Ogidi," 84; Chief Uzowulu Udo, interview by Chukwuma C. C. Osakwe, Ikenga Ogidi, 28 September 1983, in Osakwe, "Kingship in Ogidi," 110.

28. See NAE, O.P. 174/1914 ONPROF 7/1/13, "Complaint By Certain Villages of Ogidi Against Chief Amobi," 4 where Chief Nwanunu asserted that, "We never had king."

29. See footnote 1 for an explanation of this concept. See also Obiora Eugene Nwabufo, "Traditional Law and Colonial Change in Ogidi," (B.A. Thesis, Department of History, University of Nigeria, Nsukka, June 1979), 9.

30. NAE, O.P. 1520 23/2/1937 ONDIST 12/1/1082, "Biographical Note on the Honourable B. O. E. Amobi of Ogidi, Onitsha Province (Signed) C. H. Cronsdale, Ag. District Office Onitsha Division," in "Amobi (Honourable) B. O. E. Papers Concerning," 5.

31. A number of collaborators assert that the Ogidi people did not realize what was happening when Amobi made himself Igwe. According to some collaborators Amobi presented the Ogidi people with a cow, which they thought was in appreciation for the land that they had given him to build a house, but in fact he claimed that he had presented the cow to Ogidi people for his coronation ceremony as Igwe. He suggested that the Ogidi people had in fact crowned him Igwe. This collaborator further explained: "We could not do anything about the way he was crowned because he was the only learned man. He can bring the white man into Ogidi to deal with us. So we accepted him as the Igwe." Chief Nwosu Nwawulu Enwude, interview by Chukwuma C. C. Osakwe, Ikenga Ogidi, 16 September 1983, in Osakwe, "Kingship in Ogidi," 91. Another collaborator stated: "The people were ignorant of the way Amobi I was chosen as Igwe, and as such, there was no opposition to Amobi's choice and moreover to get something from the British government, you had to go through Igwe Amobi I."Chief Louis Okoye, interview by Chukwuma C. C. Osakwe, Akanano Ogidi, 13 September 1983, in Osakwe, "Kingship in Ogidi," 78.

32. Chief Nwosu Nwawulu Enwude, interview by Chukwuma C. C. Osakwe, Ikenga Ogidi, 16 September 1983, in Osakwe, "Kingship in Ogidi," 91.

33. Chief Onyeama was Warrant Chief of Eke of whom John P. Jordan wrote in his acclaimed book, *Bishop Shanahan of Southern Nigeria*

(Dublin, 1971), 136. "This particular chief would deserve a history to himself; for he was probably the only Igbo ruler whose word was law." Others say he was way way before his time."

34. Ibemesi, *Ogidi: Historical Perspective of a People,* 66.

35. NAE, OP 81 Vol II, ONDIST 7/1/7, B. G. Stone, "Report on the Villages of OGIDI and ABACHA at Present Included in the Ogidi Native Court Area of the Onitsha Division," 5; Ibemesi, *Ogidi: Historical Perspective of a People,* 67.

36. Ibemesi, *Ogidi: Historical Perspective of a People,* 62; Chief Nwosu Okudo, a.k.a Nwawulu, interview by Edward Dike Ogugua Ibemesi, Ikenga Ogidi, 6 August 1981, in Ibemesi, "Iyi-Enu Hospital," 51.

37. In fact one of Warrant Chief and King Ahebi Ugbabe's adopted children, Wilfred Ogara recalls journeying all the way from Enugu-Ezike to Iyi Enu, so that his wife could give birth. Wilfred Ogara, Ahebi Ugbabe non-biological son, interview by author, tape recording, Umuida, Enugu-Ezike, Enugu State, 25 November 1996.

38. Ibemesi, *Ogidi: Historical Perspective of a People,* 103.

39. Chief Lawrence Agulefo, interview by Chukwuma C. C. Osakwe, Ikenga Ogidi, 14 September 1983, in Osakwe, "Kingship in Ogidi," 86; Mr. M. O. Onwugbufor, interview by Chukwuma C. C. Osakwe, Ezinkwo Ogidi, 3 October 1983, in Osakwe, "Kingship in Ogidi," 116; Chinua Achebe, phone conversation with author, 1 August 2007.

40. Ibemesi, *Ogidi: Historical Perspective of a People,* 67; Chief Louis Okoye, interview by Chukwuma C. C. Osakwe, Akanano Ogidi, 13 September 1983, in Osakwe, "Kingship in Ogidi," 77; Chief Nwosu Nwawulu Enwude, interview by Chukwuma C. C. Osakwe, Ikenga Ogidi, 16 September 1983, in Osakwe, "Kingship in Ogidi," 94.

41. Ibemesi, *Ogidi: Historical Perspective of a People,* 120; Chief Louis Okoye, interview by Chukwuma C. C. Osakwe, Akanano Ogidi, 13 September 1983, in Osakwe, "Kingship in Ogidi," 79; Chief Lawrence Agulefo, interview by Chukwuma C. C. Osakwe, Ikenga Ogidi, 14 September 1983, in Osakwe, "Kingship in Ogidi," 86.

42. Chinua Achebe, phone conversation with author, 1 August 2007; Ezennia Okolonkwo Mbelu, interview by Ifeoma Catherine Onwugbufor, Ikenga Ogidi, 20 February 1992 in Onwugbufor, "Evolution of Chieftaincy in Ogidi," 109; Chief Louis Okoye, interview by Chukwuma C. C. Osakwe, Akanano Ogidi, 13 September 1983, in Osakwe, "Kingship in Ogidi," 79; Chief Akunwafor Osegbo, interview by Chukwuma C. C. Osakwe, Ezinkwo Ogidi, 19 September 1983, in Osakwe, "Kingship in Ogidi," 92; Mr. Haford C. Amerobi, interview by Chukwuma C. C. Osakwe, Uru Ogidi, 21 September 1983, in Osakwe, "Kingship in Ogidi," 108; Chief Uzowulu Udo, interview by Chukwuma C. C.

Osakwe, Ikenga Ogidi, 28 September 1983, in Osakwe, "Kingship in Ogidi," 111. Another such road project was the road from the Public Works Department to Idemili Obosi stream. The men had to collect red sand that was used in the construction of this particular road. See Chief Nwosu Nwawulu Enwude, interview by Chukwuma C. C, Osakwe, Ikenga Ogidi, 16 September 1983, in Osakwe, "Kingship in Ogidi," 93.

43. Hand written note dated April 30, 1914 from the Assistant District Officer of Onitsha, H. Rayner Eaton to the District Officer of Onitsha, outlining Ogidi peoples grievances against Igwe Amobi, NAE, O.P. 174/1914 ONPROF 7/1/13, "Complaint By Certain Villages of Ogidi Against Chief Amobi," 1 and 2.

44. Hand written note dated April 30, 1914 from the Assistant District Officer of Onitsha, H. Rayner Eaton to the District Officer of Onitsha, outlining Ogidi peoples grievances against Igwe Amobi, NAE, O.P. 174/1914 ONPROF 7/1/13, "Complaint By Certain Villages of Ogidi Against Chief Amobi," 1.

45. Ibemesi, *Ogidi: Historical Perspective of a People,* 68; Ezennia Okolonkwo Mbelu, interview by Ifeoma Catherine Onwugbufor, Ikenga Ogidi, 20 February 1992 in Onwugbufor, "Evolution of Chieftaincy in Ogidi," 109.

46. *Nzu* was a white chalk and *uli* was a dark color traditionally used by Igbo women to decorate their bodies. They also used these chalks to decorate the outside of their homes. Iyom Odenkwo Ekobi-Onwugbufor, interview by Ifeoma Catherine Onwugbufor, Nkwelle Ogidi, 25 February 1992 in Onwugbufor, "Evolution of Chieftaincy in Ogidi," 120.

47. Chinua Achebe, telephone conversation with author, 9 August 2007.

48. Amaifeobu, "Socio-Religious Importance of Ofala Festival," 11; Chief Nwosu Nwawulu Enwude, interview by Chukwuma C. C. Osakwe, Ikenga Ogidi, 16 September 1983, in Osakwe, "Kingship in Ogidi," 93.

49. Chinua Achebe, telephone conversation with author, 9 August 2007.

50. Amaifeobu, "Socio-Religious Importance of Ofala Festival," 11.

51. *Nze* means a titled man. *Ndi Nze* means titled men.

52. Florence Chinyere Ndukwe, "Burial Rites Given to Title Holders in Ogidi, Idemili Local Government Area, Anambra State," (Diploma Certificate, Department of Religion, University of Nigeria, Nsukka, June 1986), 10.

53. Ibemesi, *Ogidi: Historical Perspective of a People,* 72

54. For more on this, see Achebe, *Farmers, Traders, Warriors and Kings,* 161-173.

55. Nwosu Nwawulu, interview by Obiora Eugene Nwabufo, Ikenga Ogidi, 20 September 1978 in Eugene, "Traditional Law and Colonial Change in

Ogidi," 73; Uzowulu Ezekwesili, interview by Obiora Eugene Nwabufo, Ikenga Ogidi, 10 September 1978 in Nwabufo, "Traditional Law and Colonial change in Ogidi," 74; Ezigbo Otue Unachukwu, interview by Obiora Eugene Nwabufo, Uru Ogidi, 28 September 1978, in Nwabufo, "Traditional Law and Colonial Change in Ogidi," 76; Udozoba Okoye, interview by Obiora Eugene Nwabufo, Ikenga Ogidi, 17 December 1978, in Nwabufo, "Traditional Law and Colonial Change in Ogidi," 78; Chief Nwosu Nwawulu, interview by Ifeoma Catherine Onwugbufor, Ikenga Ogidi, 19 February 1992 in Onwugbufor, "Evolution of Chieftaincy in Ogidi," 100; Iyom Odenkwo Ekobi-Onwugbufor, interview by Ifeoma Catherine Onwugbufor, Nkwelle Ogidi, 25 February 1992 in Onwugbufor, "Evolution of Chieftaincy in Ogidi," 121.

56. Nwosu Nwawulu, interview by Obiora Eugene Nwabufo, Ikenga Ogidi, 20 September 1978 in Nwabufo, "Traditional Law and Colonial Change in Ogidi," 73.

57. Nwabufo, "Traditional Law and Colonial Change in Ogidi," 3.

58. Nwabufo, "Traditional Law and Colonial Change in Ogidi," 5

59. We will see Eze Udo and Udo in action as the circumstances that led to the Ogidi women's palaver unfolds.

60. Nwabufo, "Traditional Law and Colonial Change in Ogidi," 5-6; Udozoba Okoye, interview by Obiora Eugene Nwabufo, Ikenga Ogidi, 17 December 1978, in Nwabufo, "Traditional Law and Colonial Change in Ogidi," 78; Okeru Nnabenyi, interview by Obiora Eugene Nwabufo, Ezinkwo Ogidi, 7 August 1978, in Nwabufo, "Traditional Law and Colonial Change in Ogidi," 84; Okeru Okwesi, interview by Obiora Eugene Nwabufo, Ezinkwo Ogidi, 5 August 1978, in Nwabufo, "Traditional Law and Colonial Change in Ogidi," 86; Chief Lawrence Agulefo, interview by Chukwuma C. C. Osakwe, Ikenga Ogidi, 14 September 1983, in Osakwe, "Kingship in Ogidi," 83; Chief Lawrence Agulefo, interview by Chukwuma C. C. Osakwe, Ikenga Ogidi, 14 September 1983, in Osakwe "Kingship in Ogidi," 85.

61. Ndukwe, "Burial Rites Given to Title Holders in Ogidi," 14-15; Osakwe, "Kingship in Ogidi," 6-7; Chief Louis Okoye, interview by Chukwuma C. C. Osakwe, Akanano Ogidi, 13 September 1983, in Osakwe, "Kingship in Ogidi," 82.

62. Udozoba Okoye, interview by Obiora Eugene Nwabufo, Ikenga Ogidi, 17 December 1978, in Nwabufo, "Traditional Law and Colonial Change in Ogidi," 78; Okodo Mgbochi, interview by Obiora Eugene Nwabufo, Akanano Ogidi, 1 December 1978, in Nwabufo, "Traditional Law and Colonial Change in Ogidi," 80.

63. Nwabufo, "Traditional Law and Colonial Change in Ogidi," .7-8; Chief Lawrence Agulefo, interview by Chukwuma C. C. Osakwe, Ikenga Ogidi, 14 September 1983, in Osakwe, "Kingship in Ogidi," 83; Chief

Lawrence Agulefo, interview by Chukwuma C. C. Osakwe, Ikenga Ogidi, 14 September 1983, in Osakwe, "Kingship in Ogidi," 84.

64. Nwabufo, "Traditional Law and Colonial Change in Ogidi," 10.

65. Osakwe, "Kingship in Ogidi," 6.

66. Nwabufo, "Traditional Law and Colonial Change in Ogidi," 2; Chief Louis Okoye, interview by Chukwuma C. C. Osakwe, Akanano Ogidi, 13 September 1983, in Osakwe, "Kingship in Ogidi," 81.

67. Nwabufo, "Traditional Law and Colonial Change in Ogidi," 10-11 and 26; Nwosu Nwawulu, interview by Obiora Eugene Nwabufo, Ikenga Ogidi, 20 September 1978 in Nwabufo, "Traditional Law and Colonial Change in Ogidi," 73; Uzowulu Ezekwesili, interview by Obiora Eugene Nwabufo, Ikenga Ogidi, 10 September 1978 in Nwabufo, "Traditional Law and Colonial Change in Ogidi," 74; Udozoba Okoye, interview by Obiora Eugene Nwabufo, Ikenga Ogidi, 17 December 1978, in Nwabufo, "Traditional Law and Colonial Change in Ogidi," 78; Okeru Okwesi, interview by Obiora Eugene Nwabufo, Ezinkwo Ogidi, 5 August 1978, in Nwabufo, "Traditional Law and Colonial Change in Ogidi," 87; Chief Lawrence Agulefo, interview by Chukwuma C. C. Osakwe, Ikenga Ogidi, 14 September 1983, in Osakwe, "Kingship in Ogidi," 83.

68. Udozoba Okoye, interview by Obiora Eugene Nwabufo, Ikenga Ogidi, 17 December 1978, in Nwabufo, "Traditional Law and Colonial Change in Ogidi," 78; Osakwe, "Kingship in Ogidi," 2.

69. Nwabufo, "Traditional Law and Colonial Change in Ogidi," 11 and 26; Okeru Nnabenyi, interview by Obiora Eugene Nwabufo, Ezinkwo Ogidi, 7 August 1978, in Nwabufo, "Traditional Law and Colonial Change in Ogidi," 84.

70. Ndukwe, "Burial Rites Given to Title Holders in Ogidi," 14.

71. Osakwe, "Kingship in Ogidi," 8.

72. NAE, O.P. 174/1914 ONPROF 7/1/13, "Complaint by Certain Villages of Ogidi Against Chief Amobi," 5.

73. Iyom Odenkwo Ekobi-Onwugbufor, interview by Ifeoma Catherine Onwugbufor, Nkwelle Ogidi, 25 February 1992 in Onwugbufor, "Evolution of Chieftaincy in Ogidi," 120; Osakwe, "Kingship in Ogidi," 27; Mr. M. O. Onwugbufor, interview by Chukwuma C. C. Osakwe, Ezinkwo Ogidi, 3 October 1983, in Osakwe, "Kingship in Ogidi," 116; NAE, O.P. 174/1914 ONPROF 7/1/13, "Complaint By Certain Villages of Ogidi Against Chief Amobi," 2; Chief Lawrence Agulefo, interview by Chukwuma C. C. Osakwe, Ikenga Ogidi, 14 September 1983, in Osakwe, "Kingship in Ogidi," 86; Chief Nwosu Nwawulu Enwude, interview by Chukwuma C. C. Osakwe, Ikenga Ogidi, 16 September 1983, in Osakwe, "Kingship in Ogidi," 93; Chigioke, Ozo

titleholder, Uru, Ogidi, testimony entitled "Ogidi Palaver" in NAE, O.P. 174/1914 ONPROF 7/1/13, "Complaint By Certain Villages of Ogidi Against Chief Amobi," 6; Amobi, Igwe Ogidi, testimony entitled "Ogidi Palaver" NAE, O.P. 174/1914 ONPROF 7/1/13, "Complaint By Certain Villages of Ogidi Against Chief Amobi," 7. Igwe Amobi in his own defense claimed that it was a joint decision between him and his other chiefs to move the market. Here is his testimony: "The Market was arranged with the other Chiefs as I thought it would be a good thing, but to my astonishment they stopped the market." Amobi, Igwe Ogidi, testimony entitled "Ogidi Palaver" in NAE, O.P. 174/1914 ONPROF 7/1/13, "Complaint by Certain Villages of Ogidi against Chief Amobi," 7. This was not the only conflict Igwe Amobi had with Ogidi women. During his reign he ruled that women could no longer wear ankle bells when they were dancing, because the Igwe reserved this privilege for himself during his annual Ofala festival. Ogidi women refused to abide by this regulation, and protested this rule in a demonstration in which they marched wearing these bells. Their leaders were thrown in prison, but this did not deter them. For more on this see Amaifeobu, "Socio-Religious Importance of Ofala Festival," 11.

74. I use the terms oracle and god interchangeably because while Udo was a god, he also filled an oracular purpose in society.

75. Chinua Achebe, telephone conversation with author, 1 March 1995; Ndukwe, "Burial Rites Given to Title Holders in Ogidi," 6; Nwosu Nwaaulu, interview by Ifeoma Catherine Onwugbufor, Ikenga Ogidi, 19 February 1992, in Onwugbufor, "The Evolution of Chieftaincy in Ogidi," 103.

76. I am able to comfortably establish that this consultation must have taken place on or around March 23, 1914, by using colonial documentation, which places the Ogidi women's disturbance at Onitsha as occurring on March 25, 1914. We know that *Umuokpu Ogidi* decided to take their case to Onitsha a day after Igwe Amobi refused to grant them audience at his palace. It is a likely assumption that *Umuokpu Ogidi* after hearing Eze Udo's charge, moved to see Igwe Amobi immediately. Therefore, it is safe to say that the consultation with Eze Udo would have occurred on or around March 23, 1914. See, Hand written note dated April 30, 1914 from the Assistant District Officer of Onitsha, H. Rayner Eaton to the District Officer of Onitsha, outlining Ogidi peoples grievances against Igwe Amobi, NAE, O.P. 174/1914 ONPROF 7/1/13, "Complaint By Certain Villages of Ogidi Against Chief Amobi," 4. It reads in part, "…a previous disturbance was made in Onitsha court by the Market women of Ogidi on 25 March."

77. Chinua Achebe, conversation with author, 1 March 1995; Nwosu Nwaaulu, interview by Ifeoma Catherine Onwugbufor, Ikenga Ogidi, 19 February 1992, in Onwugbufor, "The Evolution of Chieftaincy in

Ogidi," 103; Chief Nwosu Nwawulu Enwude, interview by Chukwuma C. C. Osakwe, Ikenga Ogidi, 16 September 1983, in Osakwe, "Kingship in Ogidi," 94.

78. Nwosu Nwaaulu, interview by Ifeoma Catherine Onwugbufor, Ikenga Ogidi, 19 February 1992, in Onwugbufor, "The Evolution of Chieftaincy in Ogidi," 103.

79. Nwosu Nwaaulu, interview by Ifeoma Catherine Onwugbufor, Ikenga Ogidi, 19 February 1992, in Onwugbufor, "The Evolution of Chieftaincy in Ogidi," 104; Chief Nwosu Nwawulu Enwude, interview by Chukwuma C. C. Osakwe, Ikenga Ogidi, 16 September 1983, in Osakwe, "Kingship in Ogidi," 94.

80. Nwosu Nwaaulu, interview by Ifeoma Catherine Onwugbufor, Ikenga Ogidi, 19 February 1992, in Onwugbufor, "The Evolution of Chieftaincy in Ogidi," 104; Iyom Odenkwo Ekobi-Onwugbufor, interview by Ifeoma Catherine Onwugbufor, Nkwelle Ogidi, 25 February 1992 in Onwugbufor, "Evolution of Chieftaincy in Ogidi," 121.

81. Nwosu Nwaaulu, interview by Ifeoma Catherine Onwugbufor, Ikenga Ogidi, 19 February 1992, in Onwugbufor, "The Evolution of Chieftaincy in Ogidi," 104; Chief Nwosu Nwawulu Enwude, interview by Chukwuma C. C. Osakwe, Ikenga Ogidi, 16 September 1983, in Osakwe, "Kingship in Ogidi," 94.

82. Nwosu Nwaaulu, interview by Ifeoma Catherine Onwugbufor, Ikenga Ogidi, 19 February1992, in Onwugbufor, "The Evolution of Chieftaincy in Ogidi," 104; Iyom Odenkwo Ekobi-Onwugbufor, interview by Ifeoma Catherine Onwugbufor, Nkwelle Ogidi, 25 February 1992 in Onwugbufor, "Evolution of Chieftaincy in Ogidi,' 121; Chief Lawrence Agulefo, interview by Chukwuma C. C. Osakwe, Ikenga Ogidi, 14 September 1983, in Osakwe, "Kingship in Ogidi," 86; NAE, O.P. 174/1914 ONPROF 7/1/13, "Complaint By Certain Villages of Ogidi Against Chief Amobi," 2; Ekuwah, Ozo titleholder, Ezinkwo, Ogidi testimony entitled "Ogidi Palaver" in NAE, O.P. 174/1914 ONPROF 7/1/13, "Complaint By Certain Villages of Ogidi Against Chief Amobi," 5; Chigioke, Ozo titleholder, Uru, Ogidi, testimony entitled "Ogidi Palaver" in NAE, O.P. 174/1914 ONPROF 7/1/13, "Complaint By Certain Villages of Ogidi Against Chief Amobi," 6; Amobi, Igwe Ogidi, testimony entitled "Ogidi Palaver" in NAE, O.P. 174/1914 ONPROF 7/1/13, "Complaint By Certain Villages of Ogidi Against Chief Amobi," 7.

83. NAE, O.P. 174/1914 ONPROF 7/1/13, "Complaint By Certain Villages of Ogidi Against Chief Amobi,"2; Ekuwah, Ozo titleholder, Ezinkwo, Ogidi testimony entitled "Ogidi Palaver," in NAE, O.P. 174/1914 ONPROF 7/1/13, "Complaint By Certain Villages of Ogidi Against Chief Amobi," 5; Chigioke, Ozo titleholder, Uru, Ogidi, tes-

timony entitled "Ogidi Palaver" in NAE, O.P. 174/1914 ONPROF 7/1/13, "Complaint By Certain Villages of Ogidi Against Chief Amobi," 6; Amobi, Igwe Ogidi, testimony entitled "Ogidi Palaver" in NAE, O.P. 174/1914 ONPROF 7/1/13, "Complaint By Certain Villages of Ogidi Against Chief Amobi," 7.

84. Iyom Odenkwo Ekobi-Onwugbufor, interview by Ifeoma Catherine Onwugbufor, Nkwelle Ogidi, 25 February 1992 in Onwugbufor, "Evolution of Chieftaincy in Ogidi," 121.

85. One collaborator suggested that the women were imprisoned for 14 days, but in my calculation it must have been many more than 14 days, because according to a Hand written note dated April 30, 1914 from the Assistant District Officer of Onitsha, H. Rayner Eaton to the District Officer of Onitsha, outlining Ogidi peoples grievances against Igwe Amobi, NAE, O.P. 174/1914 ONPROF 7/1/13, "Complaint By Certain Villages of Ogidi Against Chief Amobi," 4, the women attempted a rescue their leaders from prison on April 9, 1914, which is exactly 14 days after these women leaders were imprisoned.

86. Nwosu Nwaaulu, interview by Ifeoma Catherine Onwugbufor, Ikenga Ogidi, 19 February 1992, in Onwugbufor, "The Evolution of Chieftaincy in Ogidi," 105.

87. I believe that Assistant District Officer Eaton made a mistake in his write up. In my opinion, he meant to have written April 9th, which was the date that he was writing about originally.

88. Abocha and Afudo are referenced earlier in the letter as markets. Afudo, obviously refers to the market in contention, Afo Udo market. Abocha is a bit harder to place. It perhaps is one of the much smaller markets in Ogidi.

89. Hand written note dated April 30, 1914 from the Assistant District Officer of Onitsha, H. Rayner Eaton to the District Officer of Onitsha, outlining Ogidi peoples grievances against Igwe Amobi, NAE, O.P. 174/1914 ONPROF 7/1/13, "Complaint By Certain Villages of Ogidi Against Chief Amobi," 4.

90. Out Onitsha market was located at the river bank.

91. Nwosu Nwaaulu, interview by Ifeoma Catherine Onwugbufor, Ikenga Ogidi, 19 February 1992, in Onwugbufor, "The Evolution of Chieftaincy in Ogidi," 105.

92. Chinua Achebe, telephone conversation with author, 9 August 2007. This fact is also alluded to in Hand written note dated April 30, 1914 from the Assistant District Officer of Onitsha, H. Rayner Eaton to the District Officer of Onitsha, outlining Ogidi peoples grievances against Igwe Amobi, NAE, O.P. 174/1914 ONPROF 7/1/13, "Complaint By Certain Villages of Ogidi Against Chief Amobi," 2. Specifically, Igwe

Amobi was accused of stealing £40 that Ogidi people had raised to build a church.

93. It was Igwe Amobi who introduced the wearing of the red chieftaincy cap to Ogidi.

94. Chinua Achebe, telephone conversation with author, March 1, 1995.

95. Nwosu Nwaaulu, interview by Ifeoma Catherine Onwugbufor, Ikenga Ogidi, 19 February 1992, in Onwugbufor, "The Evolution of Chieftaincy in Ogidi," 105.

96. Nwosu Nwaaulu, interview by Ifeoma Catherine Onwugbufor, Ikenga Ogidi, 19 February 1992, in Onwugbufor, "The Evolution of Chieftaincy in Ogidi," 106.

97. Anyafulu's full name was in essence a praise, which stated: "Your eye sees me, you are startled or terrified, because I defeated the masquerade." The masquerade in this praise most likely refers to both Igwe Amobi and the British District Officer.

98. Nwosu Nwaaulu, interview by Ifeoma Catherine Onwugbufor, Ikenga Ogidi, 19 February1992, in Onwugbufor, "The Evolution of Chieftaincy in Ogidi," 106.

99. Nwosu Nwaaulu, interview by Ifeoma Catherine Onwugbufor, Ikenga Ogidi, 19 February 1992, in Onwugbufor, "The Evolution of Chieftaincy in Ogidi," 107; Iyom Odenkwo Ekobi-Onwugbufor, interview by Ifeoma Catherine Onwugbufor, Nkwelle Ogidi, 25 February 1992 in Onwugbufor, "Evolution of Chieftaincy in Ogidi," 121; Osakwe, "Kingship in Ogidi," 27; Chinua Achebe, telephone conversation with author, 1 March 1995; Chief Lawrence Agulefo, interview by Chukwuma C. C. Osakwe, Ikenga Ogidi, 14 September 1983, in Osakwe, "Kingship in Ogidi," 86; Mr. M. O. Onwugbufor, interview by Chukwuma C. C. Osakwe, Ezinkwo Ogidi, 3 October 1983, in Osakwe, "Kingship in Ogidi," 116.

100. For more on strategies of female resistance in Igboland, see Achebe, *Farmers, Traders, Warriors and Kings*, 173-187.

101. Amobi, Igwe Ogidi, testimony entitled "Ogidi Palaver," in NAE, O.P. 174/1914 ONPROF 7/1/13, "Complaint by Certain Villages of Ogidi against Chief Amobi," 9.

102. Chief Nwanunu, Warrant Chief, Ikenga Quarter, testimony entitled "Ogidi Palaver," in NAE, O.P. 174/1914 ONPROF 7/1/13, "Complaint By Certain Villages of Ogidi Against Chief Amobi," 9.

Chapter 3

WOMEN AND PEASANT MOVEMENT IN COLONIAL EASTERN NIGERIA

Chima J. Korieh

INTRODUCTION

Studies of protest movements have been dominated by two important theoretical and empirical persuasions character-ized by new social movement theories in the tradition of Alberto Melucci and Alain Touraine and the political process approach associated with Charles Tilly, David Snow, Mayer Zald, and others. This binary divide has failed to incorporate less institu-tionalized forms of protest, as Michel Foucault[1] has indicated, or what James Scott calls "everyday forms of resistance"[2] and the forms of consciousness that give rise to them.

While comparative studies of protest movements have been conducted in the search for a comprehensive analytical framework, research has taken place at the margins of a more all-encompassing endeavor to explain protest movements and the intellectual traditions that sustain them in different cultural and historical contexts. Clearly, the analysis of social movements in non-western societies raises the issue of framing and how movement leaders emerge and articulate the concerns of their followers.

Attention has been drawn to the ambiguous nature of resistance, which often goes beyond domination versus resistance or institutionalized forms of power.[3] In an illuminating commentary on social movements, Irving M. Zeitlin identifies four factors that underpin most social movements. First is *discontent*, which involves the existence of widespread dissatisfaction with existing conditions. The second is the existence of an *ideology* that appeals to the discontent and through which they articulate conceived change and the process of action. The third is the existence of *leaders* who could articulate the issues, inspire the masses, spread the ideology and create an organization capable of managing the day to day activities of the movement. The fourth factor is the availability of enough *power resources*, both human and material, to challenge the prevailing social order.[4] Zeitlin's analytical framework underscores the importance of *discontent*, *ideology* and *leadership* in providing opportunity to both the instrumentalists and partisans and provides valuable insight that could be applied to specific historical examples.

Historical and anthropological research in Africa has illustrated the importance of "traditional" discourses and cultural elements in the formulation of anti-colonial discourses.[5] Such ethnographically focused studies have infused indigenous ideologies in the emergence of intellectuals. Steven Feierman, for example, points to the ability of peasants to draw upon "a rich variety of past forms of political language" in defining and achieving political objectives.[6] Central to Feierman's analysis is that peasant political movements often reflect their attempts to deal with everyday issues of survival.[7] This framework illustrates the importance of cultural elements and ideology in framing social movements.[8]

This chapter places the above commentary in the context of a remarkable revolt that occurred in the Eastern Nigerian countryside in 1929 following the implementation of the Native Revenue

(Amendment) Ordinance of 1927. The Ordinance introduced direct tax on men in 1928. Between November and December 1929, large numbers of peasant women protested the perceived extension of direct tax on women. At its peak, rural women obstructed roads, destroyed and damaged native court houses, and looted some European trading firms. They attacked the houses of the native court personnel and the British appointed warrant chiefs who were the representatives of the native population. The women "sat" on numerous warrant chiefs and demanded their resignation.[9] The scale of the movement, the organization, and the methods employed were formidable. The impasse created by the movement forced colonial troops to fire on the protesters, killing about fifty of them and wounding several others.[10] Throughout late December 1929 and early January 1930, the Birrell Gray Commission (1930), otherwise known as the Aba Commission of Inquiry, collected evidence and recommended collective punishment for the communities involved. The movement was an expression of the tensions that had been brewing since the introduction of colonial administration in the region.

It is my endeavor in this paper to explore the emergence of "popular consciousness" among peasant women focusing on the 1929 women's revolt. The paper explains how they drew upon cultural traditions and norms for framing their protest rather than the development of formal ideologies. The central argument is that movement leaders drew from a strong moral imperative of their society—a feminine and ethical one—to frame their resistance. Their consciousness was permeated by traditional notions of their position in rural life and the moral claim to certain privileges that derived from their femininity and roles as subsistence producers and providers.

BACKGROUND AND SETTING

Before the colonial period, the societies of Eastern Nigeria were not highly stratified along class and gender lines. The Igbo political structure has also been described as "stateless" and highly segmented. The most important feature of this system is the perceived lack of a formalized leadership that Victor Uchendu described as "an exercise in direct democracy" and "representative assembly."[11] In a society characterized as stateless and where the notion of *Igbo enweghi eze* (Igbo have no king) is widely accepted for many parts of Igboland, who then constituted the traditional intellectual and what was the configuration of power and authority? What vocations and leadership positions did they engage in and how did they express ideas in words or frame the word-flow that others received?

In actuality, the absence of a formalized political structure did not mean the absence of rural intellectuals. Translated literally, the term "intellectual" (*inwe ugugu isi,*) or "to posses brain power or be knowledgeable" defined traditional intellectuals among the Igbo and other Eastern Nigerian societies. Traditional intellectuals derived their power and authority through an elaborate status conferring mechanism—age, lineage headships, powerful titled and secret societies, as well as possession of certain spiritual powers. Others are based on individually achieved status and purchasing power.[12] Thus, traditional intellectuals included the native doctors, title holders such as the *ozo* and *nze*, oracular priests and priestesses, ritualists, diviners, custodians of sacred shrines, men and women elders, griots, women leaders, fortune tellers and interpreters of dreams, among others who had the knowledge and power to read and interpret sociopolitical and economic phenomenon and advance practical or spiritual solutions to perceived notions of wrongs affecting their society. These groups remained the most important sources for articulating communal ideas and ideology until Western contact.

The coming of the Europeans introduced new dynamics to African societies. From the late nineteenth century, Christian missionary education produced a new intellectual group that became teachers and bureaucrats under British colonialism from the beginning of the twentieth century. Under the British colonial policy of "indirect rule," some traditional intellectuals and western-educated leaders acted as representatives of the British administration, enforcing colonial laws and mediating local disputes that were hitherto adjudicated through a traditional system, thereby breaking with local political tradition.[13]

The new sources of identity, particularly western education and the warrant chief system, however, did not erase the traditional intellectual identity. As Raphael Njoku argues "the distinctive feature of the African intelligentsia is that it is often difficult to differentiate between an individual who has merely received a Western education and one whose mental activities merit the respect reserved for those who assume the position of 'leader of thought' in their society."[14] There was often contestation for power between the different elements within the emerging society, leading to the emergence of a counter discourse among groups whose own power and authority were threatened by the warrant chiefs. Underlying the colonial enterprise, however, was the patriarchal structure of both European and African societies. So colonialism ignored the complementary nature of men and women's roles, which fitted around rather than competed with each other.

The economic transformation of the rural economy was also an important dynamic for change. From the first decade of the twentieth century, the British colonial authority took steps to encourage the production of palm oil and kernels in Eastern Nigeria. The production of palm oil and kernels for export became the most dynamic feature of rural life even though the state acted as a "tribute-taker rather than an organizing agency for capital producers as in a developed capitalist society."[15] The commercialization of agriculture, however, provided the impetus for the emergence of peasants and often aggravated local resentment against British policy. About Eastern Nigerian women, the *Morning Post* of 26 August 1930 observed: "The women held great influence as they were largely the traders of the community. Not only did they accomplish the major part of the preparation of palm oil, but they frequently superintended the disposal."[16] The dismissal of women in the economic and political process had long-term impacts that manifested and contributed to the revolt. Explicating the 1929 women's movement is thus hampered by the obvious bias of male colonial bureaucrats and their African cohorts. In addition, capturing the voices of the rural populations during the colonial period is difficult, especially since they did not often commit their feelings to paper. Nevertheless, the report of the commission of inquiry that examined the women's revolt remains a very important source. The report mentioned the identities and actions of many of the women rioters and provides opportunity for a social analysis of peasant discourses, feelings, anger, the grief of ordinary people, long term continuities in cultural language, and how women translated their disquiet into collective action in 1929.

EMERGENCE OF PEASANT PROTEST

The perception that peasants were incapable of articulating their own ideas led Antonio Gramsci to distinguish between organic intellectuals (who originated from the working class and then became party organizers) and traditional intellectuals.[17] Although he argues that peasants were incapable of articulating their needs as intellectuals, Gramsci links intellectual discourse, production and power without a reductionist view. It is Gramsci's idea that as intellectuals become politically engaged, they continue to rely on and make use of traditional intellectuals to achieve their hegemonic dominance. Gramsci's idea has been elaborated by Stephen Feierman. In his study on Tanzania, the traditional discourses of chiefs, healers and diviners were drawn into the services of colonial authorities and modern politicians through the intermediary of the educated elite.[18] Feierman's view, however, is fundamentally different in one major respect. To him, peasants are capable of "creating their own counter-discourse" and political movements of long-term significance in the absence of centralized party institutions.[19] Feierman's perspective has the added attraction of engaging the emergence of peasant intellectuals, movement leaders and their organizational framework in specific cultural and historical contexts.

Then, what forms of discourse emerged among the African peasantry, which some scholars have described as an anomaly?[20] In colonial Africa, the impetus for social movements derived from a multiplicity of factors, including the political and economic transformation of rural societies. The incorporation of African economies into the western capitalist system was the impetus for the emergence of peasants who cultivated the land to meet their subsistence needs and state taxes. The conflict of interest between peasants and the state gave rise to a variety of protests and the emergence of men and women whom Feierman characterized as peasant intellectuals.[21] Analyzing peasant collective action and outcomes, therefore, invites analysis of a number of general problems of concern to social scientists such as the sources of political authority and legitimacy, the relationship between tradition and social movements and the influence of new political discourses that emerged in opposition to colonial institutions. Of course, intellectuals do not emerge or function in a vacuum. The intellectual tradition from which movements emerged, the role and language employed by movement leaders, and the content of the discourse have direct bearing on the social, economic and political context of protest movements in general, but particularly on how they can be shaped by culture, class, and gender.

Although some scholars have claimed that African peasants were far less "aware of their exploitation than their counterparts in Asia and Latin America,"[22] peasants in various parts of Africa were not quite oblivious to colonial policies and the demands on their income through taxes, rates, and demands on their labor. The 1929 Women's Revolt in Eastern Nigeria provides an example of how rural people were able to articulate their interest in a colonial setting.

The 1929 Women's Revolt was undoubtedly the most significant event in African-European relations in colonial Nigeria. As *The Times* of London wrote, the revolt was of "a nature and extent unprecedented in Nigeria."[23] The women's movement has been mainly analyzed as an anti-colonial political protest and a rejection of an alien system of administration.[24] Adiele Afigbo argued that the Women's War was another manifestation of the anti-colonial sentiments expressed in the *nwobiala* or Dance Movement of 1925.[25] Others have linked the women's revolt to the implementation of the "indirect rule" system in Eastern Nigeria—a system that broke with traditional political institutions.[26] The well-known authority on Nigerian nationalist movement, J. S. Coleman, argued that the women's revolt was part of the "traditional nationalism" that swept most of colonial Africa before the Second World War.[27] Nina Mba relied on the women's revolt to centralized women's resilience and contributions to the political discourse in Nigeria and demonstrates the leadership qualities of rural women in challenging the ethical and moral order of colonialism.[28] Embedded in this struggle, Nkiru Nzegwu suggests, was an attempt to exhibit a female-identified consciousness and the importance of female solidarity. Thus, women's political consciousness was directed toward the restoration of equitable gender relations that had been affected by the colonial, patriarchal social and political structures.[29] Mba and Nzegwu's analyses, like those of many other commentators, are important in many respects, but have not emphasized the peasant roots of the revolt.

These actions by women may have different significance in relation to varying discourses—peasant and nationalist. As Feierman argues, "the distinction between practical knowledge and discursive knowledge must occupy a central place in any attempt to understand peasant politics and peasant culture."[30] Feierman cautions that a course of action pursued by peasants can be analyzed in terms of whether they acted practically on the basis of tacit knowledge or whether they formulated the rationale for their action discursively—that is, placed it in context.

Our goal, therefore, is to elaborate on the peasant roots of the women's grievance and their framing strategies.[31] Women's interests in the political and economic structures created by colonialism fit well with the peasants' intellectual ideology that Feierman elaborated upon in his Tanzania study and are important in exploring the link between political and economic conditions and social movements. A peasant-oriented focus broadens and refines the understanding of the 1929 women's movement as feminist. This is critical for two important reasons. First, the analyses so far have not adequately explored patriarchal assumptions about colonial societies and the male-dominated approach of colonial development policy. Feminist/nationalist explanatory models of the movement reproduced this error. Second, the discourse on the women's movement has not been adequately grounded in the social structures and the everyday lives of rural societies. A new insight is brought to bear on the issues by discussing them in their relatedness and complexity, thereby unveiling new meanings and creating deeper understanding. The argument recognizes but also sidesteps the usual chorus of the marginalization of African women attributed to patriarchal ideals in order to engage the emergence of peasant intellectuals among women within a new political economy that adversely affected both women and men, although to varying degrees.

Four years before the 1929 revolt, women in some parts of Owerri Province, Eastern Nigeria started an anti-colonial movement known as the "Dance Movement."[32] The protest was also anti-Christianity in ideology, and the protesters called for a purification exercise to rid the society of ills.[33] The women's demands included forbidding the use of European coins and that young girls or young married women should go about naked as in the old days until they were with their first child. The message included exhortation of old customs and forbidding men from growing cassava, which they regarded as a female prerogative. The women demanded that the prices of chicken, cassava, eggs and other commodities be fixed at certain rates due to the high cost of staples. In some parts of Okigwe District, the dancing women stated that prostitutes should not charge too much for their services and married women should be allowed to have intercourse with other men without being prosecuted in the Native Courts. There were complaints about moral laxity that the women attributed to Christianity with its new moral ideology.[34] The issues raised included high bride-wealth, which prevented or delayed marriage for many young men.[35] The demands of the women can be rationalized in economic and social terms, but were also a hegemonic discourse in support of traditional values and a rejection of what was seen as foreign and European. To women, the colonial administrators, missionaries and European traders represented one entity—the foreigner whose intervention was causing economic and social upheaval. It was also an expression of female agency and women's influence as historical actors in a rapidly modernizing society. It is against this background that the tone of the 1929 movement, to which I now turn, was set.

The women's protest broke out on 23 November 1929 when a district officer, Captain John Cook, began recounting households and property for the purposes of obtaining an accurate nominal roll of villages in the Bende Division to determine taxation. The enumeration raised fears among the women of Oloko in the Owerri Province, who assumed they would be taxed like the men.[36] The movement was characterized by widespread grass roots mobilization by peasant women who employed feminine ideology and ritual symbols. Women employed protest paradigms that embodied body language, dance, songs, speech, and violent actions. The significance of the revolt lay not only in the wide area it covered (about 6,000 square miles in the Owerri and Calabar Provinces,) but also because it was led entirely by rural women.[37] The crisis attained serious proportions when rioting broke out in the commercial city of Aba, where government officials were attacked and European firms, including the local branch of Barclays bank, were looted. The rioting reached its climax at Opobo where 31 women were killed and 29 others were wounded.[38]

A week before serious rioting broke out it was reported that about 12,000 women, some coming from places almost 100 miles away, came to complain about the reported intention to impose direct tax on women to the district officer of the Aba Division. Recalling the incident, British official Henry Alexander Miller noted: "I never saw women demonstrating in that manner before. I have seen them play many a time but this was obviously entirely different and there was no doubt whatever that they were out for trouble." The account of Captain John Cook to the Commission of Enquiry on 11 March 1930 at Umudike, Umuahia is quite informative on the origin of the crisis:

> When I took over the division I found it was not certain how many males there were in the various villages in the area, and that the amount of tax that has been collected in the first year was not the same by a good difference as that collected in the next year. There were nominal rolls of males in the villages, but they were not drawn up by quarters or compounds or families, the result being that I could not fix where the men came from.[39]

Cook had carried out similar revision exercises in the Okigwe and Orlu Divisions and wanted to repeat the same exercise in the Bende Division.[40] He employed enumerators to carry out the exercise through the warrant chiefs. However, the incident started on November 18, 1929 when Mark Emereuwa, the enumerator employed by Chief Okugo, the warrant chief of Oloko, went to Ojim's compound to carry out the enumeration exercise. A scuffle arose when one of Ojim's wives, Nwanyereuwa, protested the enumeration exercise. The violent encounter between Emereuwa and Nwanyeruwa prompted her to report the incident to a group of women who were holding a meeting nearby. Ikonnia, another Oloko woman who played a prominent role in the women's movement, recalls Nwanyereuwa's outburst to the women: "How am I to count?" she said, "I am only a woman, I am not the owner of this compound. My husband is in who owns the house and you should have gone to him. Why do you come to me?"[41]

Women received the enumeration exercise with a sense of uncertainty because the census exercise in 1927 was followed by the taxation of men. The women responded to show their solidarity with her because "If one hears that another is going to be killed, we should take some steps about it, and try to stop it,"[42] Ikonnia told the Aba Commission of Inquiry. On 25 November, women began to "sit on" Okugo, demanding his resignation as warrant chief. For his role in fermenting the crisis, Okugo was fined and imprisoned for two years.[43] The imprisonment of Okugo did not bring an end to the crisis as the protests culminated in massive revolts called *Ogu Umunwanyi* (Women's War) in the Igbo and Ibibio territories. The incident at Oloko became a peasant protest in which women used the act of "sitting on a man," a traditional method of protest, on a larger scale.

The rhetoric of the women's movement had certain conditions of the society that it attempted to convert into power for the movement. This form of collective organization and militancy has its roots in long-established forms of consciousness among women, but this particular incident was defined by a sense of powerlessness and the economic crisis in the local economy. Economic changes and the implementation of income tax led to deep discontent in the region. The telegram from the Governor of Nigeria, Sir Graeme Thomson to Lord Passfield, the Secretary of State for the Colonies, on January 29 1930 provides some perspective on the level of discontent and how detached the colonial authority was from the realities of the local society. According to the Governor, the outbreak "could not have been foreseen as taxes had been paid, markets were well attended, women were cheerful and friendly, and native courts crowded with litigations. There had been no boycott of trading firms or any indication of feeling as a result of the low price of produce or dearness of imported goods... nor had there been any general protest against [the] system of buying by weight."[44] Indeed, the government did not read the writing on the wall, or what the Governor described as underlying causes, that provided favorable ground for disorder, namely: "dislike of taxation only recently introduced in these provinces, conditions of trade, low prices of produce, high prices of imported goods, change of method of buying by weight instead of by measure, cessation of presents to vendors by firms and it is alleged, dissatisfaction with some conditions of produce inspection."[45] The arrest and subsequent conviction of Okugo, the Governor concluded, "May have encouraged belief that the mob method had achieved victory which could be repeated elsewhere," and the "successful looting of Aba encouraged disorder elsewhere."[46]

The discontent surrounding the women's movement falls into three main categories. First, the government was caught in a problematic situation defined by the unpopularity of the Native Revenue (Amendment) Ordinance and the introduction of direct tax. The prospect of a direct tax on women and their response provided political opportunity that was discerned along gender, economy and collective action lines. Ikodia of Oloko summarized the prevailing feeling among women:

> We heard that women were being counted by their chiefs. Women became annoyed at this and decided to ask who gave the order, as they did not wish to accept it. As we went to various markets we asked other women whether they too had heard the rumour about the counting of women. They replied that they had heard it...We, women, therefore held a large meeting at which we decided to wait until we

> heard definitely from one person that women were to be
> taxed, in which case we would make trouble, as we did not
> mind to be killed for doing so.[47]

The sources of their outrage with tax are not hard to locate,
even though women did not pay taxes directly in 1928. The tax
system imposed a uniform rate on adult males that disregarded
income levels, and the rural poor had a hard time meeting their
tax obligations. To be sure, this was a tax on households, which
"imposed some burden on women. Some women paid taxes for
indigent spouses and sons."[48] "How do we pay tax? Tax paid by
men already affects us also," said Akulechula of Obowo.[49] Women
also considered taxation to be a male obligation.[50] According to
another woman, Mborie Amakwe of Abaja, "We are not going
to pay tax. We are women."[51] "How are we women to pay tax?
Where can we get the means from to pay it? That was our grievance and we made the demonstration to make you [government]
feel that we were aggrieved"[52] noted Akpamgbo. Nwakaji of
Ekweli, Oloko asked: "How could women who have no means
themselves to buy food or clothing pay tax?" And Uligbo of
Awon Uku, Oloko queried: "How could we pay tax? We depend
upon our husbands; we cannot buy food or clothe ourselves:
how shall we get money to pay tax?"[53] Enyidia, another leader
of the women's movement from Oloko, demanded: "What have
we women done to warrant our being taxed? We women are like
trees, which bear fruit. You should tell us the reason why we who
bear seeds should be counted."[54]

Women were infuriated by the prospects of their being taxed.
For them, taxation raised not only economic concerns, but also
what Afigbo describes as a "very strong moral and psychological
dilemma."[55] The British ideas of personal income tax touched
on certain ethical elements in the local society, particularly the
fact that women ought not to be taxed. The comparison between
women and fruit-bearing trees, according to Afigbo, "lies at the
root of certain aspects of indigenous social and ethical philosophy," which stipulate that "just as one cannot, in the interest of
human beings deal lightly with the survival of fruit-bearing trees,
one could not play with the fate of women."[56]

The prevailing conceptions of women's naturally dependent position in the social hierarchy were used by both the women and colonial officials as a benchmark to gauge the validity of their claim for economic and social change. Women used similar arguments in a metaphorical sense to protest the inclusion of women in taxation. In a mutually reinforcing manner, women used their femininity, sexuality and marginalization within the colonial society to shape their protest. Women's use of metaphors such as fruit bearing trees had potent ideological significance for both the colonial context of women's social movement and contemporary appraisals of that context. They called into place a whole range of metaphors associated with femininity, and these emotionally charged images suggest that articulating local protests and framing them calls for specific consideration of local cultural ideology.

Furthermore, women termed the existing tax policy unfair considering the effects of the depression on local producers. The discontent began to extend to another major issue of relevance to rural peasants—the price of export produce and increasing inflation. In the late 1920s, the entire world economy was in a slump due to the Great Depression. The depression caused a myriad of economic problems, including low prices for palm produce and the rising cost of imported goods. The period of the depression was by far the worst economic hardship rural farmers had experienced. Dependence on the export of palm oil and palm kernels left rural peasants vulnerable when the prices of produce dropped to their lowest levels. While rural farmers experienced a substantial decrease in income, they lacked the kinds of social programs that ameliorated the effects of the depression in Europe and the United States.[57]

Rural peasants made some efforts to protect their interests from the growing insecurity in the local economy. Caught by the fall in prices and insecure incomes, local farmers cut back production to induce price increases or adulterated products to increase volume. To increase the weight of palm kernels, producers partially cracked kernels and left part of the shell or mixed cracked kernels with uncracked ones to increase the weight.[58] As a result of these adulterations and the need to improve the quality of produce, the colonial authority introduced produce inspection to enforce quality control. However, pressure on households to meet their economic needs was ever-present, especially for women who traditionally provided the bulk of the food needed for the household.

The conviction that both the government and the European trading companies were insensitive to the needs of rural peasants was not lacking a basis in fact. From 1929, the value of palm produce dropped progressively, reaching below 70 percent of its value in previous years.[59] The low prices of palm produce and the high price for imported commodities began to take center stage in the women's protest.[60] The discontent among women culminated in petitions to European trading company officials. On 4 December 1929, for example, women gathered at Umuahia to discuss the low prices of produce. By this time, the price of a four-gallon tin of palm oil in Umuahia District had fallen from 6s and 8p to 5s. During a meeting with company agents at Umuahia, one woman leader, Nwanwanyi, noted:

> We wish to discuss the price of produce. We have no desire or intention of making any trouble but we have fixed a certain price for palm oil and kernels and if we get that we will bring them in. We want 10 shillings a tin [4 gallons] for oil and 9 shillings a bushel for kernels.[61]

In Owerri Province, the price of palm oil had dropped by over 60 percent of its value to as low as £18 per ton in 1927.[62] A district officer in the Owerri Province reported in December 1929 that women demanded the abolition of taxation on males, an increase in prices of produce (palm oil and kernels) and a decrease in the prices of imported goods.[63] In Aba District the price had gone down from 7s earlier in the year to 5s. In the Okigwe Division, women complained about the interference of produce inspectors in local trade.[64]

Attempts by the buying agents and the international trading companies to control prices forced producers to introduce price stabilization. "Can you please inform the general agents or merchants that we have to sell a tin of palm oil at 10s and a bushel of palm kernels at 7s...no products to be sold to them if they refused to accept our proposal,"[65] Obowo women in Okigwe District wrote in a petition to the District Officer. This situation affected both men and women, but it fuelled women's anger and provided a reason for their hostility to colonial institutions.[66]

While the hardships and conditions of rural society angered many women, rural discontent was exacerbated by the popular belief that the low prices of palm oil and kernels and rising inflation was a direct outcome of government policy. The Aba Commission recorded that women "were not slow to seize the opportunity whenever they were asked to state their grievances to put forward the low price of produce as one of them."[67] Akpamgbo told the Commission of Inquiry: "another matter that grieved us was in connection with the price of produce ...which was not satisfactory—we are not content with it. If we carried a kerosene tin of oil to the factories we were paid 5s for it. On the other hand, a tin of kerosene was sold to us for 9s. We made no profit...We were annoyed about all these things,"[68] It was under these hard economic times that the colonial authority introduced direct tax. Thus, the background to the women's revolt must be sought in the prevailing economic conditions in the late 1920s and the indifference shown by the colonial authority to the conditions of rural peasants.

Another source of discontent was the powerful distrust for government found in Eastern Nigeria in 1929 and the *laissez faire* attitude of the colonial authority to the impact of government policy at the local level. The *Morning Post* of 26 August 1930 acknowledged that another important contributory factor was the general failure of British civil servants to keep in touch with people."[69] This failure gave rise to the ideology through which women framed their protest. The protesters called attention to the widespread corruption that existed in the Native Administration and paralleled the rise of the new political elite with the emergence of moral decay and the wide spread exploitation of the local population. Their petitions and testimonies not only gave voice to what many described as the humiliation they received at the hands of native court members and warrant chiefs, but they also allow historians to engage their voices—what they believed were their responsibilities and the responsibilities of the colonial government to them. The desire was manifested in a growing nostalgia for the pre-colonial political order. Women capitalized on past transgressions by the government, especially the warrant chiefs, to articulate and popularize their protest. Protesters declared that the transformations that followed the European encounter had not only brought poverty, but that the warrant chief system challenged the traditional political order. As one woman declared:

> Our grievances are that the land has changed and we are all dying. It is a long time since the chiefs and the people who know book [educated] have been oppressing us. We are telling you that we have been oppressed. The new chiefs are all receiving bribes. Since the white men came, our oil does not fetch money. Our kernels do not fetch money. If we take goats or yams to market to sell, court messengers who wear a uniform take all these things from us.[70]

Women in Owerri Province demanded that current native court members be changed and suggested reforms in the political system. Corruption and abuse by warrant chiefs and native administration officials was endemic, as several of them used their positions to enrich themselves. Nwanyeruwa of Oloko, for example, told the Commission of Inquiry that Okugo "was an ordinary man" before he became the chief of Oloko.[71] According to her, Okugo became a rich man from extorting his people.[72] Okugo like many other warrant chiefs illegally levied villagers in the name of the government. Nwanyeruwa told the Commission that on one occasion Okugo collected £20 from the villagers after he told them that the District Officer had ordered that money should be collected for him to build a house. On another occasion, he told the villagers that the District Officer wanted a young wife and requested both men and women to pay the dowry. The villagers contributed £20 as dowry for the District Officer."[73] These practices were widespread, but the local people were powerless to question the warrant chiefs because of their new sweeping powers under the native administration. Those that raised their voices faced more persecution. The Commission believed that discontent over the "persecution, extortion and corruption by the native court members was another principal contributory cause."[74]

The women's protest provided fertile ground for collective action against the ruling elite. Governor Thomson acknowledged that there was widespread hostility toward some members of the native courts, especially in Owerri Province, who were believed to have aided in introducing taxes.[75] But the targeting of the native administration had deeper roots. With so many complaints and allegations of corruption and bribery, the Commission concluded: "we heard enough to be satisfied that persecution by native courts members and corruption in the native courts are a source of very considerable discontent among the people,"[76]

Ultimately, the demands for political change created a counter hegemonic discourse and consciousness among peasant women through which they defined their relationships with other segments of colonial society, especially with members of the native administration. Those who articulated women's demands were inseparable from the issue of their own identity as peasants, but their identity was also couched around their other identity as women. This enabled female peasant leaders to gain legitimacy among women as well as the colonial authority.

FRAMING IDEOLOGY AND LEADERSHIP

The discourse on the women's protest was based on deeply embedded reproduction of cultural ideologies and power relationships and drew on what Mayer Zald calls "cultural stocks of images of what is justice, for what is violation of what ought to be."[77] David A. Snow et al. point out that "the language of framing provides a valuable tool for addressing the dynamic of organized challenge and institutionalized change."[78] Frames "assign meaning to and interpret relevant events and conditions in ways that are intended to mobilize political adherents and constituents, to garner bystander support, and to demobilize antagonists."[79] Frames, in turn, generate *collective action frames*, "emergent action-oriented sets of beliefs and meanings that inspire and legitimate social movement activities and campaigns."[80]

Women drew upon pre-colonial forms of political language and relied on female-informed paradigms in framing the protest of 1929. The basis of such articulation and framing was not formed at the period in question. Feierman shows in his Tanzanian study that the social analysis of peasant discourse reveals "long-term continuities in political language are the outcome of radical social change and of struggle within peasant society."[81] Cultural elements, ritual symbols, songs, dance and social institutions women traditionally used to affect gender relations were extensively employed in the formulation of women's protest and framing of discourses.[82] The employment of ritual symbols associated with war in traditional society helped to draw the battle line between protesters and the colonial authority. Women sent leaves of the palm-oil tree (a symbol of invitation) to women in other parts of the Bende District and other places, and within a few days, about 10,000 women were said to have assembled in Oloko to "sit" on Okugo, the warrant chief of the area.

Women employed rhetorical confrontations and strategies such as name-calling and polemic rhetoric that constructed the colonial and native authority as the "enemy." Songs and dance played a vital role in the production of meanings and realities surrounding the women's protest. Women influenced both local and British official perceptions through the use of traditional forms of protests—singing and raucous behavior. The songs and narratives were framed to encourage specific perceptions of these events. These symbols and rituals, however, provide opportunity for cultural analysis that may be discerned along many directions and informed by many variables. Women composed songs embodying their grievances, as they danced, and "sat" on the warrant chiefs, or marched to the District Officer to present their petitions.[83] Women also chanted traditional male war songs, *"Nzogbu, Enyi mba Enyi"* (literary meaning elephants crushing obstacles on our way).[84]

Women stripped naked and sang war songs used for "inciting their men to battle."[85] Others danced naked, touting men to impregnate them if they were "real men" by placing their hands on their private parts. At Opobo, women wore young palm fronds of palm leaves round their necks and waists as a "sign of solidarity among the women of the different tribes and of hostile intention"[86] and chanted "What is that I smell; it is the smell of blood."[87] As one Opobo chief noted: "To wear palm leaves in old days meant that they were going to fight and I knew when the women were wearing palm leaves they were coming in to fight."[88] These rhetorical confrontations made compromise with the warrant chiefs, whose power, prestige and authority were threatened, unthinkable and induced hegemonic collaboration between the warrant chiefs and the British administration.

Despite the influence of Christianity among the Igbo, for example, many still retained the belief in the supernatural effects of witchcraft. Witchcraft is often considered forms of wickedly appropriated power or resources that can be used to "gain unfair advantage in a variety of pursuits, including business, court cases, and property disputes."[89] Witchcraft or harmful medicine was employed by both sides at Oloko. The most significant evidence of this on record was the attempt by Okugo to "harm" the women who were threatening his power and authority. Okugo employed the services of Aro medicine men to prepare *juju* to harm the women. They used earth from the spot where the women urinated and the food particles they ate during their meeting to prepare the *nsi* (bad medicine).[90] Movement leaders also took extra measures to protect their own interests and ensure the loyalty of other women. Some women who visited Oloko during the crisis were requested to swear on a *juju* that they had not engaged in looting and other violent actions. Local values accept the use of *juju* to act as moral guardian and a means of social control, for it obliges one who takes an oath to say the truth or risk dire consequences that may include death. The *juju* in this sense was used by movement leaders to reinforce their power and authority. Evil medicine (*nsi*), as employed by Okugo on the other hand, was a harmful criminal act directed at 'enemies.' Both relied extensively on traditional rituals and sanctions that were deeply embedded in local cosmology—the ideas of good and evil and their effects on humans—to either legitimize and encourage widespread acceptance of their ideas or to protect their interests.

What Feierman calls the "social position of intellectuals" is important in making sense of and articulating the ideas of those within the society who shaped discourse, "their position within the framework of domination, and the relationship between their position and the political language."[91] The changing configuration of political authority, which was manipulated by the warrant chiefs, was important in the emergence of female intellectuals who reflected upon and articulated changing conceptions of power relations. The new political environment that emerged in 1929 brought popular leadership to an important turning point, signaling the emergence of female peasant leaders and more organized rural insurgency.

Thus, organizing the 1929 protest required considerable organization and leadership. It was not enough to mobilize thousands of women to sit on warrant chiefs, disrupt the activities of European firms and the colonial administration or block highways; sustaining the movement depended on well-organized and coordinated articulation of the concerns of rural peasant women and men. Unlike many social movements, the women's revolt in 1929 cannot be described in terms of the careers, beliefs, ideologies and critical events surrounding movement leaders. Rather the idea of collective behavior as advanced by Chicago sociologist Robert Park, and subsequently by Herbert Blumer, explains how responses to social change can occur outside formal institutions and well-institutionalized processes that are advanced in the study of social movements.[92] Just as a collective ideology was the bedrock of local political and social process, so did women rely on pre-existing organizations that transformed in a unique way for the mobilization of the women. *The Morning Post* of 26 August 1930 wrote: "The most interesting feature of the riot was the fact that they had been organized entirely by women in a community, which was anything but a matriarchy."[93] Similarly, *The Times* of London wrote that: "This was essentially a women's movement, organized, developed, and carried out by women of the country, without either the help or permission of their men fold though probably with their tacit support."[94]

Governor Thomson acknowledged that the "existence of well organized women's society made spreading of the news easy."[95] There was some continuity of pre-conflict leadership as most of the women leaders were people who had played important roles in women's groups. Many of the protest leaders had also played important roles in local women's organizations and church associations. Although local church organizations were the cradle of the protest that began in Oloko, the crisis of 1929 gave existing local leaders regional prominence. Movement leaders legitimized their position in the movement by creating new discourses, including the political economy of colonialism. But they also conceptualized the protest as a movement by all women. One phrase, which was regularly used, described the movement as *ogu umunwayi* or women's war and an organizational framework that embraced *oha ndi inyom* (all women).

Oha ndi inyom could have been nothing but a short lived mob action if not for the emergence of a few women who articulated the concerns of women and framed them in a language that made it look like a moral crusade for women and peasants in general. One of the most important women to emerge who articulated women's concerns was Nwanyereuwa, who instigated the crisis itself. It was Nwanyereuwa who took the women to Emeruwa's house to sit on him to protest the extension of tax to women. She led the charge to demand the resignation of Okugo as warrant chief before he was tried and imprisoned.[96] As an older woman, she was also the voice of reason when tempers were high. Even though Okugo had assaulted the women who came to answer the alarm she raised, she advised the women not "to do any damage in Okugo's compound."[97] Nwanyereuwa played a major role not only in precipitating the revolt, but she also emerged as a leading advocate of non-violence during the protest marches. As a tacit acknowledgement of her articulate testimony and intelligence, the Crown Counsel at the commission's hearing noted of Nwanyereuwa: "You are talking like a man who is not nervous. You are talking like a lawyer."[98]

Indeed Nwanyeruwa influenced the pattern of protest in many parts of the Eastern region. She encouraged thousands of women to 'sit' on their warrant chiefs.[99] Over time, women in the Oloko area and other parts of Igboland came to regard Nwanyeruwa as a courageous leader who fought to protect women's interest regarding the tax issue. When the revolt spread, women from various parts of the region came to Nwanyeruwa for assurance that women would not be taxed. She gave out notes to various delegates stating that the district officer said that "women will not pay tax till the world ends [and] chiefs were not to exist anymore."[100]

In recognition of the leadership provided by the Oloko women, women from the Owerri Division made monetary contributions of 10s to 15s per village, which amounted to about £17 to support the Oloko leaders.[101] According to Umuaru Amachi of Umuojima in the Aba Division who made the two-day journey to Oloko, "Nwanyereuwa made a rule that money should be paid to her for her success." The money given to her was "a thanksgiving for our success in Okugo's case."[102] Nwebeme of Amabo in Aba Division was one of the delegates to Oloko. She told the Commission that they paid 10s to Nwanyereuwa in consideration of her action and the commitment she received from the government that "women are not to pay tax until the end of the world and that chiefs were not to exist anymore."[103] Nwanyereuwa told the commission the money was partly used to entertain the large number of women that frequently visited to consult with her and to support the messengers who carried the message to other towns.[104] The Aba Commission of Inquiry noted that "Nwanyeruwa became and still remains a name to conjure with [and the Oloko trio] cleverly used her as the symbol of womanhood rising against oppression."[105] Women continued to visit Oloko even after Okugo had been convicted and the rumor that women would pay tax had been dispelled.

The crisis raised the status of other Oloko women. The Oloko trio of Ikonnia, Nwannediya and Nwugo emerged during the crisis as leaders of the women's movement due to their youthful vigor, intelligence and oratory. Prior to the protest, the Oloko trio were custodians of the funds of the local women's thrift and welfare association.[106] Such a role is significant because it shows that they were judged to be reliable and trustworthy before the revolt occurred. Such qualities have been central in the emergence of local leaders among the decentralized societies of southeastern Nigeria. Ikonnia was one of the women who demanded that Okugo should be tried for "trying to get women into trouble, causing them to die by suggesting that they should pay tax."[107]

The Oloko leaders had a good deal of control over the women. Nwannediya agreed that "they were able to get them [other women] to do what they advised."[108] The letter from the District Officer gave the Oloko trio some legitimacy and the authority to address other women's groups on the tax issue. Ikonnia and the other women leaders played a role in containing the movement. The women adopted a strategy of non-violence, which may have significantly reduced death and destruction in many parts of Eastern Nigeria. Armed with the assurance from the District officer of Bende, they traveled to various parts of the region to address women.[109] Nwanyereuwa, Ikonnia, Nwannedie, Nwugo and Nwada and other women leaders traveled around the province to meet with colonial officials on the tax issue.

In addition to the use of cultural elements of the traditional society, women leaders consciously used new bureaucratic institutions such as the courts to articulate their goals. Captain John Hills, who paid tribute to their leadership qualities, often sent them to "hot spots" during the revolt to ensure that the protests did not lead to violence. In Oloko, for example, tempers ran high among women on November 30, 1929, when the District Officer refused the immediate trial of Okugo. Captain Hills was surprised that the women leaders could easily disperse the women as soon as he announced that Okugo would be tried the next day. The District Officer also sent the Oloko women leaders to Aba to stop widespread looting when women in that district looted some European factories. In Umuahia, women had massed in the town to begin to protest against the warrant chiefs. The trio addressed the women, and to the amazement of the district officer, the protest march did not take place.[110]

Other women leaders emerged in other parts of the region. In Umuokirika in the Owerri Division, Ihejilemebi Ibe emerged as a heroine of the women's revolt. Like some of the Oloko women, Ihejilemebi played a significant role in her community before the protest emerged. She had served as the head of the women's spy team during local wars and was a member of the war council. Her leadership role was called upon during the revolt. She led women to "sit" on the warrant chiefs in various communities, burning the houses of those who refused to resign and hand over their caps to her. Oral accounts collected by John Oriji say that her influence forced the warrant chief of Obohia, Chief Anyanwuagwu, to secretly negotiate a truce with her and he agreed to resign his position as warrant chief.[111] Her leadership role extended to domestic issues, including cases of spousal abuse. Women brought cases of domestic abuse to her and men found guilty were carried shoulder-high around the village and beaten by young women as a lesson to others.[112] Ihejilemebi transgressed gender boundaries. She was accorded male privileges in a male-dominated society.[113] In Onicha Ezinihitte, Owerri Division, a woman popularly known as "Mary of the Women's War," or "*Eze Ndi-Inyom*" (chief of women), emerged as an important spokesperson for the women in the area. According to Oriji, Mary was highly revered among women as a result of the war. Mary was treated as a celebrity and greeted with a lot of excitement whenever she visited any village.[114] Like other leaders of the movement, her thought and action were largely unmediated by modern political thought, but they were deeply rooted in village consciousness, which was shaped by peasant-based conflict ranging from tax and high prices to political marginalization.

Although all of the women leaders were not educated, an educated woman provided her services to the movement. Mary Okezie was a school teacher and the first Ngwa woman to receive Western education in 1915. While she did not take part in the demonstration, her sympathy was known and her literacy served the women's cause. She wrote the memo submitted to the Commission of Inquiry in 1930 by a group of Ngwa women in the Aba Division that outlined the women's concerns. In a period when very few women were educated, her education conferred a different kind of leadership to the women in Ngwa territory.[115] Madam Okezie clearly emerged as the most famous leader of Ngwa women after the revolt. She became a leading exponent of women's rights and founded the Ngwa Women's Association to promote the education and welfare of women in 1948.[116]

The structure of an all-male native court changed after the women's revolt. Some women entered the colonial bureaucracy, and some of them became members of the Native Authority. In Nguru Mbaise Native Court, a woman, Chinwe, became a member of the native court. Three women became members of the Umuapko Native Court area, while one woman was appointed to the Okpala Native Court.[117] A prominent female member of the Native Courts after the women's revolt was Ahebi Ugabe of Enugu-Ezike in Nsukka area. Ahebi was reputed for her spiritual prowess, and popularly called "Agamega" or "Female Leopard." Like the Warrant Chiefs, Ahebi was carried to the Native Court in a hammock, and the road she took to the Native Court in Ogrute village became known as "Akpata Ahebi" (Ahebi's road). Her fame and spiritual prowess also earned her a position among male elders. History tells us that Ahebi was the only woman known to have been permitted by the elders to watch the powerful *Omabe* masquerade and to have built an *Omabe* shrine in her compound.[118]

Despite their strong connection with the women, the roles of the movement's leaders as mediators between the rural women and the colonial authority increased their profile in a political structure that was dominated by men. For the movement leaders, direct engagement with the colonial authority gave them an opportunity to address their marginality in the rural political economy, which stemmed from women's peripheral access to power under the indirect rule system and the intervention of the government in peasant production. Other women used the platform to address other concerns. For example, prostitutes protested along with other women. Lucy Pepple appeared to the commission of inquiry to request that prostitutes should not be arrested "unless they were known to be suffering from sickness.[119] In some cases also, women rejected those who acted as their representatives. In Opobo, the women accused Abigail Ogolu of accepting a bribe of 6 pounds from the District Officer in order to stop the women from demonstrating.[120]

Overall, women's articulation of their protest, however, suggests a level of ideological sophistication not usually attributed to this early stage of women's protest thought. Most of these women grew up in a milieu that did not decidedly privilege anyone. But the concept of *Igbo enwe eze* with its strong sense of republicanism gradually evolved into one of privilege for the warrant chiefs and colonial bureaucrats. Movement leaders consistently set forth their ideas in the public sphere in ways that rendered them distinct from men and characterized them as an elite group among a marginalized and underprivileged people. However, protest stories were framed around the violence of the women, official restraints, and women's unruly behavior. Thus, the women were stigmatized as a danger to life, property and public order. This method of framing the women's movement invoked popular opinion against the protest and constructed the image of an unruly group of women bent on disrupting public order. However, protests proved to be essential in helping women envision themselves as important factors in colonial politics and the local social structures. For the language of rights was inescapably linked to the women's conception of their right as producers and reproducers, accountability on the part of the colonial authority and other issues they saw as essential to the creation of new moral and ethical order. The colonial government may have interpreted the women's movement as the disturbance of public order, but what both parties failed to understand was that the transformation taking place, especially the low prices for produce, was a sign of changing times that bred social conflict within the colonial society. Women, for their part, failed to recognize that their strategies were being applied to a society now governed by a very different set of rules from the kind of society they had envisioned.

CONCLUSION

Political opportunities are often deeply embedded in social movements. Political opportunity in this period is not a matter of contention, although it is deeply rooted in the economic structures of the colonial economy rather than the political institutions. The economic problematic was at the heart of the mobilization effort and the framing of the movement, although the strategies were elaborated to incorporate wider social and political concerns. While there are clear disjunctions between the rural peasant consciousness represented in the women's movement and the formal nationalist struggle in colonial Nigeria, the women's movement exhibited extensive intersection between political and economic conditions. The same is true of the attempt to conceptualize the women's movement as a feminist movement. Women did not often question the existence of the colonial authority, as one petition from a group of women stated: "We wish relations between us and government to be as cordial as those existing between us and the Reverend Fathers. If there is co-operation between us and government we shall be able to select new men to take the place of those chiefs who have been oppressing us."[121] Mobilization on a large scale in the region was not entirely new, but the 1929 women's revolt led to the transformation of the pre-conflict leadership structure, producing what can be truly known as peasant leaders. From economy to politics, the women's revolt sought fundamental change in the power relationships of rural society. But the consciousness that gave rise to the protest in 1929 was not articulated in feminist terms, but in terms of changing the existing economic and social order for the peasant class as a whole.

In the 1920s and 1930s, economic recession and growing awareness among peasants of the effect of political institutions on economic conditions invoked more spirited responses from rural peasants. The slump in palm produce prices, coincident with the imposition of taxation and coupled with the discontent caused by the taxation of men, helped fuel the revolt. There was a significant shift, therefore, from individual to collective action and ideology among women. A discursive knowledge of their action situates their movement within a combination of political and economic concerns: perceived unfairness of colonial trading patterns, price controls, and rising inflation. Whether the petitioners were economically or politically motivated, these petitions were worded in such a manner as to demand change and not to attract sympathy.

Movement leaders played a vital role in intellectual production, creating meanings and realities surrounding new events and situations during the colonial period. Women created a new level of intellectual discourse through a critical elaboration of existing traditional rituals and language. Through the selective use of language, rhetoric, symbols and the use of framing mechanisms, women influenced local perceptions of the colonial political economy and challenged the colonial authority's gendered perceptions of local societies. Women defined their movement within the metaphors, images and perceptions of the local society that called for social change. Women's strategies and framing mechanisms had a strong cultural component. Women also employed a strong moralistic identity. The moral rhetorical characteristic created a moral distinction between the women's movement and the dominant colonial order—a moral distinction that characterized the warrant chiefs and the Europeans as unethical and even wicked. Understanding Eastern Nigeria's peasant women's movement in this way has the potential to transform how we think about social movements and the emergence of peasant consciousness.

Notes

1. Michel Foucault, *The History of Sexuality: A Reader*, R, Hurley, trans. (New York: Pantheon Books, 1978).

2. James Scott, *Weapons of the Weak: Everyday Forms of Peasant Resistance* (New Haven: Yale University Press, 1985).

3. Serry B. Ortner, "Resistance and the Problem of Ethnographic Refusal", *Comparative Studies in Society and History*, 37, 1 (1995), 174.

4. Irving M. Zeitlin with Robert J. Brym, *The Social Condition of Humanity* (Canadian Edition), (Toronto: Oxford University Press, 1991), 232.

5. Terence Ranger, *Dance and Society in Eastern Africa, 1890-1970* (Berkeley, CA: University of California Press, 1975); Peter Geschiere, *The Modernity of Witchcraft: Politics and the Occult in Postcolonial Africa* (Charlottesville, VA, 1997); Jean Comaroff and John Comaroff, eds, *Modernity and its Malcontent: Ritual and Power in Postcolonial Africa* (Chicago, IL: University of Chicago Press, 1993).

6. Steven Feierman, *Peasant Intellectuals: Anthropology and History in Tanzania* (Madison: University of Wisconsin Press, 1990), 3.

7. Ibid.

8. Mayer N. Zald, "Culture, Ideology, and Strategic Framing", in Doug McAdam et al., *Comparative Perspectives on Social Movements: Political Opportunities, Mobilizing Structures, and Cultural Framings* (Cambridge: Cambridge University Press, 1996), 261.

9. When women sit on a man, they gathered at his compound, sang songs of grievances and performed other raucous behavior until the man repented and

promised to mend his ways. It is often used on men rather than women. For discussion on the act, see Van Allen, Judith "Sitting on a Man: Colonialism and the Lost Political Institutions of the Igbo," *Canadian Journal of African Studies* 6, 11 (1972): 165-181.

10. See Aba Commission of Inquiry. *Notes of Evidence Taken by the Commission of Inquiry Appointed to Inquire into the Disturbances in the Calabar and Owerri Province, December 1929* (Lagos, 1930) [hereafter, *Aba Commission* and *Aba Commission Notes of Evidence*].

11. Victor Uchendu, *The Igbo of Southeastern Nigeria* (New York: Holt, Rinehart & Winston, 1965), 41-46. There were exceptions. Some Igbo communities like Onitsha, Oguta and Nri had chieftaincy institutions in pre-colonial times.

12. Traditional tittles in Igbo society can be grouped into four main categories: (i) symbolic titles or those emanating from acquisition of wealth; (ii) those awarded due to heroic achievement, (iii) honorary awards and (iv) ascribed or titles of institutionalized social force origin. The *Duru* and *Ozo* titles are examples of status symbols among the Igbo. Their legitimacy was enhanced if conferred by the Nri since they are the direct descendants of Eri (a legendary figure regarded as the creator of the earth). An *ozo* title holder was revered and possessed a form of diplomatic immunity that was respected throughout Igboland.

13. See Adiele E. Afigbo, *The Warrant Chiefs: Indirect Rule in South-Eastern Nigeria, 1891-1929* (London: Longman, 1972).

14. Raphael C. Njoku, "An Endless Cycle of Secessionism. Intellectuals and Separatist Movements in Nigeria," in Bruno Coppieters and Michel Huysseune, eds. *Secession, History and the Social Sciences* (Brussels: Brussels University Press, 2002), 255.

15. Bill Freund, *The Making of Contemporary Africa: The Development of African Society Since 1800* (Boulder, CO: Lynne Rienner Publishers, 1998), 98.

16. *The Morning Post*, 26 August 1930.

17. Antonio Gramsci, *Selection from the Prison Notebooks*, edited and Trans, Quintin Hoare and Geoffrey Nowell Smith (New York: International Publishers, 1971), 5-9.

18. Feierman, *Peasant Intellectuals*, 18.

19. Ibid.

20. See for example, Goran Hyden, "The Anomaly of the African Peasantry," *Development and Change* 17, 4 (1986): 677-705; Robert Redfield, "Are African Cultivators to be Called 'Peasants'?" in Jack M. Potter, et al., *Peasant Society: A Reader* (Boston: Little Brown & Company, 1967). See also John S. Saul and Roger Woods, "African Peasantries," in *Peasants and Peasant Societies*: Selected Readings, ed. Teodor Shanin (Harmondsworth: Black-

well Publishers, 1971). See also Terence Ranger, "Growing from the Roots: Reflections on Peasants Research in Central and Southern Africa," *Journal of Southern African Studies* 5, no. 1 (1978): 99-133.

21. Feierman, *Peasant Intellectuals*, 18.

22. Goran Hyden, *No Shortcut to Progress*: African Development Management in Perspective (London: University of London Press, 1983), 128.

23. *The Times*, 25 August 1930.

24. See for example, M. Perham, *Native Administration in Nigeria* (London: Oxford University Press, 1937), 214; Harry A. Gailey, *The Road to Aba: A Study of British Administrative Policy in Eastern Nigeria* (London: University of London Press, 1970); and Adiele E. Afigbo, "Revolution and Reaction in Eastern Nigeria, 1900-1925: The Background of the Women's Riot of 1929," *Journal of the Historical Society of Nigeria* 3 (1966), 539-57. For feminist perspectives, see for example, Rogers Susan, "Anti-Colonial Protest in Africa: A Female Strategy Reconsidered," *Heresies* 9, 3 (1980): 22-25.

25. *Nwobia la* literally means stranger/visitor leave. This is known as the "Dance Movement." For another interpretation see "Dancing Women and Colonial Men: The Nwaobiala of 1925," in *"Wicked" Women and the Reconfiguration of Gender in Africa*, ed. Dorothy L. Hodgson and Sherry A. McCurdy (Portsmouth, NH: Heinemann, 2001), 109-129. See also Hanna Judith Lynne, "Dance, Protest, and Women's Wars: Cases from Nigeria and the United States," in *Women and Social Protest*, ed. Guida West and Rhoda Lois Blumberg (New York: Oxford University Press, 1990), 333-45.

26. U. C. Onwuteaka, "The Aba Riot of 1929 and Its Relation to the System of 'Indirect Rule,'" *Nigerian Journal of Economic and Social Studies* 7 (1965): 273-82.

27. James S. Coleman, *Nigeria: Background to Nationalism* (Berkeley, CA: University of California Press, 1960).

28. Nina Mba, *Nigerian Women Mobilised: Women's Political Activity in Southern Nigeria, 1900-1965* (Berkeley: University of California Press, 1982) and "Heroines of the Women's War," in Awe, B. ed. *Nigerian Women in Historical Perspective* (Lagos/Ibadan: Sankore Publishers/Bookcraft, 1992).

29. Nkiru Nzegwu, "Confronting Racism: Toward the Formation of a Female-Identified Consciousness," *Canadian Journal for Women and the Law* 7, no. 1 (1994):15-33.

30. Feierman, *Peasant Intellectuals*, 27.

31. For more feminist perspectives and analysis of the 1929 women's protest, see Caroline, Ifeka-Moller, "Female Militancy and Colonial Revolt," 127-57; Shirley Ardener, "Sexual Insult and Female Militancy," *Man* 8 (1973): 422-40; Sylvia Tamale, "Taking the Beast by its Horns: Formal Resistance to Women's Oppression in Africa," *African Development* 21, 4 (1996): 5-21.

32. Several colonial officials were concerned about the women's protest and officials were poised to stop its spread with the collaboration of the warrant chiefs. See especially, Nigerian National Archives, Enugu [hereafter NAE], B. 1544, CSE 3.17.15., (1925-1926), AW 80 Q, AW 2.1.57., Anti-Government Propaganda Women Dancers (1925). See also NAE, AW 80 AWDIST 2/1/56, (1919-1920).

33. See NAE 62/1925-AWDIST 2/1/57 and NAE OP. 391/1925 6/11/25 ONPROF 7/12/92, "Bands of Women Dancers Preaching Ideas of Desirable Reforms—Movement of." Kenneth Cochrane, District Officer, Bende to the Resident, Owerri Province, 9 December 1925. See also Report of the Aba Commission of Inquiry, "Memorandum as to the Origins and Causes of the Recent Disturbances in the Owerri and Calabar Provinces, Appendix III (1), 11-12.

34. Ibid.

35. NAE MINLOC 6/1/215-EP 10595A, "Intelligence Report on Obowo and Ihitte Clan, Okigwe Division, Owerri Province" by N.A.P. G MacKenzie, Assistant District Officer.

36. For most Igbo women, it was a reaction against the severe economic conditions existing in their society at this period. The enumeration exercise in Oloko Umuahia, which included women and livestock, made women suspect that they would be taxed as the men

37. Judith Van Allen, "'Aba Riots' or Igbo 'Women's War'? Ideology, Stratification, and Invisibility of Women," in *The Black Woman Cross-Culturally*, ed. F. C. Steady (Cambridge, MA: Schenkman Books, 1981), 60.

38. Notes of Evidence, Appendix III.

39. Notes of Evidence, 2.

40. Ibid, 3.

41. Ibid, 19.

42. Ibid, 21.

43. Public Record Office (PRO) CO 583/169/2, Telegram from the Governor of colonial Nigeria to the Secretary of State for the Colonies on January 6 1930.

44. Ibid.

45. Ibid.

46. Ibid.

47. Notes of Evidence, 21.

48. Interview with Linus Anabalam, Mbaise, 13 December 1998.

49. Notes of Evidence, 176.

50. Ibid., 22.

51. Ibid., 149.

52. Ibid., 82.

53. Commission of Inquiry, 12.

54. Notes of Evidence, 13.

55. Afigbo, "Revolution and Reaction."

56. Ibid.

57. For example, the United States Department of Agriculture created The Farm Security Administration (FSA) in 1937. The FSA and its predecessor, the Resettlement Administration (RA) were New Deal programs designed to assist poor farmers who suffered from the Dust Bowl and the Great Depression.

58. Interview with E. Ihediwa, Owerrenta, 24 July 1999.

59. Commission of Inquiry, Appendix III (1), 37. Figures obtained from the Supervising agent of the United African Company, Limited (Opobo).

60. Commission of Inquiry, 103

61. Mba, *Nigeria Women,* 75.

62. NAE OWDIST. 4/13/70 File no. 91/27 "Assessment Report" District Officer Owerri to the Resident Owerri Province June 1928.

63. Commission of Inquiry, Appendix III (1), 32.

64. Commission of Inquiry, 33.

65. Mba, *Nigeria Women Mobilized,* 75.

66. Interview with James Eboh, Alike Obowo, 2 January 2000.

67. Commission of Inquiry, 103.

68. Notes of Evidence, 82

69. *The Morning Post,* 26 August 1930.

70. Isichei, *A History of Nigeria,* 400.

71. Notes of Evidence, 27.

72. Ibid., 24-30.

73. Ibid.

74. Ibid.

75. Public Record Office (PRO) CO 583/169/2, Telegram from the Governor of colonial Nigeria, to the Secretary of State for the Colonies on January 29 1930.

76. Commission of Inquiry, 57.

77. Zald, "Culture, Ideology, and Strategic Framing," 266.

78. David A. Snow et al., "Frame Alignment Process, Micromobilization, and Movement Participation," *American Sociological Review*, 51 (1986): 464-81.

79. David A. Snow and Robert D. Benford, "Ideology, Frame Resonance, and Participant Mobilization," *International Social Movement Research* 1(1988): 198.

80. David A. Snow and Robert D. Benford, "Master Frames and Cycles of Protest," in *Frontiers in Social Movement Theory*, ed. Aldon D. Morris and Carol McClurg Mueller (New Haven, CT: Yale University Press, 1992), 67-68.

81. Ibid.

82. Audrey Wipper, "Riot and Rebellion among African Women: Three Examples of Women's Political Clout," in Perspectives on Power: Women in Africa, Asia and Latin America , ed. Jean O'Barr (Durham, NC: Duke University Press, 1982), 50-72.

83. Oriji, "Igbo Women."

84. Ibid.

85. Notes of Evidence, Appendix III, Edward James Crawford, Medical Officer, 11.

86. Arthur Robert Whitman, Notes of Evidence, Appendix III (14) (a) (Opobo, Abak and Utu-Etim-Ekpo), January 7 1930, 3.

87. Notes of Evidence, Appendix III, Richard Hostel Floyer, Assistant District Officer, Opobo, 23.

88. Chief Akpan Udo Lekpo of Ikot Abassi, Notes of Evidence, Appendix III (14) (a) (Opobo, Abak and Utu-Etim-Ekpo), January 7 1930, 20.

89. Gracia Clark, "Gender and Profiteering: Ghana's Market Women as Devoted Mothers and 'Human Vampire Bats,'" in *"Wicked" Women and the Reconfiguration of Gender in Africa* ed. Dorothy L. Hodgson and Sheryl A. McCurdy (Portsmouth, NH: Heinemann, 2001), 299.

90. Notes of Evidence, 25.

91. Feierman, *Peasant Intellectuals*, 4.

92. Zald, "Culture, Ideology and Strategic Framing," 263.

93. *The Morning Post*, 26 August, 1930.

94. *The Times*, 25 August, 1930.

95. Public Record Office (PRO) CO 583/169/2, Telegram from the Governor of colonial Nigeria to the Secretary of State for the Colonies on January 29 1930.

96. Notes of Evidence, 25.

97. Ibid., 26.

98. Ibid., 29.

99. Oriji, "Igbo Women."

100. Ibid. Cited by Mba, *Nigerian Women Mobilized,* 82.

101. Crown Counsel, Notes of Evidence, 133.

102. Notes of Evidence, 134.

103. Ibid., 132.

104. Ibid., 141.

105. Commission of Inquiry, 9.

106. Notes of Evidence, 20.

107. Ibid, 22.

108. Ibid., 31.

109. Ibid.

110. Mba, *Nigerian Women Mobilised,* 82.

111. Ibid, 14-16.

112. Ibid, 18.

113. Ibid, 14.

114. Ibid, 13-14.

115. Oriji, "Igbo Women."

116. Ibid.

117. Mba, *Nigerian Women Mobilised,* 96.

118. C. K. Meek *Ethnographical Report on the Peoples of Nsukka Division of Onitsha Province* (Lagos: Government Printer, 1930), 136-39.

119. Notes of Evidence, Appendix III, Lucy Pepple, 13.

120. Notes of Evidence, Appendix III, Edward James Crawford, Medical Officer, 23.

121. Ibid., 98.

Chapter 4

COLONIALISM AND THE SOCIAL STATUS OF WOMEN IN SOUTHEASTERN NIGERIA: THE IBIBIO WOMEN EXPERIENCE

Violeta I. Ekpo

INTRODUCTION

The status of women in Africa has been often interpreted as that of beasts of burden, exploited, humiliated and denigrated through the bondage of multiple births, oppressive and exploitative wifery, social inequality and political nullification. It is generally believed that Christianity and modern civilization brought social and economic liberation for the African women and wider opportunities for better education and improved social status. Yet, a closer look at the changing status of Ibibio women in the colonial society reveals that many of the contemporary discriminatory 'traditions' and 'customary' practices emerged in response to the new social, economic and political circumstances of colonization in Africa. This paper focuses on the specific role and status of Ibibio women in the pre-colonial society and how they are affected by change.

POSITION OF IBIBIO WOMEN IN TRADITIONAL SOCIETY

Studies of Ibibio folklore, cultural traditions and anthropological writings indicate that the female gender in traditional culture connoted sacredness, primordial potency and divine ritual powers for the perpetuation of the human existence and culture.[1] D. Talbot and P. Talbot cite ancient legends of matriarchal domination and female origin of the most powerful traditional societies among the Ibibio: *ekpo, ekpe* and *ekong,* the female gender which is still connected with vital secret rituals.[2] The mother concept *eka* is reflected in the most powerful deities and spirits of the Ibibio religious pantheon: *eka ekpo, eka abasi, eka ekong, eka idung,* etc. and is represented by the most powerful masks of their traditional cults.[3] Female priestesses, healers and diviners from the *Ndem, Ndam, Idiong, Inam* and other cults took vital part in the performance of sacred rituals affecting the individual and communal procreation, well-being and ritual purity.[4] The female functionaries in such ritual ceremonies used a variety of shrines and symbolic objects such as wooden pestles, pots, calabashes, carved staffs and eggs as ritual tools and as media for seeking spiritual protection and support in matters relating to fertility, virility and purity.[5]

Elderly women enjoyed special freedom of movement and privileges accorded to elders. They sat with men at village meetings, councils and societies and participated in important communal discussions and decisions on matters of life and death. Women of extraordinary character and unusual capabilities could 'marry' other women and form their own lineages.[6]

Ibibio women had a powerful influence in village, clan and lineage affairs through a number of exclusively female age sets (*nke iferi, asian ubo ikpa,* etc.), interest or co-operative labor groups such as *nka utem eyop* (association of palm oil producers), *nka urua* (market women union), *nka isip isong* (association of palm-kernel producers), *ndok ufok ebe* ("misfortunes of married life" group) etc. and through exclusively women's societies such as *ebre ikpaisong, abang, ekpa and iban isong,* which effectively organized and controlled the performance of their members' communal and domestic duties and obligations as well as the upbringing and moral behavior of women and the welfare of womenfolk.[7] These groups and associations operated under the umbrella of *iban isong* ('women of the land') organization, which was equivalent to 'women's government'. Its governing organs: *obio iban isong* (the general women's assembly), *iban isong esit* ('the hard-hearted'/women's judicial council) and *ekpa iban isong* or *ita* (the inner executive circle), exercised exclusive and ultimate powers over all women.

Their functions were parallel to those of the men's organs of government and helped to regulate all matters affecting women, at the same time jealously protecting the individual and collective interest of their members.[8] The power of 'the women's government' rested on the effective application of the methods of group consensus and social pressure, compulsory group mobilization and use of public demonstrations and strikes, supported by ultimate sacred rituals invoking female deities and the intervention of ancestral spirits on their behalf.[9] A collective strike, boycott or siege action by the entire women's body was a dreaded event by any individual or community and everything possible was done to placate the angry women and avoid a social calamity. The parallel and autonomous status of women was reflected in the allocation of special days and locations for women's activities—meetings, markets, burials, among others[10] and the accommodation of such separate activities within the communal calendar of events.

Within the family, the gender relations were anchored in partnership and reciprocity. The senior wife acted for the husband in his absence, provided leadership for the other wives and represented and controlled the entire female group on the compound. Children were considered to be their mother's responsibility and were identified within the community by her name. Married women retained their maiden names and some privileges in their parents' lineage, such as right to residence, protection and usufruct, which was also extended to their children. First daughters had special rights and obligations[11] and specific duties in the execution of their fathers' last rites.

Women were a major productive force in the Ibibio rural economy. They performed the principal part of the farm work, much of the fishing, often undertook the smoking of the fish and always the marketing, together with the making and selling of crafts.[12] At marriage, a woman was provided with some means of production (land, seedlings, tools and utensils) and/or initial trading capital (manilla currency or goods) by the husband and/or her parents (usually, her mother). She was henceforth expected to maintain herself and her children, assist her parents' extended family and supplement her husband's income through the production and sale of subsidiary products. Her time was spent entirely in outdoor activities: farming, food processing, and trading. The woman's right to independent income and personal property was jealously protected from any interferences and through her membership in women's groups and associations.[13] The colonial officers' ignorant disregard of the women's rights led to the attempt to count the women's personal effects and domestic animals and ultimately provoked the declaration of the famous 'Women's War' in 1929.[14]

Ibibio women controlled vital economic outlets—the markets. During the first half of the twentieth century, women's associations controlled market sales and attendance, held meetings and organized market activities. As their membership overlapped with that of other women organizations, they extended a strong influence outside the market limits on community issues of social and political significance. Strong and virile women unions controlled not only supply and distribution of the products, but, also, the means of production and the producers. The Idua fish-sellers' union at Oron controlled the fishing canoes and the fishermen.

Although by the nineteenth century, the main communal organs of government: the village and clan headship and the councils, as well as the major socio-political organizations (*ekpo, ekpe* and *ekong* societies) were controlled by men, Ibibio women preserved a defined and influential participation in the decision-making process though the activities of vibrant autonomous female organizations and selected representation in the main political organs.[15] Strong upright and capable women provided leadership in their communities and could occupy the headship of their extended families or villages, their influence often extending to the clan level.[16] Women were thus recognized as a vital component of the Ibibio society, which accorded them a status of respect and autonomy, reflecting their important role as mothers, wives, providers of food and agents of divine powers in the procreation and perpetuation of the community's existence and welfare.

Contrary to widely publicized views, neither the patriarchal tendencies in the African society, nor the prolific reproductive role of African women prevented them from active participation in the economic and political life of their communities.[17]

COLONIAL INFLUENCES AND EROSION OF WOMEN'S SOCIAL, ECONOMIC AND POLITICAL STATUS

Colonial rule trampled upon the inherent rights (both political and economic) of African women and enforced the doctrine of male superiority. The agents of British penetration: traders, Christian missionaries and colonial officers, handicapped by their own Victorian male-oriented background, dealt exclusively with a small section of the male population - village chiefs, traders, entrepreneurs, court clerks and native preachers. Unaware of the existence of parallel women institutions, they completely ignored the female sector of the indigenous society. The replacement of the existing multi-faceted traditional organs of government with exclusively male-dominated institutions (native courts, native authorities, district officers and warrant chiefs) at the beginning of the twentieth century totally excluded the women from the legislative, executive and judicial power and blocked off all official avenues for collective protest and seeking redress.[18] Similarly, the Christian church deprived women of spiritual authority. The Ibibio women's independence and their high visibility in communal affairs were treated as unnatural and unfeminine by the harbingers of the civilization doctrine, who aimed at molding submissive, domesticated and non-political Christian wives and mothers, suitable partners for the native preachers and teachers.[19]

"A little secular education" and a lot of Christian instructions in European "modesty and decorum," "social and moral ethics" and some domestic training in sewing, cooking, child welfare and hygiene were considered adequate for preparing the mission-trained girls for "Christian married life." The Qua Iboe mission rural evangelization and education required women to work in mission farms and maintain mission houses.[20]

Women were denied formal education and excluded from colonial civil service. Even though women were eventually recruited in the auxiliary services such as catering, nursing and teaching, the female workers were treated as appendages to their male guardians, fathers, brothers, or husbands. Male superiority was enforced in public and private, legal, administrative and political matters through regulations and practices that gave men advantages in employment, enumeration, taxation, fringe benefits, and official protocol.

The British colonial practice of demanding male guarantorship and representation in legal and official matters seriously hampered women's progress in the economic, political and social arenas because Ibibio women guarded jealously their economic independence and were trained to rely mostly on women group solidarity and cooperation in financial matters.[21]

During the colonial period, though women remained the majority of palm products producers and retail traders, they operated mostly on small-scale and individual bases in the local markets, while men enjoyed greater incentives in cash-crop production and large-scale trading as partners, suppliers and distributors. Men were able to encroach on activities traditionally reserved for women such as garri processing and retailing, palm produce distribution and marketing. Even then, Ibibio women were chiefly responsible for paying the fees and other school expenses for their children, whom they toiled to educate.

They took care of their immediate families and, often, of members of the extended families as well.

The economic depression in the 1920s and the introduction of direct taxation further worsened the women's income-earning ability and made them more dependent on men. Thus, to retain their economic independence and regain their collective influence over government policies, women became increasingly involved in various forms of anti-colonial activities in the 1920s: the anti-government women's dances, spiritual movements and numerous market riots in south-eastern Nigeria.[22]

Ekong Iban, the Women's War of 1929 (misnamed "Aba Women's Riots") represented the largest collective protest of women of various ethnic groups in the Eastern Provinces against the abrogation of their political rights and the encroachment on their economic independence. Planned and executed according to traditional strategies, it disrupted the social and economic life throughout the region and forced the introduction of new administrative and political reforms, which benefited women by exempting them from taxation.[23]

The massacre of the protesting women in 1929 effectively undermined the ability of the precolonial women's institutions to protect the collective women's interest and caused their demise, leaving governance largely to men.[24] The women's economic power base, however, remained in the local markets, where market women associations constituted themselves into active pressure groups. In times of crises, they rallied women to protest against social injustice, economic oppression and unpopular government policies. Throughout colonial rule, market-women disturbances, demonstrations and collective boycotts were widely used in protecting women's economic interests.[25]

In the early 1940s, women's branches of the Ibibio Union worked towards the educational and social advancement of women, achieving the first group sponsorship of Ibibio girls to study overseas.[26] Women branches of various development unions and local market-women associations also served as political ancillaries of the Nigerian political parties, providing votes, funds and massive popular support. Yet, Ibibio women in top party circles achieved their position either through individual initiative, or through their politician-husbands, not by being elected directly by the women's groups. They did reach back, like Emma Brown and Margaret Ekpo, to mobilize and utilize the women's group support in nationalist struggles. Women leaders like Rose Atakpo in Uyo and Nne Ndedu at Eket organized market and church women's groups, directed their welfare and economic activities and achieved respect and prestige in society. Traditional organizational and operational strategies such as ward organization and group solidarity energized women's social, economic, and religious groups. However, Ibibio women's activities remained restricted primarily to local and gender issues.

CONCLUSION

By the 1960s, woman's subordinate social status was intensified on many levels. The man was formally recognized as the head of the family, provider and leader, lord and master in his home. Dowry, which in pre-colonial times was a symbolic expression of a contracted union between two family groups, came to be regarded as an outright purchase payment. Wives became voiceless partners in marriage, often isolated from the decision-making process in their husbands' extended family. Financially, the woman was often exploited and abused, deprived of all property in case of separation or at the death of her husband. Her children and possessions were traditionally considered as belonging to her husband and his relations. She was by tradition expected to bear her husband's name, belong exclusively to his family place and union and be buried at his side when she died. In social gatherings and meetings, she could either be omitted completely, or brought in as a caterer or a protocol appendage. As a union member, she was trusted only with money and record-keeping, fund-soliciting and food-supply, but not as a leader. Petty trading was assumed to be the women's main supplementary occupation in addition to farming. Family, village and tribal allegiance was expected to prevail over gender solidarity. These are some of the many contemporary traditions which had no roots in pre-colonial Ibibio society, but were produced under colonial rule. Today, despite the officially promoted ideas of equality, these injustices are being promoted by various agencies—native courts, traditional rulers' councils, government officials and church leaders.

Inappropriate foreign notions for the exact measurement of the African woman's daily working hours, housework and child-rearing responsibilities, and leisure time are used in appalling contrast to the traditional all-encompassing activities of these women as providers of shelter, food, clothing, healthcare, education, moral and aesthetic values in the community, and in disregard to the customary added obligation of the marriage institution as an economic, social and political group contract. In the traditional rural communities women still stoically defend their freedom of movement and association, economic independence and their right to personal opinion and agency in the world around them. In some cases, they can still come out and take decisions that can impact men as well. The increasing economic pressures on women and their subsequent active involvement in revenue-yielding ventures, often as chief providers in the family, tend to support this trend.

The recent upsurge of Ibibio women's activism should then be seen as a renewed attempt to regain their traditional economic independence and active participation in the social and political decision making process, rather than as an imported innovation. In that respect, there is a need for detailed study of the actual role and position of women in pre-colonial society, as a prerequisite for the development of positive attitude and relevant strategies among African women towards the improvement of their social status. The facts strongly point out that African women have lost, rather than gained, during the last century the economic, social and political autonomy and power they had been accorded by the pre-colonial traditions and customs.[27]

Notes

1. A. Akpabio, *Ibibio Language and Customs* (Uyo: Marshall Press, 1980).

2. D. Amaury Talbot, *Women's Mysteries of a Primitive People* (1915) (London: Frank Cass, repr. 1968), 5, 193-9, 204 and P. Talbot, "Land of the Ibibios, Southern Nigeria," *Geographical Journal* 44 no. 3 (1914): 286-306.

3. Talbot, *Women's Mysteries,* 8-14, 201-2; E. A. Udo, *Who Are the Ibibio?* (Onitsha: Africana FEP Publishers 1983), 243.

4. Talbot, *Women's Mysteries,* 5-6; 15-16, 148, 191-3; 206-8; 217, Talbot, "Land of the Ibibios."; M. D. W. Jeffreys, "The Nyama Society of the Ibibio Women," *African Studies* 15, 1 (1956): 15-28

5. K. Nicklin, "The Ibibio Musical Pot," *African Arts* 7, 1 (1973): 50-55. Tabolt, *Women's Mysteries,* 177; Jeffreys, "The Nyama Society."; Judith Van Allen, "Aba Riots or Igbo Women's War? Ideology, Stratification and the Invisibility of Women," in N. Hafkin and E. Bay, eds. *Women in Africa* (Stanford: Stanford University Press, 1976), 59-85.

6. Akpabio, *Ibibio Language and Customs,* 43, E. Ekong, *Sociology of the Ibibio: Study of Social Organization and Change,* Calabar: Scholars Press 1983), 13; personal interviews.

7. Ekong, *Sociology of the Ibibio,* 101-4; M. Essang, *A Study of Oron Community - An Introductory Guide on the Cultural Heritage of Oron Society* (Calabar: PAICO, 1984), 33 36; Tabolt, *Women's Mysteries,* ch. 13; Udo, *Who Are the Ibibio?* 152-3.

8. Ekong, *Sociology of the Ibibio,* 80; Essang, *A Study of Oron Community,* 36.

9. E. O. Akpan and V. I. Ekpo, *The Women's War of 1929: A Popular Uprising in South Eastern Nigeria (Preliminary Study)* (Calabar: Government Press, 1988), 19, 55-58; V. I. Ekpo, "Characteristics of the Early Anti-colonial Women's Movement in Southeastern Nigeria," paper presented at the 37th Congress of the Historical Society of Nigeria, 18-20 May, 1992; M. E. Noah, "The Role, Status and Influence of Women in Traditional Times: The Example of the Ibibio of South-eastern Nigeria," *Nigeria Magazine* 53 no. 4 (1985); Judith Van Allen, "Aba Riots or Igbo Women's War? Ideology, Stratification and the Invisibility of Women," in Nancy Hafkin and Edna Bay, eds. *Women in Africa* (Stanford, CA: Stanford University Press, 1976).

10. Essang, *A Study of Oron Community,* 20; personal information.

11. Ekong, Sociology *of the Ibibio.*

12. Talbot, *Women's Mysteries,* 112.

13. M. E. Noah, "The Role, Status and Influence of Women in Traditional Times: The Example of the Ibibio of South-eastern Nigeria," *Nigeria Magazine* 53 no. 4 (1985); Judith Van Allen, "Sitting on a Man: Colonialism and the Lost Political Institutions of Igbo Women," *Canadian Journal of African Studies* 7 no. 2 (1972): 165-81 and Van Allen, "Aba Riots."

14. Akpan and Ekpo, *The Women's War of 1929,* 21.

15. Ekong, *Sociology of the Ibibio,* 80.

16. Personal information.

17. Nina Mba, *Nigerian Women Mobilised: Women's Political Activity in Southern Nigeria: 1900-1965* (Berkeley: University of California Press 1982).

18. Mba, *Nigerian Women Mobilised*, ch. 2; Van Allen, "Aba Riots."

19. J. Ward, *In and Around Oron Country, or, The Story of Primitive Methodism in Southern Nigeria* (London: Hammond, (nd), 66; Van Allen, "Aba Riots."

20. R. M'Keown, *In the Land of the Oil Rivers: The Story of the Qua Iboe Mission*, (1902), 97-8, 146-7 and R. M'Keown, *Twenty-five Years in Qua Iboe: The Story of a Missionary Effort in Nigeria* (London: Morgan and Scott, 1912), 163; Ward, *In and Around Oron Country*, 33, 36 and E. S. Watt, *The Quest of Souls in Qua Iboe* (London: Marshall, Morhan and Scot, 1951), 76, 78.

21. V. I. Ekpo, "Characteristics of the Early Anti-colonial Women's Movement in Southeastern Nigeria," paper presented at the 37th congress of the Historical Society of Nigeria, Calabar, 18-20 May, 1992; Mba, *Nigerian Women Mobilised*, 51, 102.

22. Ekpo, "Characteristics."

23. E. O. Akpan and V. I. Ekpo, "The Calabar Women's Revolt of 1925," in *Women in Development: Cross River State Experience* (Calabar: Media Women Publication, 1987), E. O. Akpan and V. I. Ekpo, *The Women's War of 1929*; Adiele E. Afigbo, *The Warrant Chiefs; Indirect Rule in Southern Nigeria 1891-1929* (London: Longman, 1972); Van Allen, "Sitting on a Man."

24. Van Allen, "Sitting on a Man."

25. V. I. Ekpo, "The Role of Market Women in the Nigerian Social and Political Development," paper presented to the International Association of students in Economics and Management, UNICAL chapter at the University of Calabar, Calabar, July, 1990; V. I. Ekpo, "Characteristics of the Early Anti-colonial Women's Movement in Southeastern Nigeria," paper presented at the 37th congress of the Historical Society of Nigeria, Calabar, 18-20 May 1992; Mba, *Nigerian Women Mobilised*, 101-5, 107-114.

26. M. E. Noah, *Ibibio Pioneers in Modern Nigerian History* (Uyo: Scholars Press, 1980), 112; personal interviews.

27. Noah, "The Role, Status and Influence of Women," 53.

Chapter 5

SOCIAL CHANGE AND GENDER RELATIONS IN SOUTHEASTERN NIGERIA C. 1650-1900

Raphael Chijioke Njoku
and Tomarra A. Adams

> Change is the essence of human history; under colonial-
> ism, just as in the several ages before...men and women
> had to adapt themselves and their institutions to change...
> the more interesting question for the historian to ask is
> the manner and methods by which adaptation is carried
> on.—*J.F. Ade Ajayi*

This chapter provides a broad overview of social change and gender relations in the Igbo area of southeastern Nigeria in the period beginning from about the mid-seventeenth century to the eve of British colonial rule. The study focuses on the impetus for change that came with expansions in both regional and over-seas trade relations (including the slave trade), cross-regional migrations, and the rise of Aro oracular power and the impact of these dynamics on the restructuring of power relations, gender roles, lifestyles, family systems, agricultural production, division of labor, dietary habits, social values and behaviors in the Igbo area. Most of the existing studies on gender in Africa have either been concerned with colonial influences on women's issues or preoccupied with the recent struggles for women's empowerment across the globe. Studies of colonialism have identified Western agencies—namely structures of colonial administration, cash economy, education and Christianity—as forces of social alteration in the former colonies.[1] Furthermore, the rapidly expanding scholarships on gender are often packaged in form of reactions to Western scholars' misinterpretation of African cultural practices.[2] The weight of outside influence on gender studies is even more salient in the ongoing pressures exerted by Western powers on undemocratic regimes across the world to foster socioeconomic and political structures accommodative of the interests of the marginalized in the society, including women.

The present analysis neither questions the power of European institutions in social transformation in Africa since the colonial era nor denies the increasing watchdog role Western donor institutions and civil society networks have assumed in Third World politics. The discussion is also less concerned with scholarly challenges to wrongly held notions about Africa. The point here, as J. F. Ade Ajayi has aptly underscored, is that change is the quintessence of human societies across history; at every era, men and women have responded to forces of change.[3] Without any visible and direct European influence, the southeastern Nigerian society was already experiencing far-reaching changes in the precolonial era, even though the later colonial presence proper radically accelerated and also eclipsed the pace of the previous trends. Thus, it is important to underscore African initiatives in the development of historical transformations in order to demonstrate that Africa has agency and that the various indigenous societies were not static before the era of colonialism.

Meanwhile, one must recognize the obvious methodological difficulties mitigating this area of scholarly inquiry. An African historian who aims to uncover aspects of precolonial Africa bearing evidence of indigenous initiatives is often challenged, if not discouraged, by both absence of written documents, and the arduous task of sorting through timeless and disjointed oral accounts. Yet, available anthropological, ethnographical and historical sources, when closely examined, can provide useful insights into aspects of social reordering and gender relationships in precolonial southeastern Nigeria.

Additional problems of research may be identified as the risks of anachronism and romanticism. While anachronism, as identified here means the problem of using contemporary situations to judge historical actors who lived in the past, romanticism denotes a conscious or unconscious attempt to over-exaggerate or even portray one's local history as radically exceptional from others. While most of the issues examined here dwell on Igbo history, these are not in anyway unique to the Igbo alone but pertain to some other neighboring ethnic groups in the region. Despite sharing such common attributes as language, social customs and a highly decentralized system of village-based political organization; the hundreds of independent villages that make up the Igbo area hardly conceived themselves as "Igbo" in the precolonial era. The notion of *Igboness* emerged later with the rise of nationalist movements of the late 1930s and 1940s.

BACKGROUND TO THE SOCIAL RECONFIGURATIONS OF THE SEVENTEENTH CENTURY

Internal migrations, trade, and emergence of the Aro oracular power were some of the key historical events that contributed in laying the foundation on which some major social transformations of the seventeenth century and after were grafted. While small-scale migrations have always been part of Igbo history and social formation, the fourteenth and fifteenth centuries, as L. C. Okere concurs, witnessed the movement of outside groups into Igboland. These movements brought some Bini (Benin) or Edo elements into Onitsha, Oguta, and several Ezechima village communities in western area of Igboland.[4] While these migrants who borrowed some elements of Edo political structures claim ancestral linkage with the Edo people, the name of their remote ancestor Eze Chima suggests that most of them were at least Igbo speakers who once came under Benin control. By implication, such a hydridity of cultures would impact on existing gender relations. Other cultural habits of these host communities must also be understood as a product of both Igbo and Bini practices.

Prior to the sixteenth century commercial contacts with Europeans through the Niger Delta coastal middlemen, various Igbo communities had established wide-ranging regional trade relations with their fellow Igbo and non-Igbo neighbors. Early European visitors including a Portuguese geographer in the sixteenth century, Duarte Pacheco Pereira, had reported witnessing a vigorous trade in salt, fish, and other riverine products, which the coastal people of the Niger Delta exchanged for yam, palm oil, plantain, banana, pepper, bullocks, goats and chicken from the Igbo hinterland.[5] In certain instances, these contacts were cemented by marriage, war, and oracular or ritual alliances. It is thus explicit that Igbo society and culture developed in association with neighboring societies like the Efik and Ibibio to the East, Ijo and Kalabari to the South, Edo to the West, and the Igala, Idoma and Jukun to the North. Felicia Ekejiuba has noted the profound Igala influence evident on the Ossomari's sociopolitical institutions. These were as a result of "a long period of trade contact and intermarriage" relations between the two groups.[6]

It is also noteworthy that the all-powerful *Ibiniukpabi* oracle of Arochukwu (known to the British as the Long Juju) would heavily impact on existing gender practices. Originally the oracle belonged to the Ibibio/Efik neighbors. In the sixteenth century, the Aro seized control of the oracular institution and transformed it into a more powerful instrument of terror and power. Michael Echeruo explains that one of the secrets of the Aro success at oracular hegemony in southeastern Nigeria is that the Aro custodians were careful not to directly challenge the power position occupied by the Earth goddess (*Ala*) in the indigenous religious system. Among the Igbo, the Earth goddess was the principal deity no man or woman could afford to offend or treat as inconsequential. While the belief in a Supreme Being

(*Chukwu*) has been an integral part of the indigenous belief system, *Ala* was feared and respected as the power behind production, and reproduction, including fertility, life and death, and harmony and social order. According to Echeruo, the rise of such oracular deities like *Kamalu* (god of thunder) and the *Igwe-ka-ala* of Umunneoha (which supposes that the sky is mightier than the earth) was in direct challenge to the power and authority of the Earth goddess and the belief system of the Igbo people.[7]

Given that every aspect of Igbo life was linked with the indigenous religious belief system, this trend in oracular influence implicates radical shifts on power, and gender relations. In the years that the various oracular institutions reigned, the Igbo belief system and the central role women played as spiritual leaders were gradually heading towards a new sociopolitical and economic adaptation. The individuals and groups that previously enjoyed the power and privileges attached to these institutions were also affected. While the Aro custodians of the Long Juju carefully avoided a direct challenge to the position of the Earth goddess; the domination of Aro men in the organization and running of the oracular system was significant in the sense that it prevented Aro women from appropriating spiritual, economic and political powers commensurate with that enjoyed by their men and other Igbo women elsewhere. Furthermore, wherever the Aro settled in large numbers as evidenced in their various satellite communities, including Arondizuogu, Mbano, Aguata, Ndiekerionwu, and so on, their presence as "children of Supreme God" (*Aro-Chukwu*) tended to relegate to a secondary role, the influence of diviners, mediums and medicine men and women in their host communities. In other places where Aro oligarchic control was limited such as in Nnewi, Onitsha and Asaba in particular, women continued to enjoy substantial religious, economic, and political influences through control of local trade, marriage and funeral rites, and performance of other initiation and purification rituals.

Editors Stephen Miescher and Lisa Lindsay have argued in their "Introduction" to *Men and Masculinities in Modern Africa* that gender constructions are rooted in a dialectic. According to the authors, "how men and women see and represent themselves, and how gender relations are organized and promoted, are shaped by larger socioeconomic, cultural, and religious transformations."[8] Indeed, the dynamics of social change and gender relations in precolonial eastern Nigerian society corroborates this view. In an African traditional society where the sacred and the profane were interwoven, and individuals and groups interpret and understand their world through the prism of religion, the new impulses in power relations and religion as described above, initiated new changes in individual lifestyles, family structures, and gender relations, and these continued to develop and expand in the subsequent centuries. Thus, internal developments within Igboland were both stimulated and supplemented by impulses from non-Igbo neighbors, which in turn helped define the background of a dynamic gender relation prior to the colonial era stimulus that helped in broadening the earlier contacts.[9]

THE SEVENTEENTH CENTURY DYNAMICS: POWER AND GENDER RELATIONS

In his informative study of precolonial trade in Igboland, Northrup explains that the early sixteenth century Portuguese visitors purchased palm oil along with cotton cloth, leopard skins, beads, pepper, and slaves on the Foçados River on the mouth of Niger Delta for sale at Elmina on the Gold Coast in modern Ghana.[10] The study, however, is not specific on the identity of the African suppliers of the goods who, by their initiative, opened a new chapter in southern Nigeria's economic history. What is not in doubt is that most of the products sought by the Europeans originated from the Igbo hinterland. Soon, this early commercial relations expanded to include higher demands for slaves, which continued to grow, overshadowing the other items of trade until its abolition by Britain in 1807 when the success of the Industrial Revolution in Europe radically increased the demand for palm oil produce. It is important to stress here that for the next four centuries following the early European contacts, Africans participated in the trade while also adapting their institutions in response to both external and internal stimuli.

The seventeenth century expansion in trade indirectly brought the Igbo closer within the Afro-European trading network, introduced new items of commerce and consumption, while expanding the existing regional trading networks. Although the middlemen from the coastal city-states of the Niger Delta dominated the overseas trade, the Igbo hinterland markets supplied the most sought after items of trade like palm oil and slaves. As Northrup observes, the European commercial demands at the coast would not have been sustained without a long history of internal developments during the millennium prior to 1800. In fact, "it was the Europeans who had to make the adaptation to existing African patterns."[11] It is an examination of how the impact brought by the expanding internal and external commercial activities restructured power relations, lifestyles, family system, gender roles, social values and behaviors in the Igbo area that this paper is directed.

Power is conceived as the capacity of the individual in a position of authority to influence others and the outcome of their activities. It also involves the ability to persuade or compel obedience and channel thoughts and social actions toward a targeted desire, objective or goal. Egodi Uchendu underscores that "power also means control over resources, including human resources, and of core social institutions; control that makes possible both the effective initiation of actions and decisions and the use of effective sanctions."[12] Yet, the historian who interprets power relations must also keep in mind that there are other extensive and dispersed arenas of power and control. Besides the view of strategic elite, including wealthy individuals, groups, titleholders, religious and the educated elites as people of power, the less visible categories of people like wives, girlfriends, servants and children, have also different spheres of power and influence. In an indigenous southern Nigerian society where power was widely dispersed, gender relations will be analyzed in the context of power and exercise of authority. Ways of exercising power included political participation, personal achievements and recognition, possession of uncommon skills, intellect or knowledge, as well as spiritual power.

In Igbo, as common in all patrilineal societies, men assumed a position of superiority over women. This was best expressed in the preference for male children (as primary inheritors of the family estate) over female children. Igbo society is characterized by gender differentiation as one of the dominant markers of social relations. In his *My Africa* published in 1946, Mbonu Ojike (1914-1956), a popular African nationalist, noted that in the traditional Arondizuogu society for instance, men, women, and children had their respective separate worlds of influence, even though these gendered and detached worlds operated in mutual cooperative endeavor.[13] Ojike's work corroborates pioneering work on Igbo by Olaudah Equiano, whose memoir published in 1789 remains one of the most important sources of information on indigenous Igbo social life and customs. According to Equiano, the Igbo "assembly is separated into four divisions" comprising "the married men, the married women, the young men and the maidens."[14]

How long this form of social organization has been in existence is difficult to determine. The mass of available evidence points to the antiquity of its existence in the various patrilineal and matrilineal societies of sub-Saharan Africa. However, it must not be assumed that this order was cast in a rigid and changeless order. Ifi Amadiume's *Male Daughters, Female Husbands* reveals a lot about the flexible gender system in Nnobi community in particular, and in southeastern Nigeria in general. According to Amadiume, this flexibility

> resulted not only in role ambiguity, but also in status ambiguity. In the political system there was flexibility in gender classification, which allowed the incorporation of certain categories of women into the male category, giving them positions of authority in the power structure. Daughters were, for example, regarded as males in relation to wives. Consequently, sex, in this context, did not correspond to gender.[15]

Additionally, Nwando Achebe's biography of the legendary Ahebi Ugbabe (1880-1948), (aka *Agamega* or "Female Leopard") of Enugu-Ezike, northern Igboland further supports the fact that "notions of manhood and masculinity were constructed, negotiated, and challenged by women and men."[16] In other words, although masculine power, in most instances, dominated politics and control of means of production and reproduction in Igboland, yet, in other places, female power, as reposed in such institutions as the daughters of the clan association (*otu ụmụada*), for instance, existed as a forum for the promotion and protection of women's collective interests.

There were also women's professional guilds for potters and weavers, which helped defend the interests of members including their rights to the market and continued economic independence. A lot has been written recently on the economic independence of Igbo/African women in the precolonial times.[17] This notion of independence is based largely on women's purported control of the local markets. Writing in 1920, Georges Basden, a British clergy and scholar stated that "the whole of the native trade among the Ibos are in the hands of women and by them the markets are controlled." Basden added that "Ordinarily no Ibo man takes any part in the actual buying and selling—if an Ibo man be seen buying in the market it is almost an indication that he is either a stranger or a man with no women folk to act for him."[18] Drawing from Basden's book, the subsequent studies on Igbo social life in the precolonial era have reached the conclusion that African women have always been the 'lords' of the market. Recent studies tend to assume that the observed vigorous participation of women in trade in the late nineteenth century has been the same without any change. These studies have largely ignored the basic difference between 'marketing' (*izu ahia*) and 'trading' (*igba ubiri or igba ugharama*). Thus, there is confusion over whether men actually participated vigorously in trading or not. Northrup has shed some light on this issue, which may help decipher a dynamic trading occupation rather than an assumption of a gender specific profession. According to Northrup, in precolonial Igboland, although "a large, well-attended market was very desirable, since it added to a village's prestige, most of what went on in it was 'marketing' (*izu ahia*), i.e. subsistence exchange for utility rather than for profit, which was generally in the hands of women. 'Trading' (*igba ubiri*), i.e. buying at one place and selling at a profit elsewhere, has traditionally been in the hands of the men."[19]

If this clarification is accepted, and it sounds plausible for a traditional society with limited means of transportation and the apparent dangers associated with traveling, especially long-distance journeys, then one may surmise that men were better positioned for more lucrative trading expeditions/ventures in the period before the later nineteenth century developments observed by Basden. This insight upholds Austin Ahanotu's assertion that women in Africa were mostly "preoccupied with the home economy, and were unable to accumulate wealth outside the domestic terrain."[20] However, at this point in Igbo economic history, one neither speaks of a marketing grid nor extensive ownership of private property due to what Obafemi Awolowo has identified as "insuperable physical obstacles to such acquisitions and ownership."[21]

In light of the post seventeenth century developments, the expansions in commerce and more vigorous contact with non-Igbo neighbors introduced new problems as well as new momentum for economic empowerment in the Igbo area. This impetus also affected changes in power and gender relations. One can elaborate on this with the impact of the overseas trade on the indigenous textile industry in Igboland. Originally, Igbo women controlled the textile industry, which helped them maintain some measure of economic independence in the household. Items produced and sold by the local weavers included bags, local hand fans, cotton clothes, mat, and other items. While women of Uturu, for instance, were widely known for their intricate mat designs, their counterparts in Asa, Ndoki (Akwette), Abakiliki, Nsukka, Mbieri, and Asaba were famous for their cloth-weaving skills. The highly durable indigenous textile materials had various uses, including as wearing apparels for either enhancing beauty or to meet social conventions of decency. The indigenous fabrics were also used for making bags and reclining chairs, and for dressing up masquerades believed to be visiting ancestral spirits.

Among them, the popular "Akwette cloth," whose origin has been traced by Venice Lamb and Judy Holms to the arrival of the Portuguese in the sixteenth century, remains the most popular and highly prized of the indigenous textile products.[22] According to Lamb and Holms, the expansion of the Niger Delta trade as a result of the European presence had facilitated the flourishing of the Akwette weaving industry in the late eighteenth and early nineteenth centuries. However, Gloria Chuku's recent study, which employed a variety of sources including archival and oral sources, has noted an indigenous origin of the Akwette-weaving industry. This study mentions one legendary Dada Nwankata who claimed to have learnt all her designs through dreams, worked in secrecy and introduced innovations, using European imported yarns and silks to beautify her designs.[23] By the late nineteenth century, however, the indigenous weaving suffered both corruption and decline in the face of a stiff European competition. European threads soon replaced locally grown hands-pun and hand-dyed cotton. Also European designs and patterns were incorporated into the Akwette cloths.

In connection with social change and gender relations, the transformation witnessed in the textile industry illustrates a number of points that need be highlighted. First, while women controlled the textile industry and the textile markets in the local areas, it does not necessarily mean that women were also responsible for distributing these products in far-distant regional markets. Rather men were better placed to do the long-distance and often risky trading missions across several independent and sometimes hostile villages stretching from the hinterlands to the coastal areas and vice versa. For instance, the Akwete cloth produced in Ndoki, a border community to the south, was sold in far away markets in the western and northern edges of Onitsha and Nsukka of the Igbo area respectively. Although such products may have passed from hand to hand until they reached their final destination, in which case women may have been actively involved in the distribution, women were not among the Aro traders identified by Equiano as the "stout mahogany-colored men from the south-west" or "red men living at a distance" who covered hundreds of miles on foot to bring fire-arms, gun-powder, hats, beads, and dried fish for exchange at the local markets in Isseke in the 1750s.[24]

Second, it was the men, rather than the women, who served as the conduits of change in the textile industry. This started with exchange of the indigenous fabrics and other hinterland commodities like yam, with coastal products like salt, fish and periwinkle. Gradually with the arrival of foreign textile, the men began to import into the hinterlands European threads, samples of foreign designs and patterns, and imported cotton, which they sold for profit. This insight lends support to Northrup's more nuanced account of trade among the Igbo in the precolonial era which explains that 'trading' (*igba ubiri*)—that is "buying at one place and selling at a profit elsewhere, has traditionally been in the hands of the men."[25] The local weavers adopted the new items of importations to transform the *modus operandi* of the indigenous textile industry.

While the commercial expansions undercut the local textile industry and thus displaced women from this source of livelihood and societal recognition, it also provided those in the western riverine communities of Asaba, Onitsha, Ossomari, Illah and other Ika Igbo areas, with the possibilities to acquire wealth and social influence through trade. With time, the achievements of these women were recognized with the highly influential female chieftaincy institution known as the *omu* or "queen mother." As a forum for the promotion and protection of women's interests, the *omu* institution offered the women the opportunity to appropriate enormous power and social recognition.

The origin of the *omu* institution, which was a parallel institution of authority to the kingship (*obi*) institution of the Onitsha, Asaba, Illah, and Ossomari communities, possibly coincided with the period when the early Portuguese traders first arrived in the delta in the 1480s. However, the scanty information available may not be enough to argue for a direct connection between the early beginnings of the overseas commercial relationship and the development of the female chiefship. Historians of Africa "who seek to reconstruct the early history of a preliterate and acephalous people" as Adiele Afigbo underscores, "can easily fall victim to either wild romanticism or sterile skepticism."[26] Nina

Mba speculates that the *omu* society may have either "developed at the same time with the obiship or was introduced much later as a result of Igala influence."[27] Since the cost of taking the title was enormous, it is most likely that the expansion of the overseas trade over the succeeding centuries provided some women traders with an opportunity to expand their businesses and gradually accumulate the wealth and societal recognition later to be associated with the *omu* titleholders. The successes of these exceptionally talented women also changed social influence and gender relations. Chuku's study provides us with an insight into the rights and privileges of an *omu* titleholder in Onitsha:

> The *Omu*, like the king [of Onitsha], wielded enormous power and authority. Once the *Omu* was installed, she was handed her staff of office by the king. She possessed all the insignia of royalty such as the sword and fan. She had her own palace and could not be deposed by the king. She performed rededication (*ofala*) just like the king and, her funeral was marked by a human sacrifice as in the king's funeral. *Omu*'s council members (*Otu Ogene*) held similar positions and could be bestowed titles as the king's council members (*Ndichie*).... The Omu controlled all markets and virtually all trade in Onitsha. All the women were under her authority.[28]

Ekejiuba, whose biographical sketch of Omu Okwei (1872-1943) of Ossomari remains one of the most detailed on the topic, adds that the "Omu, the chairman of the Council of Women and the official queen of Ossomari reigns side by side with the King... In addition to her royal status, the Omu has military, religious and administrative functions. She is the field marshal and her war canoe must lead others in any military expedition."[29] Thus, the fact that *omu* titleholders controlled an enormous amount of material resources had significant implications for social and gender relations. First and foremost, the size of this new form of wealth, often created with slave labor, was formerly unknown in the indigenous society. By implication, it corroborates Obafemi Awolowo's critique of the notion of traditional African socialism as a grossly misunderstood concept. In his *The People's Republic*, Awolowo argues that capitalism was not alien to Africa; insisting that until the introduction of paper money, the wealthy African wisely maintained a retinue of dependents whose services were vital in moving his cows, bags of cowries or iron bars and other bulky and perishable items that served as stores of value in times of crisis. This need, Awolowo argues, was responsible for the pre-colonial African's practice of socialism rather than "any adherence to the principles of socialism of which they [the Africans] were never conscious."[30] The *omu*, a good example of Awolowo's targeted critique, exploited male and female labor (free or bonded) for capitalist accumulation. One may rightly perceive the size of wealth created by the 'queen mothers' as an expansion of the indigenous propensity towards capitalist accumulation.

Second, the practices of the 'queen mothers' and their wealth raises questions about the myth of men's exploitation of female labor in traditional African system of production. In a related but different study, Susan Martin asserts that within "most hinterland Igbo societies, the key to a man's success in commercial palm production lay in control of women's labor. Martin claims that women did most of the job in palm oil processing and cassava cultivation, but their male household heads were able to claim ownership of the product."[31] Such a sweeping charge brings to mind a similar allegation brought by Mary Slessor of the Church of Scotland Mission on gender relations in Arochukwu in precolonial times. On her arrival in 1903, Mary Slessor had expressed alarm at what she perceived as excessive degree of women's dependency in the social system. "They have no proper status in the community, being simply the creatures of man to be exploited and degraded—his laborer, his drudge, the carrier of his kernels and oil, the boiler of his nuts. A girl child not betrothed by her guardian [sic] lacks the protection of the law. She can, if not attached to some man, be insulted or injured with impunity."[32] Elsewhere I have argued that Slessor's perception was that of an outsider, and therefore open to over-exaggeration. The truth remains that the structure of gender relations that existed in precolonial Arochukwu society must be examined and understood in the context of the indigenous modes of production and structures of power. The gender practices were constructed for family disciple and social control.[33]

The power and influence associated with the position of the female chiefship as outlined above demonstrates that caution must be applied in the reading of a local culture by outsiders such as Slessor. The commercial expansions of the post-seventeenth century provided a stimulus, which helped generate a new social trend that enabled some women gain prominence in society. These women enjoyed enormous prestige, political influence and power that were far beyond the reach of most Igbo men. According to Ekejiuba's 1967 study, the *omu* titleholders in Ossomari owned slaves, merchant vessels, and enormous commercial concerns.[34] Pursuing this point from a different angle in an anthropological work on Onitsha published in 1972, Richard Henderson concluded that the queen mother had at times so challenged the authority of "the king that she has threatened his position."[35] Indeed, the *omu* chiefship declined in the late nineteenth century following a serious power tussle between the king of Onitsha and a very radical *omu* of the town, known as Nwagboka (1884-1886), who was crowned an *omu* by the Obi of Onitsha, Anazonwa I.[36] Although the cause of the discord is not clear to contemporary historians, the rift between queen mother and the king was so deep that at her death in 1886, the Onitsha monarch refused to appoint her successor, bringing to an end the *omu* institution in Onitsha. A contemporary social historian may observe that today among the Igbo, Onitsha women are widely regarded by their neighbors as highly liberated and money conscious. While the degree of love for money may differ from individual-to-individual and thus making a sweeping generalization wrong, it is important to link this observed peculiarity among Onitsha women to the social history of the *omu* institution and women's commercial influence in the area.

If the expansion in commercial relations produced a new genre of rich women, it also brought about the emergence of a new class of wealthy men (or *ogaranyas*) in Igboland. This was particularly witnessed in those Igbo areas like Aniocha, Ngwa, Arondizuogu, Bende, Owerri, Mbieri and Arochukwu, to mention but a few. A number of individuals from these areas mostly exploited the opportunities created by the trade in slaves and palm oil for accumulation of personal wealth. With expansions in the volume of the import and export trade, the profit wealth that came with it turned the new men into arrogant and often informal but lawless political patrons.[37] In their different studies, Richard Ohizu, Elizabeth Isichei, Felix Ekechi, and Don Ohadike have all made a brief reference to the *ogaranyas* of the late eighteenth and nineteenth centuries as a new social force that challenged the traditional structures of power and values in their respective communities.[38] These previous studies also highlight the increased recourse of the 'new men' to militarism in the Igbo area. According to Ohadike, one of the "most notable changes of the mid nineteenth century in the western Igbo area was the sudden expansion of domestic slavery and a rise of new class of slave owners that elbowed out the elders and age grades as the effective rulers of the society."[39] These were the individuals who banded into the formidable *ekumeku* armed resistance against British colonial intrusion in the western Igbo area.

Indeed, militarism was only one out of other ongoing social issues; the full impact of the new class of wealthy men or "robber barons" on gender and family structures has not yet been assessed. Ohizu, in his *The Original History of Arondizuogu from 1650-1960* noted that some of these "important men in Arondizuogu used to marry 20-40 wives and each of the wives had her own private house in the very compound" [sic].[40] While neither monogamy nor polygamy was alien to precolonial Igbo society in particular and Africa in general, the new practice of acquiring dozens of wives and the capacity to provide them with private houses and other needs marked a new social phenomenon in gender relationships. First, it represented a sphere of informal power claimed by these individuals. According to John Illife in a related but different study, "the large complex household headed by a Big Man surrounded by his wives, married and unmarried sons, younger brothers, poor relations and dependents, and swarming children" represented a "key colonizing group."[41] Second, it marked a shift in values as parents encouraged their male children to aspire to the *ogaranya* status. Parents also pushed their female children to welcome marriages with the 'new men'. In his memoir, Equiano had observed that in the 1750s such propensity to violence was not unknown to Igbo women. "All are taught the use of weapons; even our women are warriors, and march boldly out to fight along with the men. Our whole district is a kind of militia."[42] Thus, while the Aba women's war (*ogu umunwanyi*) of 1929/30 have been over flogged in the extant literature, it may be important to explore a possible connection between the women's predisposition to protests and violence and the societal trends emerging from the preceding centuries.

Third, the emergence of the *ogaranyas* marked a new trend in consumption patterns, which included an increased appetite for sex and food. As Michael Schatzberg argues in a different but related study on sub-Saharan Africa, the standard idea "that power is designed to induce changes in behavior and that it is often met with resistance," differs from its African context. "Power and politics in African societies often have more to do with consumption than transformation.... Power concerns the capacity to consume, or the ability 'to eat'" as often encountered in local idioms and discourses. Correlating food, corruption, sexuality, size, and power as aspects of politics and everyday life in contemporary Africa, Schatzberg concludes that "one is powerful if one can "eat"; the more one eats, the more powerful one becomes.[43] Although Schatzberg's study is concerned with contemporary Africa, the conclusion reached provides a vivid idea about the importance of size and consumption ability in the precolonial era. As the careers of the *ogaranyas* reveal, such patterns of consumption capacity implies a continuity of tradition in social change.

In general, with the rise of the new men, one may also identify a significant change in eldership, family structure and gender relations. As Leith-Ross' study on women's view of polygamy in the early colonial period suggests, some first wives in such large households readily welcomed the new trend in acquisition of multiple wives by their husbands. Such an attitude of accommodation by the senior wives was on the grounds that an addition of each new wife meant an increase in the number of people under the control of the most senior women in the households. It is noteworthy that in the colonial period when both the European churches and colonial administration condemned polygamy, some Igbo women rose in protest against what they came to perceive as the abandoning of the old order.[44]

Like every polygamous family, quarrels and petty bickering were not uncommon to the emergent larger households. This in turn brought about problem of family control. In the Ngwa area for instance, men with dozens of wives found it nearly impossible to satisfy their wives' sexual needs. The concubinage (*iko mbara*) practices emerged in the period before the turn of the twentieth century as an institution that permitted extramarital affairs. Husbands turned a blind eye to wives who kept companions as a way to satisfy their sexual needs. The legal husbands of these lecherous women accepted the children that resulted from such relationships. According to Victor Uchendu, "through concubinage a woman can get a husband to share his [husband's] 'exclusive sexual right' with a paramour chosen by the bride and acceptable to the bridegroom."[45] This new practice was in sharp contrast to the serious consequences of adultery in most parts of Igbo area in the period before 1750s. According to Equiano's eyewitness account, at least before the turn of the nineteenth century, adultery "was punished with slavery and death." Such forms of harsh punishment, he believed, existed "throughout most of the nations of Africa, so sacred among them is the honor of marriage bed, and so jealous are they of the fidelity of their wives."[46] Thus, the *iko* practice among the Ngwa represented a crucial shift in values and marriage/family practices in the Ngwa area. In some other places like Nnobi, the elders responded to the trend in sexual laxity and breakdown in family obedience with new rules stipulating that "on such and such days any people fighting, quarrelling, or crying will give a fowl as an indemnity." In instances where such fines failed to secure the elusive peace, "the head of the family also uses another" strategy "called *afolaja*, to maintain peace in the family." The term *afolaja* is difficult to translate into English. Literally translated, perhaps the closest phrase to it may be "do not abuse sacrifice" or never abuse sacrifice or privilege." This is a kind of charm known also as "accept advice" (*onye adumara kwe*). This therapy was believed to add some mystic force into the voice of the family head and could compel obedience within the nuclear family.[47]

Among the Aro, the new impetus in commercial transaction and wealth structure also affected the existing division of labor and gender relations. What is well known in the literature on Aro is the extension of Aro commercial network across southeastern Nigeria as the slave trade expanded. It is important to note that the frequent absence of most Aro men from home created new problems which often required strict measures in order to maintain family discipline and social control. In fact, the seemingly domination of women, which Mary Slessor had observed in Arochukwu in the early colonial period was part of a new social construct aimed at instilling obedience in the family and kinship systems. Different but related studies of migrant labor in Southern Africa have shown that families with absentee husbands or fathers are often susceptible to role swap, dissent, rebellion, and moral breakdown.[48] Among the Aro of whom trading, especially long-distance trading, was the major occupation for men, certain steps were taken by elders to maintain social control and instill family obedience and social conventions. These included objections to Aro women contracting unions to non-Aro men. Also a strict widowhood practice was recommended as a way to guard against women's rebellion to existing mores.

Having secured their homes with these laws, Aro men felt secure to travel, while the women assumed greater responsibility in family management, agriculture, and other matters. Before the nineteenth century changes, Leith-Ross explains that Igbo women hardly took their younger children to farms or markets. Rather, at the earliest age, care of babies was instilled in the young children's mind. "These children take their position as nursemaid very seriously; even the small boys will be seen wiping the baby sister's nose with utmost care and quickly twisting a little grass together so that it should not sit down on the bare ground."[49] The author considers this as one of the most attractive features of Igbo family life. While Leith-Ross' study is concerned with the early colonial period, it may also be surmised that with the frequent absence of husbands and younger men from home, wives had to employ the extra available hands in the farms, as well as in the homes. For instance, grandparents began to offer more help with childcare.

Across the entire Igboland, as the palm oil trade became the main economic stay of the Igbo people in the nineteenth century, palm kernel, a by-product of oil processing, acquired commercial value in the 1870s. In southern Nigeria, at least before the nineteenth century, oil palm trees belonged to the kinship group under the control of elders. However, women dominated production in the industry, especially since they were free to collect the ripe-fallen nuts, which they processed primarily for household consumption or for exchange by barter with other commodities needed by the members of a household. The situation changed radically with the unparalleled demand for palm produce from industrializing Europe in the late eighteenth and nineteenth centuries. With this grand commercialization of palm oil, men began to demonstrate vested interest in its production. Soon men claimed control over palm oil production and commercialization while palm kernel was left as a compensation for women. In an ethnographic study in 1933, British scholar and Assistant District Officer J. G. C. Allen observed that as soon as the people appreciated the economic value of palm oil and kernels, there were changes in its regulations, ownership pattern, methods of production, and organization of the trade. "The majority of palm trees in the village were now reserved for the community, no matter whether they [grew naturally] or have been planted by the individual...a certain day was set apart once in 20 days, when every member of the community may cut as much produce as he desired."[50] The money realized from this effort was used for community works such as road construction and other needs.

Susan Martin has observed that the expansion in the overseas trade introduced radical changes to hinterland Igbo farming systems. Although archaeological excavations have revealed the antiquity of iron technology in the Igboukwu area of eastern Nigeria, dating back to the first millennium B. C. E., it appears that metallurgical knowledge was not widespread in the area. The expansion of metal works throughout southeastern Nigeria probably was a later development. What is not clear, however, is whether this expansion in metallurgy preceded the sixteenth century commercial expansion or was facilitated by the new trade stimulus. According to Martin, the importation of "iron tools made it easier for the Ngwa and others to clear tracts of virgin forests, and a wide range of new crops was introduced.

Many of the new crops, in particular the cocoyam (*ede*), became known as 'women's crops', meaning that women harvested them as well as performed their routine work of planting and weeding. Women's workloads probably increased as a result of this innovation. Previously, the local diet had been heavily dependent on the yam, which men harvested in addition to their main task of land clearance."[51] Other popular items of food include beans (*akidi*), Indian corn (*oka*), plantain (*abirika* or *ogede*), and a local specie of banana popularly known as *inine*. Ohadike has underscored some aspects of the pangs of dietary adjustment associated with the entrance of foreign food items into the indigenous society. Initially, most men refused to eat either cassava or cocoyam on the grounds that it was reserved for women. However, it largely took the event of 1918-1919 worldwide influenza and the crop failures that followed for most Igbo men to accept cassava and cocoyam as substitutes for yam. This dramatic acceptance of foreign food items was part of the increasing trend already adopted by women. By way of implication, the switch to women's crops put more power into their hands as cooks and domestic managers. Traditionally, Igbo women used their role as cooks for both bargain and protest against perceived ill treatment or injustices in the family or larger society. Until now, the effectiveness of this bargaining strategy was largely limited by the ease with which a husband could live on roasted yam, which was easy to prepare from his sitting room (*obi*). With the acceptance of the new food items like cassava (which takes an elaborate preparation to be turned into *fufu*), women gained more power over men's stomachs—and by implication extended control over the entire household.

Generally, the centuries of commercial exchange between the people of southern Nigeria and the Europeans affected the Ijo, and Ibibio coastal people more than their counterparts in the Igbo hinterlands. Writing on the social impact of the palm oil trade on women in 1937, Leith-Ross aptly observed that:

> The development of an economic crop, in contradistinc-
> tion to that of a food crop, had disturbed the peasant's
> natural harmony of mind. Desire was on every side, in
> every form: desire for education, for jobs, for money;

> desire for bicycles, for boots, for silk handkerchiefs; desire
> for power, importance, influence; desire for more food,
> more crops, more children, and above all, . . . better prices
> for palm oil.[52]

While Leith-Ross's study mostly applies to the first and second decades of the colonial era, the point on taste for foreign products and desire for more acquisitions also applies to the late precolonial era. Early on, Equiano had stressed that the manners of his Igbo people were "simple" and their "luxuries few." Adding that the "dress of both sexes [was] nearly the same" consisting of "a long piece of calico, or muslin, wrapped loosely round the body."[53] Major differences in taste and fashion began to emerge late in the period after the eighteenth century following the influx of European manufactured goods. The modesty and simplicity of Igbo women in dressing began to disappear as the desire for cheap European fabrics increased.

Finally, as Afigbo has argued, "probably the most important impact of this trans Atlantic trade factor on Igbo history was the rise of a number of indigenous Igbo business oligarchies whose livelihood came to rest, if not entirely at least mainly on the activities linked to this trade. The most prominent among these was the Aro oligarchy. So much has been written on the Aro role on the history of the Igbo and their neighbors. Meanwhile less has been said about the impact of the Aro slaving oligarchy on gender and cultural practices in non-Aro societies. According to Leith-Ross, with the emergence of the Aro slaving oligarchy, a young girl who failed to attain maturation stage of menstruation "would have been given (not sold) to a passing Aro to be sold as a slave)."[54] The Igbo precolonial society was often known for its comeliness and practice of euthanasia. As Equiano added, deformity was indeed unknown amongst the people. However, the choice of giving off women with biological deformities to slavers was, for sure, a later eighteenth century development that touched every aspect of the people's life and customs.

CONCLUSION

This chapter was intended to give a sense of social change and gender relations in southeastern Nigeria in the period before 1900, which marked the formal beginning of British colonial rule. It first provided a cursory but insightful idea on the background to the dynamic forces of social change occurring centuries before the coming of the European colonialists. The foregoing reveals that change and adaptation has been a constant part of the indigenous society long before 1900. It also highlights the fact that patriarchal power, as often misunderstood, is not hegemonic, but rather fluid. In their contact with other cultures before the colonial intrusion, the Igbo established dynamic sociocultural and commercial relations with their various neighboring groups, which involved exchange of ideas, institutions, trade goods, and other material cultures. Although the impacts of these exchanges were not evenly experienced throughout Igboland, their implications were nonetheless significant in the sense that the more recent colonial and postcolonial developments on gender relations did not emerge in a vacuum. Over time, the precolonial trends reordered power structures, agricultural practices, family structures, ritual practices, gender relations, and individual lifestyles. While the colonial rule hastened the pre-existing dynamics and attempted to obscure the indigenous initiatives, the precolonial trends formed the basis on which the colonial and postcolonial developments are fostered.

Notes

1. See for instance Jean Allman, Susan Geiger, and Nakanyike Musisi (eds.), *Women in African Colonial Histories* (Bloomington: Indiana University Press, 2002).

2. See most of the collected essays in Obioma Nnaemeka (ed.), *Female Circumcision and the Politics of Knowledge: African Women in Imperialist Discourses* (Westport, Conn.: Praeger, 2005).

3. J. F. Ade Ajayi, *Tradition and Change in Africa: The Essays of J. F. Ade Ajayi*, edited by Toyin Falola (Trenton, NJ.: African World Press, 2000), 156-7. For a similar view, see also Sally Falk Moore, "Changing Per-

spectives on Africa: The Work of Anthropology," in Robert H. Bates, V. Y. Mudimbe and Jean O'Barr (eds.), *Africa and the Disciplines: The Construction of Research in Africa to the Social Science and Humanities* (Chicago and London: The University of Chicago Press, 1993), 6.

4. L. C. Okere, *The Anthropology of Food in Rural Igboland: Socioeconomic and Cultural Aspects of Food and Food Habit in Rural Igboland* (Lanham: University Press of America, 1983), 26.

5. Duarte Pacheco Pereira, cited by David Northrup, "The Growth of Trade among the Igbo before 1800," *Journal of African History* 13, 2 (1972), 220. See also David Northrup, *Trade Without Rulers: Precolonial Economic Development in South-Eastern Nigeria* (Oxford: Clarendon Press, 1978), 28; and A. G. Hopkins, *An Economic History of West Africa* (New York: Columbia University Press, 1973), 87.

6. Felicia Ekejiuba, "Omu Okwei, the Merchant Queen of Ossomari. A Biographical Sketch," *Journal of the Historical Society of Nigeria* 3, 4 (June 1967), 635.

7. Michael, J. C. Echeruo, *A Matter of Identity, Ahiajoku Lecture 1979* (Owerri, Nigeria: Ministry of Information, Culture, Youth and Sports, 1979), 19-20. For a similar idea, see John Nwachimereze Oriji, *Ngwa History: A Study of Social and Economic Changes in Igbo Mini-States in Time Perspective* (New York: Peter Lang, 1991), 49-50.

8. Stephan F. Miescher and Lisa A. Lindsay, "Introduction" in Lisa A. Lindsay and Stephan F. Miescher (eds.), *Men and Masculinity in Modern Africa* (Portsmouth, NH: Heinemann, 2003), 2.

9. For a detailed study on this, see Adiele Afigbo, "Igboland Before 1800," in Obaro Ikime (ed), *Groundwork of Nigerian History* (Ibadan: Heinemann, 1980), 73-88. See also the National Archives Enugu (hereafter NAE) for the anthropological work of C. K. Meek (ADO), File No. OP.206D ONPROF 7/14/75. "Nsukka Division, Onitsha Province" (1927).

10. Northrup, *Trade Without Rulers*, 23.

11. Northrup, "Trade among the Igbo," 22.

12. Egodi Uchendu, "Women, Power, and Political Institutions in Igboland," in Akinwumi Ogundiran, *Precolonial Nigeria: Essays in Honor of Toyin Falola* (Trenton, NJ.: Africa World Press, 2005), 203.

13. Mbonu Ojike, *My Africa* (New York: The John Day, 1946), 135. This form of social system is well documented in colonial records. See for instance NAE. File No. OW4363-9/1/860 RIVPROF, "Aro Marriage Customs" (1939-1940).

14. Olaudah Equiano, *Interesting Narrative of the Life of Olaudah Equiano or Gustavus Vassa the African Written by Himself* vol. 1 (New York: W. Durrell, 1789), 36.

15. Ifi Amadiume, *Male Daughters, Female Husbands: Gender and Sex in an African Society* (London and New Jersey: Zed Books, 1987), 51.

16. Nwando Achebe, "'And She became a Man': King Ahebi Ugbabe in the History of Enugu-Ezike, Northern Igboland, 1880-1948," in Lisa A. Lindsay and Stephan F. Miescher (eds.), *Men and Masculinity in Modern Africa* (Portsmouth, NH: Heinemann, 2003), 53. For a brief but lively discussion on the career of this tough woman who was perceived as a man during her lifetime, see also John N. Oriji, " Igbo Women from 1929-1960," *West African Review* 12, 1 (2000), 7.

17. For instance see Bastian L. Misty, "'Vultures of the Market Place': Southeastern Nigerian Women and Discourses of the *Ogu Umunwanyi* (Women's War) of 1929)," in Jean Allman et al (ed.), *Women in African Colonial Histories* (Bloomington, IN.: Indiana University Press, 2002), 206-81; Gloria Chuku, "Women in the Economy of Igboland from 1900-1970: A Survey," *African Economic History* 23 (1995): 37-50.

18. Georges T. Basden, *Among the Ibos of Nigeria* (1920; reprint London: Frank Cass, 1966), 194. See also G.T. Basden, *Niger Ibos: A Description of the Primitive Life, Customs, and Animistic Beliefs and Customs of the Igbo People of Nigeria* (1938; reprint London: Frank Cass, 1966).

19. Northrup, "Trade among the Igbo," 226.

20. Austin M. Ahanotu, "Social Institutions: Kinship Systems," in Toyin Falola (ed), *African Culture and Societies Before 1885* (Durham, North Carolina: Carolina Academic Press, 2000), 52.

21. Obafemi Awolowo, *The People's Republic* (Ibadan: Ibadan University Press, 1968), 209.

22. See Venice Lamb and Judy Holms, *Nigerian Weaving* (Lagos: The Shell Development Company of Nigeria, 1980), 237-8.

23. Gloria Chuku, *Igbo Women and Economic Transformation in Southeastern Nigeria, 1900-1960* (New York: Routledge, 2005), 68; Adiele Afigbo, *Igbo History and Society: The Essays of Adiele Afigbo* edited by Toyin Falola Trenton, NJ.: African World Press, 2005), 221-57. See also Adiele Afigbo and C. S. Okeke, *Weaving Tradition in Igboland* (Lagos: Nigerian Magazine, 1985), and also Adiele Afigbo, "Textile Art and Culture in Southern Nigeria," *Nigerian Heritage: Journal of the National Commission for Museum and Monuments* 7 (1998), 11-20.

24. Equiano, *Interesting Narrative*, 38.

25. Northrup, "Trade among the Igbo," 226.

26. Afigbo, *Igbo History and Society*, 167.

27. Nina Emma Mba, *Nigerian Women Mobilized: Women's Political Activity in Southern Nigeria, 1900-1965* (Berkeley: University of California Press, 1982), 22.

28. Chuku, *Igbo Women*, endnotes, 250. See also Mba, *Women Mobilized*, 23.

29. Felicia Ekejiuba, "Omu Okwei, The Merchant Queen of Ossomari: A Biographical Sketch," *Journal of Historical Society of Nigeria (JHSN)* 3, 4 (1967): 645.

30. Awolowo, *People's Republic*, 209.

31. Susan Martin, "Slaves, Igbo Women and Palm Oil in the Nineteenth Century" in Robin Law (ed.), *From Slave Trade to 'Legitimate' Commerce: The Commercial Transition in the Nineteenth century West Africa* (Cambridge: Cambridge University Press, 1995), 180-1.

32. W.P. Livingston, *Mary Slessor of Calabar: Pioneer Missionary* (New York: George H. Doran Company, 1916), 225.

33. See Raphael Chijioke Njoku, *African Cultural Values: Igbo Political Leadership in Colonial Nigeria, 1900-1966* (New York: Routledge, 2006).

34. Ekejiuba, "Omu Okwei," 633-46.

35. Richard Henderson, *The King in Everyman: Evolutionary Trends in Onitsha Ibo Society and Culture* (New Haven: Yale University Press, 1972), 375. For more on this, see Simon Ottenberg, *Igbo Religion, Social Life and Other Essays by Simon Ottenberg* edited by Toyin Falola (Trenton, NJ: Africa World Press, 2006), 217-23.

36. Henderson, *Everyman*, 314. See also Mba, *Women Mobilized*, 25; and Ahanotu, "Social Institutions," 53.

37. Elizabeth Isichei, *A History of the Igbo People* (New York: St. Martins Press, 1976), 102-3.

38. Richard Ohizu Igwebe, *The Original History of Arondizuogu* (Aba, Nigeria, 1962), 60; Isichei, *Igbo People*, 103-4; Don C. Ohadike, *The Ekumeku Movement: Western Igbo Resistance to the British Conquest of Nigeria, 1883-1914* (Athens: Ohio University Press, 1991), 30-1; Felix K. Ekechi, *Tradition and Transformation in Eastern Nigeria: A Sociopolitical History of Owerri and its Hinterland 1902-1947* (Kent, Ohio: Kent State University Press, 1989), 145-6.

39. Ohadike, *Ekumeku Movement*, 30.

40. Ohizu, *Original History*, 60.

41. John Illife, *Africans: The History of a Continent* (Cambridge: Cambridge University Press, 1995), 94.

42. Equiano, *Interesting Narrative*, 40.

43. Michael G. Schatzberg, *Political Legitimacy in Middle Africa: Father, Family Food* (Bloomington: Indiana University Press, 2001), esp. 38-41.

44. Sylvia Leith-Ross, *African Women: A Study of Ibo of Nigeria* (1937 reprint; New York and Washington: Fredrick Praeger Publishers, 1965), 269.

45. For a detailed study on this, see Victor C. Uchendu, "Concubinage Among the Ngwa Igbo of Southern Nigeria," in F. C. Ogbalu (ed.), *The Igbo As Seen by Others* (Nsukka, Nigeria: University of Nigeria Publishing Company, 1988), 144.

46. Equiano, *Interesting Narrative*, 35.

47. Leith-Ross, *African Women*, 227.

48. See Teresa A. Barnes, "The Fight for Control of African Women's Mobility in Colonial Zimbabwe, 1900-1939," *Signs* (Spring 1992): 586-608; Elizabeth Schmidt, "Farmers, Hunters and Gold –Washers: A Reevaluation of Women's Roles in Precolonial and Colonial Zimbabwe," *African Economic History* 17 (1988): 45-80; "Negotiated Spaces and Contested Terrain: Men, Women and the Law in Colonial Zimbabwe, 1890-1939," *Journal of Southern African Studies* 16, 4 (1990): 622-48.

49. Leith-Ross, *African Women*, 104.

50. J.G.C. Allen (A.D.O.), NAE. EP 7021 CSE 1/85/3708-10, "Ngwa Clan, Aba Division," 1933.

51. Martin, "Women and Palm Oil," 177-8.

52. Leith-Ross, *African Women*, 166.

53. Equiano, *Interesting Narrative*, 36.

54. Leith-Ross, *African Women*, 104.

Chapter 6

BRAZILIAN WOMEN IN LAGOS, 1879-1882

Lisa A. Lindsay

Beginning in the mid-1800s, groups of free Africans from the northeastern Brazilian state of Bahia made the return journey to Africa and settled in Lagos and other port cities of the West African coast.[1] Some of them had been deported after an 1835 slave rebellion in Bahia, but the majority emigrated voluntarily and purchased their own passage. There were few such immigrants at first, but their numbers grew rapidly after Great Britain annexed Lagos in 1861. Primarily artisans and traders, they formed a semi-autonomous class that, for the most part, spoke Portuguese and adhered to at least some aspects of Catholicism. Although they originally intended to reintegrate into African society, these immigrants assimilated slowly. The Brazilians in Lagos comprised a distinct community until well into the twentieth century.

In addition to tracing in broad outlines the history of Brazilian settlement in Lagos, this essay will highlight the experiences of women migrants as revealed in legal proceedings. In particular, I will focus on four cases from the Lagos Supreme Court between 1879 and 1882 that involved members of the Brazilian community. Testimony in these cases reveals a great deal about the domestic situations of the women involved, both before they left Bahia and after settling in Lagos. Additionally, the cases depict four resourceful women who used migration and community networks in attempts to modify their living conditions and maximize their economic prospects.

Freed Africans from Bahia began to travel to West Africa in the late 1830s.[2] Those implicated in the 1835 slave revolt were ordered to be deported, and shortly thereafter an ordinance was passed that required all freed Africans to leave the state. Slaves who purchased their own freedom or were manumitted also made the voyage.[3] Immigration in the 1840s was light, at least in part because of the realistic dangers of both crossing the ocean and landing in Lagos. After enduring a second Atlantic crossing, emigrés faced robbery and even resale into slavery by the captains of the ships in which they traveled. Local chiefs and kings also demanded a hefty tax from all who entered the territory.[4]

The numbers of immigrants began to increase during the 1850s because of factors in both Bahia and Lagos. In Brazil, government authorities offered powerful incentives to emigration in continued efforts to reduce the free black population.[5] In West Africa, both native and European authorities saw potential economic and political benefits of Brazilian immigration, and they took steps to assure repatriates' security upon landing. In 1847, King Kosoko extended a guarantee of their safety, although he continued to levy taxes for each entry into his territory. In 1851, Lagos became a British consulate, and thereafter Counsel Benjamin Campbell persuaded Dosunmu, the new Lagos king, to remove the tax on repatriated Brazilians.[6] Records in the Lagos Land Registry indicate that Dosunmu also made thirty-eight land grants to Brazilian immigrants between 1858 and 1860.[7]

Lagos had become a hub of the Atlantic slave trade in the early nineteenth century. With Great Britain's efforts to abolish the trade in favor of "legitimate" items like palm oil, the pace of Lagos's growth quickened. To protect its economic interests and suppress the slave trade, Britain bombarded Lagos in 1851 and established a colonial administration. The island was formally annexed ten years later. In the 1850s, Christian missionaries arrived to build churches and schools, and liberated Yoruba slaves from Sierra Leone joined those from Brazil. In 1853, there were 130 Brazilian families living in Lagos.[8] With the continued growth of trade and immigration from the interior and elsewhere, the city's population swelled to about 35,000 in 1880.[9] Out of this number, approximately 2,500 were Brazilians.[10]

In the 1840s and '50s the Brazilian community in Lagos was composed of people from a variety of backgrounds, not just freed slaves. There were European-descended Brazilian slave traders; their mixed-race offspring; their servants, who became free upon their owners' deaths; white captains of slave ships; and freed African emigrés, mostly of Yoruba descent. Additionally, small numbers of repatriated Cubans became part of the Brazilian community. Interestingly, this varied group was in some sense perceived as homogeneous by the native Lagosians. The Yoruba name for Brazilians, *agudá*, meant, at the same time, *Brazilian, Catholic,* and *white.* This term remained in use even after most "white" Brazilians left the colony: the Brazilian quarter of Lagos was called *Popo Agudá* throughout the century.[11]

While some Brazilian traders and slave dealers became wealthy and powerful, the survival of the Brazilian ex-slaves, especially during the 1840s and '50s, was precarious. They faced re-enslavement and plunder upon landing and the challenge of earning a living after arrival. Even after British administrators extended protection to the immigrants, they landed with very little capital and faced commercial competition from both indigenous Lagosians and Sierra Leonians. During this early period, the Brazilians' prevailing ambition seems to have been to earn a living and secure their safety. Their hard work and strong community support helped them to establish themselves in unfamiliar surroundings. Those newly arrived lodged together or with more established friends or relatives until they got on their feet. Wills in the Lagos Probate Registry indicate that for many repatriates, their ship-mates and other friends from American slavery became their only family in Lagos, and it was to these close friends that possessions were bequeathed.[12]

The 1850s and '60s saw changes for both wealthy slavers and newly arrived freed people. One of the first casualties of the British presence were the predominantly white Brazilian slave dealers and their non-white employees, whom Counsel Campbell expelled between 1854 and his death in 1857. A clear message was sent to the rest of the Brazilians that involvement with slavery would not be tolerated. In exchange for Campbell's promise of protection, the remaining Brazilians were required to "abandon all connection with Slave Traders, and abstain from Slave Trade," as well as to "learn our Anti-Slave Trade language."[13]

The remaining repatriate population, while certainly containing variation, was more uniform than earlier. As before, cohesion was provided by language, religion, and cultural practices imported from Bahia. Additionally, these Brazilians were primarily engaged in trade and skilled work. Commerce was the primary route to wealth in early colonial Lagos. Although fewer Brazilians than Sierra Leonean immigrants reached the top echelon of merchants, many were engaged in smaller commercial endeavors.[14] There were a handful of wealthy traders who utilized ties with Brazil to build up international trading houses, while others were petty traders and local representatives of Brazilian commercial firms. João da Rocha, for example, had attended mission school in Ilesha before his capture by slavers in about the 1840s. Returning to Lagos in the 1870s, he became an important trader and leader of the Brazilian community in ensuing years. His children were firmly among Lagos's African elite by the turn of the century.[15]

A larger group than the merchants comprised independent skilled artisans—carpenters, masons, tailors, and dressmakers who were noted throughout the colony for their handiwork. Prisco da Costa came to Lagos in 1867, having learned carpentry in Brazil. He became a prosperous master builder and merchant in Lagos and was identified in 1890 as "one of the leaders of the Brazilian young men."[16] Some Brazilians, like members of the Martins family, [17] found work for colonial officials, although the language barrier and competition from Sierra Leonians kept most out of government service. These examples are necessarily more elite than other Brazilians, simply by the fact that their names appear in records and newspapers. Many more repatriates, although they pursued these or similar occupations, struggled to make their livings in Lagos.[18]

Brazilian women, like Yoruba women generally, were heavily involved in petty trading. They also earned money as washer-women, seamstresses, and sellers of Afro-Brazilian food. Brazilian women appear not infrequently in colonial court and probate records. Like their male counterparts, some became quite wealthy while others struggled to earn their livelihoods. In the booming land and credit market of late nineteenth century Lagos, some female traders became money lenders, like Maria da Conceicao, who sued to recover her debts in 1877 and 1888.[19] Many more women, however, had debts of their own, and a woman known as Felicidade in the 1879 inheritance case, *Francisco Augustino vs. Antonio Ariba*,[20] was probably more typical. She was captured, taken to Brazil, and redeemed and married by a man there. In 1871, after a brawl in which her husband knocked out one of her teeth, Felicidade sailed to Lagos. There, she lodged with Ariba, a relative from the Nigerian interior, until she could borrow money to buy her own house. She earned her living by selling fried plantains in front of Ariba's house, and when she died her property consisted of some clothes and a few plates. Three years after her death, her husband Francisco Augustino returned to Lagos and sued Ariba for her remaining property.

Felicidade's interest in buying a house in Lagos, as well as her husband's desire to claim her property, reflects the importance of land and resources in the Lagos economy. As Kristin Mann has pointed out, access to credit was imperative for initiating trade, and this access frequently depended upon land for collateral.[21] From the 1850s, Lagos saw a drastic commodification of land and extension of credit. Felicidade borrowed money to buy a house; the next step would have been to use her house and any savings to invest in small-scale trade.

Felicidade's case also illustrates the use of immigration between Brazil and West Africa to redefine one's domestic situation. For her, Lagos offered an escape from an abusive husband and a chance for independence. The 1882 case, *Manoel B. Moreira vs. Constancia Maria do Rosario*[22] also depicts a woman's attempt to ameliorate her domestic situation through migration. Rosario was married to Bonifacio Moreira in a Catholic ceremony in Brazil. The two, plus Moreira's son Manoel, immigrated to Lagos probably in the early 1870s. There, Moreira converted to Islam and married two other women. In 1878, Rosario moved back to Brazil. She told the court that her re-migration was because she missed her son, while Manoel testified that she and her husband had argued. One can easily imagine marital friction ensuing from Bonifacio's conversion and adoption of polygyny, but both motivations may have played a role. By the time Moreira died in 1880, his other two wives had also left him. Manoel was left to pay for the funeral and repairs to the house, where he continued to live. He wrote of the death to Rosario, and two years later she returned to Lagos and claimed possession of Bonifacio's house. Manoel refused to relinquish it unless she reimbursed him for funeral and home improvement expenses. They could not agree, and Manoel sued Rosario. The court ruled that she was to reimburse Manoel and then take possession.

According to court testimony, when Manoel first refused to transfer the house to Rosario, she turned to community elders and then to a prominent African civil servant, J. A. Otonba Payne, for redress. Payne, who had ties to the Brazilian community and later married a woman who may have been related to Rosario, decided in her favor.[23] In this use of community-based mediation, Rosario's case resembles one from 1929, also involving the Brazilian community, recounted by Kristin Mann.[24] In this instance, a woman brought her unfaithful and abusive husband before a family tribunal rather than the colonial court. Mann points out that few women brought cases to court. Resolving disputes within kin and community fit more closely with the values of the participants and avoided the expense and publicity associated with colonial adjudication. Rosario also attempted to avoid the colonial court, and it was Manoel who brought the matter before civil authorities.

In Re Phillip Simon alias Ojo Ladile, deceased, illustrates several of the phenomena described above.[25] It shows contestation over the ownership of a house, as well as migration as an opportunity to redefine a woman's domestic situation. Maria

Francesca emigrated from Brazil in 1867 with Phillip Simon, his wife Silvara Bon de Jesus, and his two children, and all five lived together upon arrival in Lagos. Simon had not married the mothers of his two children, but he had married Silvara in a Roman Catholic ceremony in Bahia. Silvara died in 1872; when Simon died seven years later Maria Francesca had been living with him as his wife and taking care of him. According to his will, Simon left his house to her. His two children, Seraphim Philip Simon and Leonarda de Seville Bon de Jesus, sued to prevent the implementation of the will on the grounds that Maria Francesca was not married to their father. Further, they and two other witnesses implied that she had forged the will. The case record is not clear and leaves open several possibilities. Perhaps Simon did write a will leaving his house to Maria Francesca; perhaps he only promised it to her but never wrote the will; perhaps he never intended for her to inherit his property. In the absence of a will, Simon's property would have been divided according to Yoruba tradition among his brothers, wives, and children; with the will presented, Maria Francesca became the principal heir. The case record ends with an order that the registrar of the court administer the estate.

At least in the nineteenth century, the Brazilian community assimilated into Yoruba society slowly. Language and religion differentiated them from their neighbors, as did their Brazilian traditions. Additionally, many Brazilian families cultivated an image of middle-class respectability that was frequently noticed by European observers. In 1847, for example, John Duncan described the Brazilians in Whydah (Dahomey), as "the most industrious people I have found,"[26] while six years later Counsel Campbell described them as "industrious and well-conducted people."[27] An English missionary in Lagos wrote in 1881 that the immigrants "form an important element [in society], on account of their . . . higher average intelligence, as compared with those who have not been out of the country."[28] The Brazilians, according to Governor Alfred Moloney in 1887, "represent an orderly, industrious and respectable portion of this community and set generally a good example as citizens."[29]

The 1880 criminal case *Reg. vs. Christopher Lisboa da Silva*[30] illustrates this aspect of the Brazilian community. Sabina da Silva, a seamstress and the daughter of a well-off trader, charged Christopher with libel after he posted public notices that cast doubt on her morality. Christopher had lived with the Silva family previously, and there had never been anything remarkable about his relationship with Sabina. After he moved out, however, he propositioned her in the street. When she refused his advances, he vowed revenge. During the next few days, his friends threw stones at her and slapped her. That Sunday, several flyers, written in Portuguese and English, appeared on pillars near the Catholic Church and the Silva house on Bamgbose St. Although the court record does not contain exactly what was written, it suggests that the papers made insinuations about Sabina's virginity. After hearing testimony from an Arabic scholar who said he was paid by Christopher to write the notices, the court sentenced the defendant to three months of hard labor.

This case seems to differ from the other three in two respects. First, it is the only one brought by a woman herself. Second, it does not involve material property; it relates to the woman's honor. On closer examination, though, these differences may not have been so great. Although Sabina did press charges, it was probably the case that her father, Gaspa da Silva, encouraged her to do so or at least that he paid the court costs. One should note, also, that a woman's reputation, certainly in "respectable" Christian circles, could and did translate into material benefits. One can only speculate on this particular case, but it seems likely that a stain on Sabina's honor could not only have had repercussions for her marriage possibilities, but could have marred the respectability of her kin and community. This could have motivated Sabina and her father to pursue the case.[31]

These Supreme Court records raise more questions than they answer. First, how much can we generalize on the basis of them, for female Lagos residents and for Brazilian immigrants? In some respects, the cases involving Felicidade, Maria Francesca, and Constancia Maria do Rosario reinforce descriptions of late nineteenth century Lagos. In particular, they highlight the economic importance of possessing a house and land and the efforts undertaken to obtain them. Additionally, they point to networks of resources and credit that linked families and individuals.

In other ways, the testimony of Sabina da Silva, Francisco Augustino, and Constancia Maria do Rosario points out some of the particularities of the Brazilian immigrant experience. Silva's case shows the importance of respectability in the aspirant middle-class Catholic Brazilian community. Further, it indicates widespread literacy and close social contact among this group. Augustino's and Rosario's cases illuminate the circumstances under which friends and family members migrated together to Lagos and their living situations upon arrival. They also reveal the continuing links between Africa and Brazil, ties that provided an "escape hatch" in case of unsatisfactory arrangements. Fluid domestic and religious affiliations, frequently changing with changed residence, are also revealed for some members of the Brazilian community.

This essay has explored some aspects of Brazilian women's domestic and economic lives on the basis of records of the Lagos Supreme Court. In particular, some of these records show the linkages between migration and domestic renegotiation, the social and economic bonds among the Brazilian community, and the importance of land and credit for establishing one's household in Lagos. More research is necessary to shed light on the experiences of women and immigrants in the colony, however. In addition to the questions posed above, we need to explore the changes in women's and immigrants' positions over time, periodizing their experiences in the context of Lagos's history. Further, we should probe more deeply the continuing contact between residents of Lagos and Bahia to find evidence of cultural adaptation, on one hand, and trans-Atlantic continuity, on the other.[32] In this way, the Brazilians in Lagos can link the histories of Africa and the Americas, helping us to learn more about both.

Notes

1. This paper was prepared for and presented at the conference on "Women in Africa and the African Diaspora: Bridges across Activism and the Academy," held in Nsukka, Nigeria, in July 1992. I have updated

the bibliographic references but otherwise largely left the paper in its original form. Funding for the research on which it was based was provided by the University of Michigan Center for Afroamerican and African Studies-Ford Foundation project and University of Michigan's Rackman Graduate School. I would like to thank Frederick Cooper, Kristin Mann, João Reis and Rebecca Scott for their help with my graduate school research on Brazilian repatriation to Lagos.

2. Most of the repatriates had been born in Africa. In Lagos, however, they referred to themselves, and were referred to by others, as Brazilians. In this paper, I will use the terminology of nineteenth century Lagos and call them Brazilians, repatriates or immigrants.

3. For characteristics and numbers of emigrants from Bahia, see Jerry Michael Turner, *Les Bresiliens: The Impact of Former Brazilian Slaves Upon Dahomey*, Ph.D.diss., Boston University, 1975, 67-68. I published what I knew about Brazilians in Lagos in my 1994 article, "'To Return to the Bosom of their Fatherland': Brazilian Immigrants in Nineteenth Century Lagos," *Slavery and Abolition* 15 (1994): 22-50. Also see Robin Law, "The Evolution of the Brazilian Community in Ouidah," in Kristin Mann and Edna G. Bay (eds.), *Rethinking the African Diaspora: The Making of a Black Atlantic World in the Bight of Benin and Brazil* (New York: Frank Cass, 2001), 22-42; J. Lorand Matory, "The English Professors of Brazil: On the Diasporic Roots of the Yoruba Nation," *Comparative Studies in Society and History* (1999): 72-103; and other references in the notes below. On the 1835 slave revolt in Bahia, see João José Reis, *Slave Rebellion in Brazil: The Muslim Uprising of 1835 in Bahia*, trans. Arthur Brakel (Baltimore: Johns Hopkins University Press, 1993).

4. FO 84\1002, Campbell to Clarendon, January 21, 1856. FO 84\1031, Campbell to Clarendon, June 6, 1857; FO 84\950, Campbell to Clarendon, May 4, 1854; FO 84\920, Campbell to Clarendon, Dec. 28, 1853.

5. For the conditions of freed people in Bahia, see Manuela Carneiro de Cunha, *Negros Estrangeiros: Os Escravos Libertos e sua Volta a Africa* (São Paulo: Editora Brasiliense, 1985), 68-74.

6. Brazilians' treatment under Lagos and British authorities is described in FO 84\920, Dec. 28, 1853 and May 4, 1854; FO 84\1031, June 6, 1857 and CO 147\59, Moloney to Holland, July 20, 1887.

7. Dosunmu Crown Grants, Lagos Land Registry. I am grateful to Kristin Mann for this information. For more on land transfers in early colonial Lagos, see Kristin Mann, *Slavery and the Birth of an African City: Lagos, 1760-1900* (Bloomington: Indiana University Press, 2007), ch. 7.

8. FO 84\920, Campbell to Clarendon, Dec. 28, 1853.

9.   Kristin Mann, "A Social History of the New African Elite in Lagos Colony, 1880-1913, Ph. D. diss., Stanford University, 1977, 28.

10.   CO 147\59, Moloney to Holland, July 20, 1887.

11.   Antonio Olinto, *Brasileiros na Africa* (Rio de Janeiro: Ediçoes GRD, 1964), 162.

12.   See for example, the will of Idowu (a.k.a) Francisca Martin, died on July 26, 1891. Lagos Probate Registry, Vol. 1, 142-143.

13.   Campbell to Clarendon, FO 84\920, Dec. 28, 1853. The other conditions imposed on the immigrants were to "regard Akitoye (installed by the British) as the rightly King of Lagos," provide the consulate with the names of all the heads of Brazilian families in Lagos and send their children to missionary schools.

14.   Jean Herskovits Kopytoff, *A Preface to Modern Nigeria: The "Sierra Leonians" in Yoruba, 1830-1890* (Madison: University of Wisconsin Press, 1965), 95-9, 169; and da Cunha, 120-33.

15.   Interview with Chief Mrs. A. Y. Oyediran, Lagos, 12 August 12, 1991. Also see Mann, *Slavery and the Birth of an African City*, 126.

16.   *Prisco Francisca da Costa v. Maria de Jesus,* Lagos Supreme Court, Judges Notebooks, Civil Court (hereafter JNCC), 171-177, 27 August 1890. These records are located in the tower of the High Court, Lagos. I am grateful to the Registrar for permission to use them.

17.   See for examples, entries for D. J. Martins, E. J. Martins, F. G. Martins, G. N. Martins and P. J. Martins in the 1894 and 1897 Lagos Civil Establishment Lists Lagos Blue Books, Nigerian National Archives, Ibadan (hereafter NAI).

18.   For the occupation of the Brazilians immigrants, see Campbell to Clarendon, FO 84\976, August 30, 1855 and Kopytoff, 169.

19.   *Re William Thomas George,* Judge's Notebook, Police Magistrate's Court, Lagos, 111, July 12, 1877; *Maria da Conciecao v. D. Hughes Taylor,* JNC, case no. 5, Jan. 17, 1888 and Feb. 7, 1888. Only a few fragmentary records from the Police Magistrates Court have been found in the tower of the Lagos High Court building. For a discussion of women's involvement in the Lagos credit market, see Kristin Mann, "Women, Landed Property, and the Accumulation of Wealth in Early Colonial Lagos," *Signs* 16 (1991): 682-706.

20.   JNCC, vol. 2, 64-68, 18 Feb 1879.

21.   Kristin Mann, "Trade, Credit and the Commodification of Land in Colonial Lagos," paper presented at the conference on New Perspectives on Colonial Africa, University of Illinois, March 29-31, 1987; "Women, Landed Property"; and *Slavery and the Birth of an African City*.

22.   JNCC, vol. 5, 101-2, 31 Oct. 1882.

23. Kopytoff, 296.

24. Kristin Mann, "Women's Rights in Law and Practice: Marriage and Dispute Settlement in Colonial Lagos," in Margaret Jean Hay and Marcia Wright (eds.), *African Women and the Law: Historical Perspectives* (Boston: Boston University, 1982).

25. JNCC, vol. 2, 114-121, 19 June 1879 and 23 June 1879.

26. John Duncan, *Travels in Western Africa, in 1845 and 1846, Comprising a Journey from Whydah, through the Kingdom of Dahomey, to Adofoodia, in the Interior,* 2 vols. (London: Richard Bentley, 1847), 185.

27. Campbell to Clarendon, FO 84\920, Dec. 28 1853.

28. J. Buckley Wood, "On the Inhabitants of Lagos: Their Character, Pursuits, and Languages," *Church Missionary Intelligencer* 6 (November, 1881):690.

29. Moloney to Holland, CO 147/59, 20 June 1887.

30. Judges' Notebook, Criminal Cases, vol. 2, pp. 446-451, 7 June 1880.

31. See Kristin Mann, "The Dangers of Dependence: Christian Marriage among Elite Women in Lagos Colony, 1880-1915," *Journal of African History* 24 (1983): 17-56, especially pp. 43-47 and *Marrying Well: Marriage, Status and Social Change among the Educated Elite in Colonial Lagos* (Cambridge: Cambridge University Press, 1985).

32. For examples, see Matory, "English Professors" and *Black Atlantic Religion: Tradition, Transnationalism, and Matriarchy in the Afro-Brazilian Candomblé* (Princeton, NJ: Princeton University Press, 2005), as well as Mann and Bay, eds., *Rethinking the African Diaspora*.

PART II

TRADITION, CULTURE AND POLITICS

Chapter 7

WOMEN, RITUALS AND POLITICS OF PRECOLONIAL YORUBALAND

Biodun Adediran and Olukoya Ogen

The publication of LaRay Denzer's "Yoruba Women: A Historiographical Study," appears to have stimulated considerable scholarly interest in the role of women in pre-colonial Yoruba society.[1] Some of the major works in this regard include Modupeolu Faseke (1998), J.D.Y Peel (2002), Stephen Arifalo (2003), Oyeronke Olajubu (2003), and K.M. McIntosh (2007). In spite of these major advances in Yoruba gender studies, studies about colonial and post-colonial women continue to receive more attention largely because of the paucity of information on the pre-colonial period. Indeed, Denzer laments the fact that scholars have not really investigated the role of women in pre-colonial Yoruba society.[2]

Historiographically, the relative neglect of Yoruba women in the prevailing literature has a long tradition. For instance, Samuel

Johnson's *History of the Yorubas* (1921), which is the most comprehensive written account of the Yoruba in pre-colonial times, deals only marginally with women. This in itself is a reflection of the fact that by the middle of the nineteenth century, when the history and traditions of the people were being reduced into written form, women were no longer as prominent as they used to be in the society. For instance, they featured sparingly in the negotiations that brought peace to Yorubaland following a century of internecine warfare,[3] and they were hardly in the forefront in the attempt to establish Western civilization. Indeed, in such cases as in the western Yoruba states of Ketu and Sabe where women collaborated with European administrations to establish colonial rule, their roles were regarded as aberrations of normal conventions.[4]

It is, however, interesting to note that the more one reads the various local histories on different Yoruba areas, the missionary and travelers' accounts of the nineteenth century, as well as the 'Intelligence Reports' and 'Assessment Reports' compiled by European administrations in the early twentieth century, the more convinced one becomes of the fact that women were not as passive in Yoruba traditional society as they are represented in written literature. Of course this has been amply demonstrated in works that deal with the role of Yoruba women in rituals.[5] Bolanle Awe and Stephen Arifalo have even attempted to draw attention to the positive contribution of Yoruba women particularly in politics, though Arifalo's work is largely on the colonial and post-colonial period.[6] Denzer also submits that Yoruba women occupied a significant position in the socio-political and economic structure of traditional Yoruba society; the work is, however, more or less an assessment of the existing historiography on Yoruba women.[7] Again, Faseke focuses primarily on the role of women in traditional Oyo-Yoruba socio-political and economic superstructure.[8] Though the work represents a veritable contribution to the literature on Yoruba studies, it says little or nothing about the status of Yoruba women and gender power relations in eastern Yorubaland.

WOMEN, RITUALS AND POLITICS IN PRECOLONIAL YORUBALAND

The cultural dynamics of the social construct of gender in Yoruba religious worldview is the focus of J.D.Y Peel.[9] He concludes that religious practice in Yorubaland was highly gendered. In the same vein, Oyeronke Olajubu explores the interplay of gender and power relations in Yoruba indigenous religious and Christian traditions.[10] In spite of the work's brilliant analysis, its primary focus is on the role of women in Yoruba religious practices. Finally, K. M. McIntosh attempts a comparison of the economic role of Yoruba and Baganda women during the pre-colonial and colonial periods.[11] As noted earlier, an easily discernible trend in the available literature is the excessive focus on the colonial and post-colonial periods. But most significantly, these works have failed to properly articulate the nexus between the ritualized and political roles that women performed in traditional Yoruba society. This chapter is of the opinion that adequate cognizance must be taken of the fact that in traditional Yoruba society, religion and politics did not exist in water-tight compartments. It further contends that even though womanhood in pre-colonial Yorubaland was ritualized, women were, through their control of religious activities, able to influence political activities. In fact, religion and politics were inseparable simply because the religious role of Yoruba women reinforced their political status. Unlike previous works on the role of women in Yoruba pre-colonial society, the scope of this work is also relatively wide. Essentially, it covers the ritualized and political status of women mainly in pre-colonial Ife, Oyo, Idaisa, Ondo and Ikale. This spatial coverage is, of course, without prejudice to the other numerous kingdoms in Yorubaland that are mentioned in this chapter.

In historical times, the Yoruba-speaking peoples of West Africa exhibited strong patrilineal tendencies. This has contributed to the notion that women played a very little role in politics. But there are indications that the Yoruba also exhibit matrilineal tendencies.[12] Some Yoruba myths and rituals make it clear that women, at some time in the past, enjoyed a high status in some parts of Yorubaland.[13] Oduduwa, the putative progenitor of the Yoruba, is regarded as a female deity.[14] A look at the early history of Ile-Ife, considered to be the cradle of Yoruba civilization, reveals that up till about the twelfth century A.D., women exercised considerable influence in all spheres of life. Among those who contributed to the emergence of Ife as the first centralized polity in Yorubaland were women such as Olokun, Yemoo, Aje, Osara, Moremi, and Luwo among others.[15] These outstanding women dominated social and economic activities and influenced the direction of political development.

Indeed, Ife art, particularly the potsherd culture, and the representation of female features in Ife art objects are indicative of the fact that women were not as relegated to the background in the remote past as they later came to be. Thus, the Ife pre-dynastic experience appears to support the claim that there was a time in the distant past when Yoruba society was matrilineal or when women had suzerainty over their male counterparts.[16] That period must be the period now identified in Yoruba history as the pre-Oduduwa period which tentatively could be dated to the pre-twentieth century A.D. Between then and the 16th century; the Yoruba country was engaged in series of revolutions which resulted in the formation of centralized states. During this process, women were presumably relegated to the background.

The traditions of state-formation during the post-Oduduwa period suggest that men were primarily accorded the rights to wear beaded crowns, the symbol of political authority in the Yoruba culture area.[17] In cases where women succeeded to the leadership, they were often deposed with an interdict making female reigns illegal. Thus, the period when most of the Yoruba kingdoms were established saw the ascendancy of men in politics and the gradual erosion of the political power of women.

By the sixteenth century, the political system in the Yoruba country had been fairly well established. Virtually all the major Yoruba kingdoms had been established. Of these, the Oyo kingdom of the *Alaafin* probably represented the best-known example. Its structure of administration has been well and exhaustively discussed,[18] showing the *Alaafin* as a personification of the state with a machinery in which male officials predominated but not to the total exclusion of female officials. Indeed, early Oyo history indicates that women were once forces to be reckoned with. Oyo traditions record the regency of two women—Iyayun, mother of *Alaafin* Kori who was a minor,[19] and Adasobo, mother of Ofinran who was also a minor.[20] There are also indications in extant traditions that such early kings of Oyo as Orompoto and Ajiboyede could have been female rulers. However, after the resettlement of Oyo-Ile in the early sixteenth century following a period of forced exile, the influence of women declined considerably and seems to have been confined largely to the palace.[21]

Through the various roles they played in the palace organization, women were inextricably linked with state policies and politics.[22] In fact, Peter Morton-Williams identifies the *Ayaba* (wives of the king) as a distinct social category in pre-colonial Oyo, an indication that though confined to the palace, they constituted an important force in state affairs.[23] The palace was the nucleus of Oyo administration and the nexus of the state. Historical reconstructions of the physical organization of the palace at Old Oyo indicate that women occupied a prominent position. J. D. Clarke, who carried out some archaeological excavations at the site of the old Oyo palace, indicated that the women section was a very large one with many compounds, one of which had ten carved posts.[24] The present Oyo palace, which was presumably structured after the one at Oyo-Ile, contains a number of chambers devoted exclusively to the women of the palace.[25] *Kaa Agbo* was the medicinal chamber of the *Alaafin* in which women priestesses predominated; *Akanti* was the courtyard where the *Alaafin* relaxed with his wives; *Ile Osanyin Kekere* was reserved for the female servants of the *Alaafin's* wives; *Kaa Ile Igba* contained the sleeping apartment of the favorite wives of the *Alaafin,* while the aged wives of the preceding kings occupied *Kaa Omole Iya Oke.*

It would appear that the number of women who inhabited the palace was more than the men since all palace officials as well as civil chiefs and rulers of important chiefdoms had official mothers; all shrines within the palace had priestesses and all cult organizations in the town had female representatives in the palace. The early nineteenth century European traveler Hugh

Clapperton was so overwhelmed by the number of the *Alaafin's* female attendants that he declared that "it was impossible to count the number of his ladies, they were so densely packed and so numerous."[26] Richard Lander, who attempted a guess, put the number at 2,000. This was at a period when the Oyo kingdom was at an advanced stage of decline.[27]

From the various discussions one could classify the palace women of Oyo into six.[28] First, there were the *Iya Afin* (Mothers of the palace), whom Johnson refers to as 'the ladies of rank' of whom he identified eight major and seven minor ones. Then there were the priestesses, eight of whom are regarded as principal ones on the basis of the crucial roles they played in the peaceful ordering of Oyo society. In the third group were the scores of women loosely referred to as *Ayaba*, usually made up of wives of the reigning *Alaafin* and wives of his predecessors, whom he had to inherit on ascension. Then, there were the female *Ilari* (titled royal servants), whose number corresponded to that of the male palace officials and of whom Johnson identifies 48 principal ones. In addition to these, there were the numerous princesses and in the last group, maids, servants and slaves of the *Alaafin* and his wives. Though largely confined to the precincts of the palace, these women, particularly those in the first four groups, in between them, had substantial input into state affairs.

From the choice of an *Alaafin*-elect through his demise, women played crucial roles in his private and public life. At the installation of an *Alaafin*, women dominated the rituals, particularly those connected with his initiation into the cults of the ancestors at *Oju Aganju, Abata* and *Ipadi*. It is in fact one of the 'mothers of the palace', the *Iya Kekere*, that crowns him. Once an *Alaafin* was installed, these women continued to play prominent roles in his physical and spiritual upkeep. As Peter Morton-Williams observes, "no man was ever alone with the king, and whatever other men might be there, at least one *Ayaba* would always be in attendance, and she would rank senior to the man received in audience and command his deference."[29] It was as if men could not be trusted with the safety of the *Alaafin*! In fact, the personal attendant who ensured the *Alaafin's* domestic comfort and was constantly by his side when he appeared in public was a female official, the *Are Ori Ite;* while the person who kept all the medicinal powders and concoctions for the physical well-being of the *Alaafin* was also a female official, the *Iya Ile Agbo.*

Of the numerous women of the palace, the *Iya Oba,* as the official mother of the *Alaafin,* was a highly privileged member of the royal household. She was also the official mother of the *Basorun,* the highest-ranking non-royal chief. These positions gave her some controlling influence over both royal and non-royal affairs. Another very influential woman was the *Iyalagbon,* mother of the *Aremo* (crown prince) and head of a large section of the palace. But much more powerful than either of these two was the *Iya Kekere* who, although ranked below the *Iya Oba,* was head of the scores of officials (both male and female) called *Ilari,* for it was in her apartment that each *Ilari* was created and the guardian spirit was kept. In this capacity, apart from ensuring the safety of the *Alaafin,* the *Iya Kekere* had a restraining influence on most palace officials including the *Osi Efa,* the most influential palace official. In addition, the *Iya Kekere* wielded immense power because she was in charge of the king's treasures, the royal regalia including the crown and other state paraphernalia. These latter duties put her in a position that gave her approval for all state receptions.

The spiritual upkeep of the *Alaafin* was also entrusted to women. Though basically not priests, the *Iya Oba, Iya Naso, Iya Monari* and *Iya Afin Iku* controlled two major cults—those of *Orun* and *Sango.* The *Iya Oba* was the only other person present with the *Alaafin* when the *Basorun* divined the king's spiritual condition to determine whether or not the *Alaafin* was fit to continue as king. As the official mother of both, she was in a position to reconcile the differences between the royal and non-royal segments of society. Priestesses were in charge of major shrines associated with the *Alaafin's* spiritual well-being: the *Iya Ile Ori* was in charge of *Ogun,* the royal deity, and, as the official in charge of the king's *Ori* shrine, appropriates the king's god of fate. This makes her almost as important as the *Iya Oba,* for in Yoruba belief, the *Ori* (head/fate), which underlies the belief in pre-destination, is the most important element in the identity of an individual and the essence of human existence.[30]

All shrines had female officials attached to them whether or not they had priests. The duty of the female officials was usually to represent the king's interest and ensure that the deities in the care of men were properly propitiated. In many other cases, the female officials themselves performed the propitiation ceremonies. Thus, although the worship of *Ifa* was basically a male affair, the *Iya Mole* was the *Alaafin's* personal *Ifa* priestess and head of all *Ifa* priests; the *Iya Mode* propitiated the spirits of the king's ancestors and had charge of *Bara*, the royal mausoleum; the *Iya Ile Oduduwa* propitiated the spirit of that deity for the *Alaafin;* the *Ode* headed all the hunters and propitiated *Ososi*; the *Obagunte* represented the *Alaafin* in the *Ogboni* house; the *Iya Ile Eye* headed the cult of *Esu* (the Yoruba trickster god in charge of fortune and disaster). She was also in control of the priests and officials that controlled commercial activities and additionally controlled the activities of witches, the powerful women who, in Yoruba belief, owned the world. Other deities of importance in the Oyo pantheon such as *Orisanla, Yemonja, Osun, Osin,* and *Eri* had priestesses resident in the palace.

The Oyo example indeed confirms the observation that women were physically prominent in rituals, and Drewal is on the right track when he suggests that "all Yoruba cults, even those described as male, have one powerful female official."[31] Thus, in different parts of Yorubaland women, especially those above the age of puberty are initiated into powerful cultic groups such as *Egungun (Iya Agan)*, the bull roar cult *(Iya Oro)*, the *Gelede* cult *(Iyanla)*, and the *Ogboni (Erelu)*. The peculiar case of Oyo could be because the far-flung nature of the state precluded a detailed examination of the activities of women outside the metropolis. Indeed an examination of other Yoruba states, which were not territorially as expansive as Oyo, reveals that women were equally active in other spheres of life.

One such state is Idaisa, a Yoruba kingdom located in present-day Benin Republic. Women were so prominent in all aspects of Idaisa life that, in spite of its very small size, it is not unlikely that the kingdom had the longest list of female chiefs in Yorubaland. This is because at every level–lineage, compound, quarter, village, town and state, every male chief must have a female counterpart, which Adediran referred to as "mother" and attached the prefix *Ina* (mother) to his title.[32] The functions of these women were primarily secular as they were expected to play conciliatory roles that would ensure the well-being and proper functioning of their male counterparts; but the conception of a female chief as a 'mother' to her male counterpart suggests that the relationship has a ritual connotation. Motherhood in Yoruba belief is associated with mystic powers, which control the forces that shape human destiny and order the society.[33]

As suggested elsewhere by Adediran, the prominence of women in the administrative system of pre-colonial Idaisa was due to the roles they played in the political development of the state.[34] For instance, it is believed that Idaisa owed its independence from Oyo overlordship to a woman whose activities is reminiscent of those of Moremi of Ife legend. Contrary to earlier speculations that the Idaisa case might have been influenced by Dahomey, it would appear that it was actually one of the aspects of Oyo administration that Idaisa kings who had earlier served as royal hostages in the Oyo court introduced to the area. This latter suggestion is based on the fact that, like in Oyo, most of the female chiefs were chosen from the royal household and all of them were attached to the palace. What is, however, certain in the Idaisa case is that in the pre-colonial period, women had equal rights as men to the throne, and descendants of princesses could become *Jagun* (king).[35]

Whether a female ruler was on the throne or not, the female chiefs constituted an important fulcrum of state administration. For instance, the affairs of the dynastic group were almost totally left in the hands of the female chiefs, the significance of this will be realized when it is known that Idaisa was a highly centralized state dominated by the royal lineage. The Idaisa female chiefs were resident at Esepa, the royal quarter in Igbo-Idaisa (Dassa-Zoume, the state capital). But as each had a male counterpart resident in other quarters of the town, they were well-informed about the goings on in the larger society. Indeed, no male chief could voice an opinion without prior consultation with his female counterpart. For instance, any state decision that emanated from the palace was the consensual opinion of the male chiefs headed by the *Jagun* and the female cabinet headed by the *Ina-Jagun*. This is because of the belief that the female chiefs had the control of the inner essence (*Ori*) of the male chiefs. Given this situation, female chiefs actually formulated state policy, since what the male chiefs expressed as their opinion was often the opinion of the *Ina*. Even the king as head of state could not discountenance with the opinion of the *Ina-Jagun*. Usually the oldest woman in the palace, the *Ina-Jagun* was the embodiment of the history and customs of the royal lineage. To bring an ambitious *Jagun* under control, therefore, it was usually the *Ina-Jagun* rather than the council of state that the Idaisa citizenry looked up to.

The position of the women chiefs was further enhanced by the fact that they had some restraining influence on the ritual priests. In a perpetually turbulent society built on compromise among diverse groups, the *Jagun* depended on some religious institutions to rule.[36] These included a number of deities particularly *Nana Burukuu* and *Ogun*. The priests of these could precipitate crises by withholding their services or declaring the *Jagun* incompetent to rule; but such actions were made difficult by the fact that each priest had to get the consent of his *Ina* who was a member of the royal lineage. Thus, the women chiefs were the actual guarantors of peace and stability in Idaisa society.

Unlike the Oyo and Idaisa examples, where the female chiefs were from the royal lineage or strongly attached to the palace, there were states where the female chiefs were non-royal secular chiefs resident in different parts of the capital or even dispersed all over the state. This is particularly true of states in eastern Yorubaland, of which Ondo serves as a good example. In Ondo, the position of women is deeply entrenched in the traditions and beliefs of the people. The society itself exhibits strong matrilineal tendencies; women had rights to land and land was transmissible by and through them.[37] The Ondo kingdom is believed to have been established by a woman, Pupupu, who was deposed in favor of a male ruler, Airo, from whom successive kings (*Osemawe*) of Ondo since about the 16th century have descended. The reason for the change of dynasty is said to have been due to the fact that Pupupu was no longer capable of carrying on with the civil duties of a head of state.

One version of the traditions says that she devoted more attention to the feeding of chickens, a possible indication that she was more preoccupied with mundane issues. Another version states that she became too old to perform her duties. In both cases, it is clear that Pupupu suffered from some inadequacies. Even then, in all available versions of the traditions, the contributions of Pupupu to the establishment of a solid foundation for the Ondo kingdom continued to be acknowledged.[38] It could therefore not be argued that the deposition of Pupupu was on gender chauvinistic basis and that the Ondo males were simply reluctant to be ruled by females. What in fact appears to be the case is that political issues became so complex that militant leaders were required. This conjecture seems apposite for the expansion of Oyo and Benin into the region during the period, and compounded the problem of political stability faced by the dynastic group from the pre-dynastic Idoko and Ifore peoples.[39] The possession of militant rather than pacific characteristics with which women were associated was, therefore, a *sine qua non* for the exercise of political leadership.

But women continued to be significant in Ondo politics as shown by the institution of the *Lobun*.[40] The term *Lobun* means "head of the market" and its institution after the deposition of Pupupu from the *Osemaweship* suggests that women then had control of economic affairs. The position of the *Lobun* was particularly enhanced by her role as the chief priestess of *Aje*, the goddess of prosperity. In fact, as the titular head of all markets in the kingdom, the *Lobun* controlled a vital sphere of the life of the kingdom. She gave her consent before a new market could be established in any part of the kingdom and had to perform purification rites for prosperity in all markets. Since most of the markets were located in rural areas, the *Lobun* presumably had some authority over the practice of agriculture. She could sanction goods going to the markets, and since these were mostly farm products, farmers tried to remain in her favor.

More than her economic roles, the *Lobun* was virtually the power behind the throne and, in effect, co-ruler to the *Osemawe*. She had her own palace, held her own court and had her own line of chiefs complimenting that of the *Osemawe*, with each male chief having a female counterpart.[41] This group of female chiefs is known as the *Opoji*. But while the male chiefs could act as a restraint on the power and activities of the *Osemawe*, the *Lobun* towers high above all other female chiefs, such that the reverence given to her was virtually more than that given to the *Osemawe*.[42] Because of the matrilineal tendencies of the Ondo society, women formed a major pressure group and their control was crucial to the peaceful ordering of the society. The *Lobun* could mobilize the women to foment trouble, and Ondo traditions remember powerful *Lobun*, such as Ogunsuntokun, Osungbeni and Lomiyike, who not only reigned with the *Osemawe* but actually ruled. Definitely, the contents of the *Lobun's* power and authority far transcended those of the *Iyalode* of central Yorubaland.[43] The *Osemawe* often sought the *Lobun's* advice and consent on major issues, which the women chiefs would discuss at the *Lobun's Ugha* (palace). Through her advice to the *Osemawe*, the *Lobun* was able to influence the decision of the male chiefs. The views of the women were transmitted to the *Osemawe*, who was expected to reconcile them with those of the male chiefs and achieve a consensus acceptable to the *Lobun* before announcing them.

Also, the *Lobun* played crucial roles in the installation of all chiefs (male and female) as well as in the selection and installation of an *Osemawe*.[44] She played what is regarded as the most sacred part of the installation process and indeed, without a reigning *Lobun*, an Osemawe could not be installed. On the other hand, a *Lobun* could not be installed during the lifetime of an *Osemawe* but after the demise of one.[45] This ensured the independence of the *Lobun* and prevented the appointment of a puppet to the position. The Ondo believed that the absence of a *Lobun* could have serious repercussions, hence the death of a *Lobun* often brought tension and recriminations against the *Osemawe*. For instance, when *Lobun* Ujinmade died barely four years after the installation of Adekolurejo (d.1991) as *Osemawe* in 1976, the Ondo requested that the Oba should also die to allow for the installation of a new *Lobun*. This was openly expressed in a song that tended to precipitate civil strife.

> *Oba wa Utiade o*   Oh our king Utiade
> *Se duo ku o*   why not die now
> *Di oje Lobun je*   so that a *Lobun* may be installed

Furthermore, in pre-colonial Ondo Kingdom, women were prominent in the Yoruba cult of *Esu*. Apart from being a communal god, every household had an *Esu* shrine located at the entrance to each house because it was widely believed that *Esu* could ward off any mishap. In fact, as a result of *Esu*'s perceived benevolence and protective ability, women were involved in sacrifices made outside the town wall so that *Esu* could protect the town from foreign enemies and natural disasters.[46] Even though the Ondo case now stands as a unique one, there are indications that it was not the only Yoruba state in eastern Yorubaland where women played prominent roles in politics.

The religious and political activities of women in Ikaleland in the southeastern part of the Yoruba country also deserve some attention. One of the most striking attributes of Ikale's pre-colonial socio-political system was the institution of women chiefs. In the pre-colonial period, the Ikale established several kingdoms, fourteen of which were prominent. In eleven of the kingdoms, the female chieftaincy institution is known as the *Jima* chieftaincy. In the other three kingdoms, Erinje, Osoro and Irele, this institution of female chiefs is known as *Liseri, Liha Lobon* and *Iyalode* respectively.[47]

The *Jima* was regarded as an *Oloja Obiren,* (female king) or head of women, with all the paraphernalia of office in pre-colonial times.[48] Among the Ikale and Ilaje sub-groups of the Yoruba, *Oja* connotes town, and *Oloja* refers to the leader or head of the town.[49] Each kingdom had its own *Jima,* who was more or less the minister of women affairs. She was also involved in the religious ceremonies that accompanied the installation and burial of the *Oloja*, and members of the *Ijama*. The *Ijama* society formed the highest executive, legislative and judicial council with the *Oloja* in Ikaleland.

The sociological explanation for the power and respect accorded women in Ikaleland has been traced to "the manner in which succession to rights is traced not exclusively or even predominantly in the male line but both male and female lines."[50] Beyond this, there is an economic explanation. The *Jima* exercised economic functions that centered on a firm control of trade and market activities, especially the regulation of trade and settlement of trade disputes. The *Jima* was assisted by other female chiefs such as *Laara, Joolu, Ane, Libara, Raluwoye, Ogwapemoye, Efunyo, Obayanmuwa, Oghomobi,* and so on.[51]

Although the profound economic functions of the *Jima* showed that women were supreme in trading activities, yet there is abundant evidence on women's remarkable political and religious functions as well. For instance, women were supreme in the rituals associated with the worship of *Ayelala,* the goddess of retributive justice. *Ayelala* performed socio-judicial functions by exposing and punishing evil-doers, criminals, witches and wizards.[52] The comments of B.J.A Mathews, an early twentieth century British colonial official in Ikale, about *Ayelala* are significant:

> Ayelala is a good juju and protects the town, and it has the special power of detecting criminals, witches and the users of bad medicine. A person caught by Ayelala will confess all his past offences, and his body will then swell up and he will die.[53]

Indeed, the *Ayelala* cult, which was dominated by the women folk, was the most revered cult in pre-colonial Ikaleland and its influence was pervasive in religious traditions.[54]

According to Verger, women were instrumental to the origin of Yoruba secret cults.[55] In fact, Peel rightly argues that religious practices in Yorubaland were strongly gendered with women preponderant in the cult of most *Orisa.*[56]

As Faseke observed, to a large extent women dominated and controlled virtually all facets of religious life in traditional Yoruba society. In some rituals such as that of *Orisa-oko,* an elderly woman usually represented the deity.[57] In the worship of *Sango,* the Oyo-Yoruba god of thunder, women were the most involved. Indeed, men who happened to be *Sango* worshippers must usually dress like women, plait their hair and assume women posture.[58] Such men must first be married to *Sango* and should never marry a *Sango* priestess because they were both co-wives of

Sango. The rituals associated with the festival of *Osun* in Osogbo provide another example. During the festival, a female virgin, guided by an elderly woman, had to carry a basin containing the basic materials connected with the annual rituals associated with the worship of the *Osun* goddess.[59]

At first, all these could be interpreted to mean that as Yoruba society was becoming militarized and complex, the subtle nature of women made them inadequate to cope with the burden of leadership and they had to be limited to less rigorous activities, such as the performance of rituals. But these were not mundane activities and women continued to be a force to reckon with in the decision-making process of the various kingdoms which emerged. As a matter of fact, it appears as if their pronounced religious visibility gave them added political advantage in many Yoruba kingdoms.

Apart from the afore-mentioned Yoruba kingdoms, there are also traditions of women rulers and female religious leaders in Ilesa, Akure and Ekiti Kingdoms.[60] In Akure, there were powerful women pressure groups, such as the *Apate Ukoji* and *Eseri.* Arifalo identifies some female monarchs in pre-colonial Akure, such as Eyearo (1393-1419), Eyemoi (1705-1735) and Amaro (1830-1841).[61] The Akure case is unique in one respect; it shows that unlike the other Yoruba kingdoms, especially Ife, Oyo and Ondo, women monarchs still held sway in the eighteenth and nineteenth centuries. Though no explanation has been offered for this exceptionality, it appears reasonable for now to suggest that in Akure and the Ekiti Kingdoms of eastern Yorubaland, the practice where a female regent succeeds an *Oba* is reminiscent of a once influential role which women played in the society. In virtually all these states, there are long lists of female chiefs whose roles compliment those of the male and whose heads are referred to as "kings." They are also installed with the pomp and pageantry befitting an *Oba* and surrounded with an aura comparable to that of a divine king.

Interestingly, women were also highly influential in most of the new Yoruba states that came into being in the nineteenth century. In Ibadan and Abeokuta for instance, the office of the *Iyalode* was very powerful and important.[62] The *Iyalode* wielded considerable socio-religious, economic and political power. She represented all women in the Council-of-State and was a kind of queen or first lady. Anna Hinderer, a nineteenth-century British missionary stationed in Ibadan, describes the position of the *Iyalode* in the following words:

> These Yoruba people have some very nice arrangement about their form of government. I found out that there was an 'Iyalode,' mother of the town to whom all women palavers are brought before they are taken to the king. She is in fact a sort of queen.[63]

CONCLUSION

This chapter examined the ritual and political functions of women in pre-colonial Yorubaland. The discussion showed that it will amount to an understatement to state that women in pre-colonial Yorubaland were allowed participation in government as a "token."[64] It also frowns at the view that gender constructs were non-existent in traditional Yorubaland.[65] However, it will equally be an exaggeration to assume that the content of the power and authority that women exercised in pre-colonial times actually surpassed that of men. As implied in a cross-section of the traditions examined, the patriarchal inclinations and political as well as military vicissitudes of post-Oduduwa Yorubaland accounted for a drastic reduction in women's political power. Thus, in spite of its seeming patriarchal nature, Yoruba pre-colonial society was still highly gender conscious. Women were greatly respected for their role as mothers, for their leverage in rituals and religious matters, for their importance in agricultural production, and for their almost complete domination of the trade and exchange sectors of Yoruba pre-colonial economy. It is indubitable that all these, especially women's religious roles, conferred on them considerable political influence.

Notes

1. LaRay Denzer, "Yoruba Women: A Historiographical Study," *International Journal of African Historical Studies* 27, no. 1 (1994): 1-39.

2.   Ibid., 1.

3.   I.A. Akinjogbin, et al., *War and Peace in Yorubaland, 1793-1893* (Ibadan: Heinemann Educational Books, 1998).

4.   See A. I. Asiwaju, *Western Yorubaland Under European Rule, 1889-1945* (London: Longman, 1976).

5.   C. Odugbesan, "Feminity in Yoruba Religious Art," in *Man in Africa*, ed. M. Douglas and P. M. Kaberry (London: Tavistock Publications, 1969); Henry Drewal, "Art and Perception of Women in Yoruba Culture," *Cahiers d'études Africaines* 68 (1978): 545-567; J. R. O. Ojo. "The Symbolism and Significance of Epa-type Masquerade Headpieces," *MAN* 13 (1978): 455-470; M. Faseke, "The Role of Women in Traditional Yoruba Society: A Review," in *Culture and Society in Yorubaland*, ed. Deji Ogunremi and Biodun Adediran (Ibadan: Rex Charles, 1998), 149-156; Oyeronke Olajubu, *Women in Yoruba Religious Spheres* (Albany: State University of New York Press, 2003).

6.   Bolanle Awe, "The Iyalode in the Traditional Yoruba Political System," in *Sexual Stratification: A Cross-cultural View*, ed. A Schlagel (New York, 1977), 144-160; S. O. Arifalo, "The Evolution of Women in Nigerian Politics," in *Essays in Contemporary Nigerian History*, ed. S.O. Arifalo and Gboyega Ajayi (Lagos: First Academic Publishers, 2003), 99-121.

7.   Denzer, "Yoruba Women."

8.   M. Faseke, "The Role of Women in Traditional Yoruba Society: A Review," 149-156.

9.   J.D.Y. Peel, "Gender in Yoruba Religious Change," *Journal of Religion in Africa* 32, no. 2 (2002): 136-61.

10. Olajubu, *Women in Yoruba Religious Spheres*.

11. K. M. McIntosh, "A Comparison of Baganda Women in Uganda and Yoruba Women in Nigeria during the Pre-colonial and Colonial Period," paper presented at the Department of History, Obafemi Awolowo University, Ile-Ife, 17 June 2007.

12. P. C. Lloyd, *Yorubaland Law* (Oxford: Oxford University Press, 1966); D. Bender, "Agnatic or Cognatic: A Re-Evaluation of Ondo Descent," *MAN* 5 (1970): 71-87.

13. P. Verger, *Notes sur le culte des Orisa et Vodun à Bahia* (Dakar: IFAN, 1957).

14. E. G. Parrinder, *The Story of Ketu: An Ancient Yoruba Kingdom* (Ibadan: University Press, 1967), 14-15; Verger, *Notes sur le culte des Orisa et Vodun*, 448.

15. J. A. Ademakinwa, *Ife, Cradle of the Yorubas*, 2 vols. (Lagos, 1958).

16. U. Beier, "The Historical and Psychological Significance of Yoruba Myths," *ODU* 1 (1955), 1; Verger, *Notes sur le culte des Orisa et Vodun.*

17. Samuel Johnson, *The History of the Yorubas* (Lagos: C.M.S. Press, 1921), 7-8; A. Aderemi, "Original Sons of Oduduwa Crowned by Oduduwa," National Archives, Ibadan, File No. Oyo Prof. I/203, 1931.

18. Johnson, *The History*, 140-78; Peter Morton-Williams, "The Yoruba Kingdom of Oyo," in *West African Kingdoms in the 19th Century*, ed. D. Forde and P.M. Kaberry (London: International African Institute, 1967), 48-66; R.C.C. Law, *The Oyo Empire, C.1600-1836* (Oxford: Clarendon Press 1977), 61-82; S. O. Babayemi, "Oyo Palace Organization: Past and Present," *African Notes* 10, no. 1 (1986): 4-24.

19. Johnson, *The History*, 155.

20. R. S. Smith, "The Alafin in Exile: A Study of the Igboho Period of Oyo History," *Journal of African History* 6, no. 1 (1965): 64.

21. Ibid.

22. Babayemi, "Oyo Palace Organization: Past and Present," 12-14.

23. Morton-Williams, "The Yoruba Kingdom of Oyo," 50-51.

24. J. D. Clarke, "A Visit to Old Oyo," *The Nigerian Field* 7 (1938): 139-143.

25. B. I. Omole, "The Oyo Palace: An Historical Analysis of Its Organisation," *The African Historian* 8 (1976): 31-57; Babayemi, "Oyo Palace Organization: Past and Present," 7.

26. Hugh Clapperton, *Journal of a Second Expedition into the Interior of Africa* (London, 1921): 36-37.

27. Richard Lander, *Records of Captain Clapperton's Last Expedition to Africa*, vol. 2, (London, 1830), 191.

28. Johnson, *The History*, 64-67; Morton-Williams, "The Yoruba Kingdom of Oyo," 64-65; Omole, "The Oyo Palace," 43-44; Babayemi, "Oyo Palace Organization," 5, 12-14.

29. Morton-Williams, "The Yoruba Kingdom of Oyo," 65.

30. Wande Abimbola, "The Yoruba Concept of Human Personality," in *La Notion de Personne en Afrique en Afrique Noire* (Paris: Éditions du Centre national de la recherche scientifique, 1971), 73-89; Wande Abimbola, *Ifa: An Exposition of Ifa Literary Corpus* (Ibadan: Oxford University Press, 1976), 113-16.

31. Henry Drewal, "Art and Perception of Women in Yoruba Culture," *Cahiers d'études Africaines* 68 (1978): 547.

32. A. A. Adediran, *The Frontier States of Western Yorubaland* (Ibadan: IFRA, 1994).

33. Verger, *Notes sur le culte des Orisa et Vodun.*

34. A. A. Adediran, "The Structure of Administration of Pre-colonial Idaisa," *Anthropos* 79 (1984): 57-60; A. A. Adediran, "Idaisa: The Making of a Frontier Yoruba State," *Cahiers d'études Africaines* 93 (1984): 71-85.

35. M Palau-Marti, "Notes sur les Rois de Dasa," *Journal des Africanistes* 27, no. 2 (1957): 197-209.

36. Adediran, "The Structure of Administration of Pre-colonial Idaisa," 60.

37. Lloyd *Yorubaland Law*, 15-17.

38. Olatunji Ojo, "Slavery and Human Sacrifice in Yorubaland: Ondo c. 1870-94," *Journal of African History* 46, no. 3 (2005): 382.

39. A. Obayemi, "The Yoruba and Edo-speaking Peoples and their Neighbours before 1600 A.D," in *History of West Africa*, vol. 1, ed. J. F. Ajayi and M. Crowder (London: Longman, 1985): 283-285; Adediran, *The Frontier States of Western Yorubaland*.

40. A. F. Bridges, "Intelligence Report on Ondo District of Ondo Division," NAI, File No. COS.26/4/30172, 1934.

41. Ibid., 14.

42. Ibid., 10-11.

43. Bolanle Awe, "The Iyalode in the Traditional Yoruba Political System," in *Sexual Stratification: A Cross-cultural View*, ed. A Schlagel (New York: Columbia University Press, 1977), 144-60.

44. S.O. Bada, *Iwe Itan Ondo* (Igbehin: Adun Press, 1959), 15-17; Ojo, "Slavery and Human Sacrifice," 384.

45 J. K. Olupona, *Kingship, Religion and Rituals in a Nigerian Community* (Stockholm: Almqvist & Wilksell International, 1991).

46. Ojo, "Slavery and Human Sacrifice," 385.

47. Olukoya Ogen, "The Ikale of Southeastern Yorubaland, 1500-1900: A Study in Ethnic Identity and Traditional Economy," (PhD Thesis, University of Lagos, Akoka, Lagos, 2006), 91-92.

48. B.J.A Mathews, "Ikale Assessment Report," NAI, CSO 26/4/30030, Vol.1, 1932: 175-76.

49. Ogen, "The Ikale of Southeastern Yorubaland," 208-9.

50. A. Obayemi, "The Yoruba and Edo-speaking Peoples and their Neighbours before 1600 A.D," in *History of West Africa*. vol. 1, ed. J. F. Ajayi and M. Crowder (London: Longman, 1976), 224.

51. B.J.A. Mathews, "Ikale Assessment Report." NAI. CSO 26/4/30030; Vol.1, 1932, 175-176; Ogen, "The Ikale of Southeastern Yorubaland," 91-92.

52. Eben Sheba, "Aale: A Deterrent Symbol and Communication Device among the Ikale Yoruba of Nigeria," *Journal of the Institute of Cultural Studies* 7: (1999): 10-16.

53. Mathews, "Ikale Assessment Report," 149-50.

54. Ogen, "The Ikale of Southeastern Yorubaland," 336-37.

55. P. Verger, "Grandeur et Décadence du culte de "Iya mi Osoronga" (ma mère la sorcière) chez les Yoruba," *Journal des Africanistes* 35, no. 1 (1965): 141-243.

56. Peel, "Gender in Yoruba."

57. Faseke, "The Role of Women," 152.

58. J. L. Martory, *Sex and the Empire that is No More: Gender and the Politics of the Metaphor in Oyo Yoruba Religion* (New York: Berghahn Books, 2006), 7.

59. Faseke, "The Role of Women," 152.

60. M. A. Fabunmi, *Ife Shrines* (Ile-Ife: Ife University Press, 1970); N.A.C. Weir, "Intelligence Report on Akure District," NAI, File No. CSO 26/30014, 1934, 10; S. O. Arifalo, "The Evolution of Women in Nigerian Politics," in *Essays in Contemporary Nigerian History*, ed. S.O. Arifalo and Gboyega Ajayi (Lagos: First Academic Publishers, 2003).

61. Arifalo, "The Evolution of Women in Nigerian Politics," 100.

62. Faseke, "The Role of Women," 150.

63. Anna Hinderer, *Seventeen Years in the Yoruba Country: Memoirs of the Wife of David Hinderer* (London, 1872), 10.

64. Awe, "The Iyalode."

65. Oyeronke Oyewumi, *The Invention of Women: Making an African Sense of Western Gender Discourses* (Minneapolis: Minnesota University Press, 1997).

Chapter 8

GENDER RELATIONS IN IBIBIO TRADITIONAL ORGANIZATIONS

Ihuoma F. Abaraonye

This paper examines the way gender notions were perceived in the traditional organizations of the Ibibio people of Southeastern Nigeria. It analyzes gender relations as they operated within the traditional Ibibio Organizations. It will also discuss how gender was constituted and experienced by individuals through some of the organizations. Gender concept as a tool for understanding the position of women was revisited by Jane Flax[1] and Lynda Birke,[2] who argued that gender is not narrow and should not be limited to distinctively feminist issues, the situation of women, or the analysis of male domination. Hence Birke insisted that gender is something which human beings constantly reconstruct throughout their lives, both with respect to themselves and to other people around them.[3] Gender, then, includes the way we understand the meaning of that whole interaction in its social, political, religious and economic context. Thus, gender lacks a fixed essence, since it also refers to social divisions or the collective experience of gender. Experiencing gender means experiencing our individual bodies and their functions in a social context and the shared social assumptions that derive from that experience.

THE IBIBIO PEOPLE

The Ibibio-speaking peoples occupy what is known today as Akwa Ibom State of Nigeria. They are believed to number about six million, according to the population projections of 1989.[4] Ibibioland is low lying and flat, with heavy rain in the wet season and high humidity the rest of the year. The main food crops are cassava and yams, vegetables, pumpkin and *Afan*—a forest plant which grows wild. Goats, fowls and dogs are reared. Fishing is practiced in coastal and riverine settlements. Farming remains the main traditional occupation. However, many Ibibio these days live in large cities and pursue modern occupations. The indigenous social structure is based on segmentary lineage principle, whereby a group of extended families made up of exogamous patrilineages trace descent from a common male ancestor. The system is patriarchal, though women exercise considerable power through their membership in secret societies and title organizations which are the actual power behind the government in Ibibioland. As in the case of a man, a woman's position and importance in her village/clan is solidified by advancement in age, intelligence, wisdom and experience.

Gender and Traditional Organizations

In this section, we will be considering a patterned, normative order that served as the basis of society and through which the life of society's members was collectively organized. This order contains differentiated values and particularized norms—rules binding upon its members. As a collectivity, it displays a patterned conception of membership that distinguished between members and non-members of the organization.[5] Based on these assumptions, we will select some key organizations in Ibibio-

land for this discussion and classify them under the following
sub-headings: socio-political and religious, age and sex groups,
occupations and quasi-trade unions.

Socio-Political and Religious Organizations

The *Ekpo* and *Ekong* (warrior) societies were prominent for
their governmental roles in pre-colonial Ibibio Society, although
today most of these functions have been removed to modern
executive and legislative arms of government. Consequently,
the societies have assumed purely social roles. The term *Ekpo*
means 'ghost'. The Ibibio differentiate between *Ukpa Ubugko
Ekpo* (ghost of the dead) from *Ekpo Ndem Isong* (the spirit of
the earth's deity) and from *Ekpo Nyoho* (the masqueraded ghost).
The Ibibio despise *Ukpa Ubugko Ekpo* because it is believed to
be a wondering spirit of the dead who had found no rest in the
spirit world. *Ekpo Ndem Isong* is the spirit of the earth's deity and
a representative or messenger of the ancestors, while *Ekpo Nyoho*
is the earthly representative of the deity and more often seen.
This means that Ibibio people regard *Ekpo Ndem Isong* and *Ekpo
Nyoho* as spirit beings. *Ekpo* was predominantly male but admitted women, because oral tradition has it that, in ancient times,
women were solely entrusted with the secrets of nature; therefore
it originated and controlled most of what we know today as male
organizations.

Membership of *Ekpo Ndem Isong*—the highest governing
body—was officially restricted to only titled men in the district (*Ikpaisong*) whose identities remained hidden until death.
This cult served as the grand jury over cases involving sacrilege,
like serious crimes or murder. A case brought to this jury often
earned the offender a death sentence; hence this cult was actually
dreaded. *Ekpo Nyoho* served as the executive arm of the judiciary,
enforcing laws and maintaining justice and social control. They
also served as an instrument of social stratification and a source
of religious entertainment due to their performances during festivals and funerals of members.

Special privileges went with the membership of this cult. Members were entitled to palm groove, which they harvested until death. It then reverted to the society and could protect women, children and male non-members during the *Ekpo* season among others.

Ekong society was an association of warriors who have distinguished themselves in battle by bringing back an enemy's head. Fathers initiated their talented daughters, but the membership title was not inheritable upon redemption. All members were entitled to the society's special privileges.

Idiong Cult

Idiong cult was made up of sorcerers, diviners, visionaries, native doctors and herbalists. They could predict the future and foretell events. They gave rulers advice concerning their community. Thus, because they had the last say over matters affecting the community and prescribed how to deal with difficult matters, they were very powerful in policy and decision-making processes. Their calling to *Idiong* was a natural selection process termed '*Nkpo sop*' (spirit possession), which started with a series of misfortunes, acute headaches or partial insanity. Such a person consulted an *Abia Idiong* or *Abia Mfa,* who were reputed for their ability to see and communicate effectively with the spirits and ancestors. They were vital in the revelation of wrong doers, thereby helping in social control and the administration of sanctions.

Members of this cult were men and women. All those naturally called to this society possessed supernatural powers and wielded much influence in the community, and their services were sought by members and leaders of the community. *Idiong* could be acquired by apprenticeship.

IBAN ISONG

Iban Isong, meaning women or daughters of the land, was a cult and a club. Due to the influence of Christianity, it today operates more as a club with its social functions greatly enhanced.

Every adult female of the village was regarded as a member of *Iban Isong Idung*. As a governing body, it assumes an executive and judicial form which contradicts Teken N. Tamuno's assertion in his article "Before British Police in Nigeria" that:

> Women as a whole assumed a less active role in the enforcement of customary law. Whereas, a man, entrusted with police duties could take action against women as well, a woman, with some exceptions, when engaged in enforcing customary law or good behavior acted within the ranks of people of her sex.[6]

Of note is that Tamuno's exceptions, for instance the priestess of *Nzeanzo (Mbamto)* in Bachama, Bata and Mbula area of Yola Province, are common examples in Ibibioland among *Ibiong* and *Ndem* priestesses. The activities of the *Ebre* and *Iban Isong* in collective action are a neglected issue in Tamuno's writing.

Iban Isong is the mother and most powerful of all the women's organizations in Ibibioland. In the Oruk Annang area of Annang sub-group, *Iban Isong* operates alongside another powerful ancient female organization called *Ekpo Nsabok,* whose members could tap palm wine and drink on equal grounds at *Eke Ukot* (palaver shade) with men—a very secret group whose members are known at death. *Iban Isong* had the right to impose any form of sanction on offending members and such sanctions were acceded to by the village head.[7]

When *Iban Isong* assumed the name *Iban Isong Esit* ("Hard-hearted, strong-willed women"), their actions were usually directed at men. *Iban Isong Esit* were elderly, very stern in their judicial proceedings, and left no stone unturned until they brought an offender to complete humiliation and often times to death. Suffice it to say that the leaders were often the oldest women of the group referred to as *Eka Iban* (mother of women), *Obong Iban* (chief of women), or *Ofong Enwimani* for Oron area. Members were middle-aged and or older. They could belong to other male and female organizations, like *Inam. Abang* (pot) is an association within *Iban Isong,* the inner core, that is restricted to full members of *Iban Isong* who could afford it. It is popular in Oron, Mbo and Uruan riverine areas.

In pre-colonial times, *Iban Isong* was strong in all the clans but stronger today in the riverine areas. Their rule cuts across gender. When *Iban Isong* had to perform, nobody—man or woman—was allowed to pass through the area of operation. Their major objective was to protect every woman in the clan from physical and verbal oppression from male and female members of the community. A man reported his wife secretly to the *Ekpo* cult for discipline, and women reported their husbands who talked rudely about their sexual anatomy to the leaders of *Iban Isong*. The leaders would summon the offender and bid him to apologize with a heavy fine—depending on the gravity of his offence—or face the music of their action. They never sympathized with stubborn men who proved recalcitrant after committing such a grevious crime against *Iban Isong Esit*. The leaders would fix a date for the trial of such an offender and trailed him to ensure he slept in his house that night. At about the first cock crow, *Iban Isong* would surround the man's compound and wake him up with the sound of their leader's gun shot in the air or the shrill cry of their leader. This signaled action for *Iban Isong*. They would bring the man out of his house, surround him, ensure that nobody else remained in the compound, strip him and force him to sit in a central place, to ensure he looked at them. Sir Justice Udo Udoma, whose mother and grandmother were leaders in *Ebre* and *Iban Isong* respectively, said that they rubbed charcoal on their bodies and held objects made in the shape of a uterus in their hands, ordering the male offender to look at them. They washed vagina in a basin of water and forced the male offender to drink it. They would invoke the supreme God of the Sky (*Abasi Ibom ke Ikpa-Eyong*), who created and endowed women with sexuality that enabled both male and female to come into the world to smite him and deny him children. They would invoke *Ndem* (water goddess) and *Abasi Isong* (earth goddess) to kill him anytime he attempted sexual intercourse with a woman. They would subsequently throw the water at the offender's doorstep and leave.

The offender usually died shortly after this visit. In fact, *Iban Isong Esit* action is still dreaded by eye-witnesses. To them, the only difference with *Ekpo* cult in the execution of justice is the method; *Ekpo* was outright whereas *Iban Isong Esit* used the incantation and curse method from which death usually occurred within a fortnight after such a visit. The family fell into serious misfortune. It was in this way that Ibibio women won respect from their men.

EBRE

Ebre club was exclusively for women, both old and young, married into a community. It derived its name from the water yam, which only women cultivated and served as an ingredient in most rituals. *Ebre* was ritualistic and performed specific functions.

They performed their rites once every year during *Ebre* harvest season, in which time they appeased the *Abasi Isong* (earth goddess) and *Ndem* (water goddess), who ensured fertility for both men and women. Nicklin observed that, nowadays, *Ebre* rituals are performed secretly at night due to Christianity.[8] Their social functions include dancing in the market square during the debut of maidens from *Mbopo* (fattening house), new entrants into their group, and the death of a member or leaders of their community. No thief could become a member of *Ebre*. Their law stipulates that no member, no matter how poor, should steal. Hence any woman caught stealing was paraded round the village with the stolen items tied to her neck and beaten up and forced to sit on a heap of soldier ants. The person was instantly dismissed and ridiculed the rest of her life, if she survived the harshness of this punishment. *Ebre* restricted their judicial functions to women.

INAM

This is a rite-of-passage for the elderly, wealthy and influential men and women. In order to qualify for initiation into *Inam* society, a person must be morally upright and purified, about seventy years of age, a member of the major secret societies, and his/her daughters must have gone through *Mbopo* rites. This society prepares members for death or life in the spirit world.

The *Inam* exalted its members to the status of a semi-diety in the years immediately preceding his death, but if he died in the fatting house following his initiation, it was regarded as an abomination and treated as such. The holder of *Inam* title was accorded an elaborate "second burial" and the construction of a conspicuous *Ngwomo* (shrine) for the temporary abode of his spirit after death.

Inam initiation is renewed after every seven years for seven consecutive times, with children born into such families being named after such subsequent renewals. *Inam* were revered because they bestowed blessings and could rescue children from *Ndem* for parents who make constant sacrifices to appease *Ndem* to ensure the preservation of their children's lives.

AGE AND SEX GROUPS, OCCUPATIONAL AND QUASI TRADE UNIONS

A woman's life experience from childhood, puberty, womanhood, maturity and old age is regulated through a number of organizations: age sets like *Asian Ubo Ikpa* (association of unmarried girls) and *Mbopo* (introduction into womanhood); interest groups like *Okutama* (debut), *Ndok Ufok Ebe* (humiliations of married life), and *Ebre*; occupational and quasi-trade unions like *Nka Urua* (market women association), *Nka Isip Isong* (pal kernel processors), and *Nka Utem Eyop* (palm oil processors); religious cults like *Ndem, Inam, Idiong, Ndam;* and societies like *Abang, Ekpa and Iban Isong.* This last group organized and appropriated communal tasks, maintained high moral standards among women and between women and men, propagated cultural heritage, perpetuated the community's existence, and provided mutual assistance, child care and health education.

The *Mbopo/Nkuho* (riverine Ibibio) or *Ngwo-gwo* (Annang) systems was a female rite-of-passage, marking a change in status from girlhood to nubile womanhood. It was a system whereby young girls were inducted into womanhood, equipping them with knowledge of skills and resources and ensuring their maximum contribution to their community. Girls' induction and education were carried out by the *Ndam* or *Nyama* society, who committed the *Mbopo* to their deity, *Nya-Ama,* for protection.

Ekpa Iban Isong was the highest judicial system in women's government but embedded within *Iban Isong Idung*. Elderly and powerful women leaders could be admitted into major male societies, such as *Ekpo, Ekpe and Ekong,* which were reputed to have been originated by women in ancient times. Hence, matriarchal features are still retained in the rituals and hierarchy of the major traditional male organizations in which the mother image *Eka* looms large and powerful.

A married woman belonged to both her natal and marital lineages, and her interest was protected by both groups as wife and daughter. Their taboos and religious provisions worked to her advantage. Before Christianity came to Ibibioland, women retained their maiden names in marriage. Collective actions by women aimed at village and clan heads and/or their councils could take the form of ridicule, satirical songs, boycotts, and strikes, like 'sitting on.' This was the case in 1926 when Itu women sat on the clan head to release land for the building of the leper colony, and also in 1906, when Eket women boycotted the beach and withdrew their canoes from business until the European trading firms were forced to withdraw a six pence tax imposed on canoes.[9] These demonstrations were methods of communication aimed at seeking redress and checking abuse and the denigration of womanhood through theft, adultery, pre-marital pregnancy, disruption of public peace, maltreatment or non consultation of women in major decisions affecting them. Occasionally, women collectively refused to cook food, care for children, or grant sexual favors to their husbands, which immediately forced men to reconsider their positions on an issue.

Maltreatment by husbands occasionally earned them humiliation because such women collectively organized to ridicule their husbands with sorrowful songs and satires, thus constituting themselves into *Ndok Ufok Ebe*.

CONCLUSION

It is evident that gender concept in Ibibioland was complex and revolved around a patterned normative order through which the life of Ibibio people was collectively organized. Personal identity thus began with one's initiation into the girls' club (*Asian Ubo Ikpa*) or young men's club (*Mkparawa*). Leadership qualities— like good moral behavior, oratory skills, wisdom, experience, and knowledge—marked one for higher ranks. Such individuals played key roles with age and maturity in important religious cults and societal functions and could conduct community rites connected with fertility, virility and protection. They could, irrespective of sex, sit at discussions on an equal basis at the *Efe Ukot* (palaver house), where vital information to the community was disseminated. Women and men had great influence as healers (*Abia Idiong*), seers and diviners (*Oku Idiong*), shrine keepers and priestesses (*Oku Ndem* or *Oku Mbiam*), and so forth. They underwent special preparations before death and were elevated after death to revered status as ancestors whose protection and support were sought after through the media of woodcarvings (*Ekpu oro*), shrines (*Iso Eka Ekpo*), mother images and symbols (*Udung* and *Nyin Udung*), and mortar and pestle. Thus gender is experienced through one's biology as well as through different collective organizations to which one belonged in the society. It is at this level of the lived experience of our biology that both similarities and differences between women become manifest. Hence, gender is embedded in complex interactive processes that change during the lifetime of a person and between individuals over historical time as social and historical contexts of individual lives change.

Notes

1. Jane Flax, "Postmodernism and Gender Relations in Feminist Theory," *Signs: Journal of Women and Culture* 12, no. 14 (1987): 621-43.

2. Lynda Birke, *Women, Feminism, and Biology: The Feminist Challenge* (Sussex: The Harvester, 1986).

3. Ibid., 103.

4. Akwa Ibom State on the Move, 1989.

5. Ekong E. Ekong, *Sociology of the Ibibio* (Calabar, Nigeria: Scholars Press, 1983), 93.

6. Teken N. Tamuno, "Before British Police in Nigeria." *Nigeria Magazine* 39 (1966): 102-16.

7. Ekong, *Sociology of the Ibibio*, 102.

8. Keith Nicklin, *Collected Works: African Arts and Material Culture Studies* (BAR Int. Series, 1981-90), 120.

9. Information from oral interviews held at Eket, Nigeria in 1990 and 1991.

Chapter 9

WOMEN, POLITICS, AND SOCIETY AMONG THE ÌGBOMÌNÀ-YORÙBÁ

Funso Afolayan

Much has been written on state formation and warfare in pre-colonial Yorubaland.[1] While women are occasionally alluded to as playing important roles, there is yet no comprehensive exploration of the contributions of women to Yoruba history and society before the colonial era.[2] This study of the role of women among the Ìgbomìnà-Yorùbá is an attempt to contribute towards the bridging of this gap and the remedying of a major deficiency in Yoruba studies. Using the Ìgbomìnà as a case study, the paper attempts to identify and examine the role of women in Yoruba society before the era of European conquests.

MYTH, GENDER, AND THE YORUBA COSMOS

Women featured prominently in the cosmological myths of the Yoruba. Various myths and folklores attest to the presence of women in various capacities at the beginning and subsequent phases of Yoruba history. A popular story connected with Ọsun, the Yoruba goddess of fertility and romantic love, shows the indispensability of women in the creation and maintenance of the Yoruba social and economic order. According to a well-known version of this story, recorded and recollected in the Ifa Odù, Olodumare, the Yoruba Supreme God, sent seventeen Odù or deity to go to the earth to establish cosmic order. Of the seventeen divinities sent, sixteen were males, while only one, Ọsun, was a female. The reasons for this disproportionate representation were not given. But it is very clear in the story that Osun was neither to be ignored nor treated as just one among equals. As the only female personage in the group and thus the voice and representative of half of humanity, she gained her a status and importance far out of proportion to her single representation. This fact, of course, was not immediately obvious to the sixteen male divinities, who promptly connived together to ignore and sideline Ọsun.

Thus, on arrival on the earth, the sixteen male Odùs, decided to exclude Ọsun from their deliberations, plans, and efforts. The sixteen made spaces and carved out specific jurisdictions for each and everyone of themselves, but made no provision for Ọsun. Ọsun, the gentle but coyish queen of love, also known as Ọsun Seegesi, the pre-eminent hair platter, with the coral beaded comb (olóoyà iyùn), assumed a philosophical attitude of "wait and see" wondering how these men hope to succeed without her participation and help. Unbeknown to the other divinities, Olódùmarè had made Osun the custodian of the hidden power of witchcraft (àjẹ).

> They all decided not to contenance Ọsun in their deliberations.... They never knew she was an àjẹ (witch)

When they were coming from heaven, God chose all good
    things;
He also chose their keeper, and this was a woman.
All women are *àjẹ́*.
And because all other Odù left Ọsun out, nothing they
    did was successful.[3]

After a long period of energetic but fruitless efforts in which
nothing but chaos and calamities attended their ways, the sixteen
male Odùs returned back to Olódùmarè to express their frustration and inquire as to the reason for their collective failure to
establish order on earth. In response Olódùmarè chastised them
for conspiring together to exclude Ọsun, the only female Odù,
from their plans and actions. He informed them that, unbeknown to any of them, he had endowed Ọsun with the power
of *àjẹ́* (witchcraft), which makes her the custodian of ritual and
cosmic powers, without whose support and secret knowledge
nothing the male Odùs did could ever prosper. After making
them to acknowledge their complicity in the exclusion of Ọsun
from their company, Olódùmarè charged them thus:

"You are all intriguers
That one (Ọsun) you left behind
If you do not bring her here,
There will be no solution to your problems
If you continue this way, you will always fail."
They then returned to Ọsun, and addressed her:
"Mother, the preeminent hair plaiter with the coral-
    beaded comb.
We have been to the Creator
And it was there we discovered that all Odù were derived
    from you (Ọsun)
And that our suffering would continue
If we failed to recognize and obey you (Ọsun)."[4]

The above Ifa verses show that women were active participants at the very beginning of Yoruba history. It is also clear that
Olódùmarè intended complimentary relations between men and
women. By making women the custodian of ritual powers which
puts them in a position to bolster or thwart the efforts and designs
of men, he affirmed the importance of women in the ordering of

social and political relations among the Yoruba. Yoruba traditions of origin and creation myths that tend to exclude or suppress evidence of women's active participation may need to be given a more critical look. Contrary to generally accepted traditions, there are many extant myths of origins that portray Odùduwà, the eponymous founder of the Yoruba as a female rather than a male figure. While this claim has remained controversial, the persistence of the claims in several myths and folklores attest to the centrality of women at the beginning of Yoruba history.

Equally instructive is the fact that over the centuries, women continued to serve as the primary repositories of Yoruba myths and ritual knowledge. As Karin Barber shows in her illuminating study of praise poems among the Yoruba, women were and remain the most prolific and versatile preserver and transmitter of *oriki* or praise poems or chants. *Oriki* is a genre of Yoruba oral literature made up of appellations and attributions, composite collections of epithets, pithy or elaborate that are often discursive and compelling, and are addressed to a subject. This could be an individual, a group, a lineage, a community, or a deity. In addressing the essential elements of their subjects, *oriki* are designed to simultaneously define and evoke them. They are performative rites in which women are the most versatile and most celebrated reciters and performers. Resilient, loaded with symbols and metaphor, and often transgressive and subversive, *oriki* preserves and transmits within its various purviews and forms, values, morals, norms, history, and a wide variety of knowledge and information. Through *oriki*, identities are delineated, negotiated, constructed, deconstructed, and affirmed, with significant consequences for the validation (and at times, repudiation) of social and political rights, obligations, and prerogatives. Ubiquitous and pervasive, instructive and entertaining, *oriki* are a regular and important feature of Yoruba social and ceremonial lives.[5]

WOMEN, ECONOMY, AND RELIGION

The story began with the home. As with most human societies, women in Ìgbomìnà had the major share of domestic responsibilities. From infancy through puberty to adulthood, she was schooled and socialized to fulfill certain and specific designated societal roles. The most important of these roles are fulfilled through marriage. Marriage is considered an honorable institution, to which every child, male or female, is expected to aspire. Though not for the weak hearted or the lazy soul, marriage is considered a necessity for anyone to live a fulfilled life and be a useful member of society. Prolonged bachelorhood or extended spinsterhood is considered akin to a curse and thus frowned upon. These perspectives can be seen reflected in this verse from the *Ifa* Odu of Osetura:

> Aini obinrin ko se e dake lasan
> Bi adake lasan, enu ni yo ni
> Nini ejo, aini oran
> Enia ko l'obinrin
> O to ko Kawo l'ori sokun gba oja lo
> Ki ise oran aseju
> Oran asesa ko [6]

> Having no wife calls for positive action
> To keep quiet is to invite trouble and inconveniences
> Having a wife is as difficult as having none
> A man without a wife
> Should cry and weep publicly in the market place
> It is neither an extreme action
> Nor an over-reaction.

At marriage, the woman was expected to leave her natal home for that of her husband. Honor and convention would not permit her to return to take residence in her natal home, except in dire circumstances of abuse, neglect, accusation of witchcraft and, in extremely rare cases, divorce.

Divorce was a rare phenomenon in traditional Yoruba society. This was due largely to the nature of Yoruba marital relationship. Marriage was defined not just as a union between a couple, but also as a union between two families. The couple just happens to be the arrow heads of that union. Thus, the woman is seen as being socially (though not conjugally) a wife to everyone, male and female, in her husband's family. Consequently, everyone already present or born into the family, irrespective of age or gender, refers to the new wife as "Iyawo mi" or "my wife", and treats her socially as such. This invariably puts the onus for ensuring the success of the marriage on the shoulders of everyone. When a man decides to divorce his wife or in some rare cases vice versa, he is not just divorcing an individual, he is simultaneously severing the many ties created between his own extended family and the extended family of his spouse. Thus, in the same way that the choice of a marriage partner is not always an individual decision, so the decision to break up a marriage union is a family and communal one, with far-reaching implications and consequences for all the members of the two extended families or lineages involved.

Marriage, of course, does not completely severe a woman's ties with her natal patrilineage. While she is not expected to return to reside there again for any length of time, she is still regarded as a member of her natal family, an *Omo-osu* (female children of the patrilineage), and remains privy to and influential in major events and decisions regarding the welfare and progress of her natal household. She continues to attend her family or lineage meetings and events, participate in its rituals and ceremonies, and receive the respect as a female "husband" of incoming wives to her lineage. In her new home, however, the woman remains a necessary outsider, whose presence is crucial for procreation and thus the continuity of her husband's lineage, but whose outside kinship origin and blood ties and continuing connections to her natal family make her loyalty and commitment to her husband's family suspect. However, with time and as the woman gives birth to children, especially male children, her status and integration into her husband's family are enhanced and strengthened.[7]

By nature and nurture, the major burden of child bearing and child rearing rested more on women than on men. Cooking, washing, house chores, and sanitation were traditionally recognized as women's duties. The woman was also held responsible for the socialization of her children. Hence in Yoruba folklore, a wise child is usually referred to as the child of the father while a foolish child is described as the child of his mother. Usually girls stayed at home or followed their mothers to their trades, such as pottery, weaving, and dyeing, and received much of their education from them. Boys on the other hand followed their fathers to their work; usually farming, hunting, or smithing. They were not expected to be actively involved in cooking, washing, or sweeping. Thus early in life a form of gender asymmetry or complimentarity with regard to roles and functions is created, imbibed, and sustained.[8]

In pre-colonial Ìgbomìnà, women played prominent roles in the political economy of the society. In theory, just as the woman was expected to be primarily responsible for the bearing and raising of children and the carrying out of other domestic chores, the man was expected to be the primary bread winner and provider for the family. In practice, however, things were more complicated. The polygamous bent of traditional Yoruba society, meant that each woman received what she could obtain from her husband, while working hard at her particular trade and occupation to supplement and augment whatever she has for the upkeep and training of her own children.[9] Only few women, apart from wives of royalties and powerful chiefs, can afford to sit at home content with domesticity and with no trade or income earning work of her own. For the vast majority of Yoruba women, active engagement in trade, either at home, like weaving and dyeing, or outside the home, was the norm. Women thus constituted an active part of the working force. Farming was the most important economic activity in pre-colonial Yorubaland. While Ìgbomìnà women, unlike the women of Indonesia, the Ijaw, and the Igbo of southeastern Nigeria, were not known to be active farmers; they were not left out altogether. Though they contributed little to the early stages of farming such as clearing, ridging, planting, and weeding they were fully involved in and indeed dominated the last stages of the farming activities. These involved the harvesting, processing, carrying, storing, and marketing of the farm products. Among the Ìgbomìnà, unlike their northern Fulani neighbors, domestic animal husbandry, which usually involved the raising of goats, sheep, pigeon, and chicken (to name the most prominent), rather than cattle, was considered a female domain.[10]

In the area of crafts and manufacturing women were dominant in weaving, beer brewing, hair dressing, soap making, cloth dyeing, bead making, and pottery. The women of Idọfian, Igbo Owu, Ila, and Oyo were especially noted for their dexterity in cotton manufacturing. In all these places weavers experimented successfully with a variety of cotton cloth. Ila became so successful with the broadloom weaving system that weavers came all the way from Oyo to learn and to master the art.[11] Pottery was also a highly lucrative business. It brought wealth and influence to its practitioners. Ìgbomìnà women also dominated local and long distance trade. This dominance, which antedated and survived the nineteenth century Yoruba wars and the wealth it conferred, gave Yoruba women a degree of economic and political influence beyond the bound of tradition and culture.

In the sphere of religion, women were also prominent. There were female deities in virtually all the settlements. In the leading Ìgbomìnà town of Ila, the *Imarugbo* ritual was performed annually by the Ọràngún in memory of the mother of Igbonnibi, an early Ọràngún and the founder of present Ila. The great importance attached to this ritual which was called *'imarugbo'* ('honoring the elderly woman') is a recognition of female contribution to Ila's evolution and an acknowledgment of the dependence of royal (masculine) authority upon the procreative power of women (Pemberton 3rd, 1986: 228). Similarly in Omu Aran, the *Orugbo* female deity and annual festival were associated with an ancient Queen mother who had distinguished herself in various ways in the socio-political evolution of the town. The goddess was expected to protect the town against invasion and pestilence and ensure the fertility of both the earth used for farming and of women in the town. Other examples of female deities were: *Ayaba* in Iwó and Idofian; *Omideyi* in Omu Aran and Oke Ode; *Osin*, in Omupo; and *Ita* in Igbaja.[12]

Beside deification, women were also prominent as priestesses to many deities and participated actively in the veneration of others. Most of the *aworo* (officiating ministers) of *sango* and *orisa oko*, where these deities existed, were usually women. In cases where some of the officials were men they usually dressed and plaited their hair like women. Mention must also be made of other powerful female officials connected with other deities such as the *Iya Agan* of the egungun cults, the Iya Orò in the Orò cult, and the *erelu* in the *Ògboni* cults where all these cults existed. The upkeep and maintenance of ritual spaces such as altars and sacred groves fell squarely on the shoulders of women. Women also had charge of keeping custody, cleaning, painting, and dressing the various symbols and images in the ancestral and lineage shrines or altars.[13]

WOMEN, POLITICS, AND STATE FORMATION

In many societies, the realm of politics was generally and universally viewed as a male province. With few exceptions women were not usually seen as leading political actors and are often generally treated as being politically irrelevant.[14] But a deeper understanding of the political process cannot ignore the contributions of women to Ìgbomìnà politics and society. Over the years and all over the Yoruba country, women featured prominently as founders of states and dynasties. The traditions of Ife, Oyo, Ilesa, Akure, and Ado Ekiti, to mention just a few, speak (though often with reluctance) of female rulers.[15] Extant traditions in parts of western Yorubaland depict Oduduwa, the eponymous founder of Yorubaland, as a woman. The founder of the western Yoruba state of Ketu (now in Benin Republic) is said to have descended from a female scion of Oduduwa.[16]

In Ìgbomìnà, women have been known to play active roles during the foundation and early development of the various kingdoms. Ila, the earliest and for long the most important Ìgbomìnà kingdom, was said to have been founded by a woman, Adetinrin, a daughter of Oduduwa, who is also remembered in some extant traditions as the first Ọràngún or ruler of the town. Nevertheless, at Ila, the Adetinrin legend is generally admitted with some reluctance and elaborations are not easy to come by.[17] This is not surprising. It is only a reflection of the patriarchal nature of Yoruba society and the gendered slant of its world view. This position becomes more plausible when it is realized that the two other princes, the Olowu and the Alaketu, whom Johnson recorded as being of female origins had to secure their claims to royalty through some devious stratagems.[18] In the case of Adetin-rin, the mother of the Ọ̀ràngún, it involved an elaborate scheme on the part of Adetinrin amounting to an incestuous engagement with her father, Oduduwa, which eventually compelled the latter to grant this impetuous daughter her heart's desire, a crown.[19] The impression one gets from the traditions is that female succession to the highest office of the state, in an essentially patrilineal society, was unusual, if not abnormal, and thus had to be specifically conferred and ritually validated.

Beyond the foundations of the kingdoms, women continued to play important roles in Yoruba history. Oyo Empire, the most powerful of the Yoruba states, preserved traditions of female rulers (*oba obinrin*). The most widely acknowledged of these female alafin was Ọrọmpọtọ, the twelfth Alaafin on Johnson's *History*, who appeared to have reigned during the Ighoho exile period. Ọrọmpọtọ was noted for her warlike qualities and her military conquests. The rearguard of her large army is said to have consisted of 1000 horsemen and 1000 foot soldiers.[20] Another not widely known but implicitly confirmed in some traditions was Gbagida, listed as Onisile by Johnson.[21] Two other women, who probably served as rulers, were Adasobo, Ofinran's mother, and Bayani, Sango's sister.[22] In Ila, where we have no record of any subsequent female ruler, after the first Ọ̀ràngún-birin (female Ọ̀ràngún), Adetinrin, there are traditions of women who wielded considerable influence in royal and state affairs, most especially as it relates to succession to the highest office in the state. During the reign of the second Ọ̀ràngún, Amotagesi, the kingdom was faced with a series of crises emanating from internal civil strife and external aggressions. The most pronounced was the war with the Olowu which lasted seventeen years. Amota's army was squeezed by the more experienced Owu forces and the kingdom was on the verge of total collapse when desperate attempts were made to harness the hidden but potent and untapped feminine 'powers' of the state. This, the traditions continued, involved the Ọ̀ràngún ritually transforming himself into a beautiful woman, who permitted "herself" to be captured by the Olowu, who in turn found this beautiful captive irresistible and took her in as his favorite wife. Hints from other versions of the tradition show that in all probability, the new wife was either the Ọ̀ràngún himself, who became a surbodinate ruler under the Olowu, or a younger wife of the Ọ̀ràngún or a beautiful maiden deployed by him to allow herself to be captured to become the wife of the Olowu. Whatever the nature of her identity, mustering her beauty and feminine wiles, the new wife soon warmed herself into the Olowu's heart, eventually "seducing" the sovereign to reveal to her the secret of his victorious army. While the Olowu was away at war, she escaped from the palace and the town, transformed "herself" back to a man and returned to Ila. With this, the secret of the *Olowu's* army was exposed, the *Olowu* himself was disarmed, his army was defeated, and Ila was saved. This victory and more especially the contribution of women to the survival of the state is commemorated annually at the rite of *Sakungbengbe*, which normally takes place on the 12th day of the annual *Aworo Ose* festival. On this day, Chief Ọdọọde, representing the Ọ̀ràngún, dresses in a full woman regalia (like Amota who was believed to have transformed himself into a woman) and in the company of the senior queens of the palace marches to the market shrine of Amota to perform the ritual in honor of Amota and in commemoration of other Ila heroines. This ritual thus annually reenacts a critical period of Ila history in which royal (masculine) power was inadequate to defend the town and recourse had to be made to the hidden or covert power of womanhood for the survival of the state.[23] The *Sakungbengbe* festival re-echoes a similar festival at Ile Ife, the Edi festival, celebrated every year for seven days to commemorate the sacrifice of Móremí. An Ife princess of spectacular beauty who allowed herself to be captured by the Igbo warriors who were then harassing the emergent Odùduwà migrant group at Ife. While in captivity, Móremí discovered the secret of her people's enemies, escaped back to Ife and passed her discovery to the Odùduwà group, who eventually routed the Igbo. Before embarking on her dangerous mission of espionage, Móremí had sought the assistance of the goddess Esinminrin, pledging to grant her anything she would demand if she crowned her mission with success and rescued her people from defeat and conquest. After the triumph of the Odùduwà group Móremí returned to Esinmirin, who in turn demanded Olúorogbo, Móremí's only child. For risking her life to save her people and for subsequently sacrificing her only child for the same purpose, Móremí entered into Yoruba folklore as the most revered and most celebrated woman among the Yoruba.[24]

Beside Ila, women also featured prominently in the political traditions of other Ìgbomìnà societies. Ajase traditions acknowledge Oyinmola, a woman and a disconsolate daughter of the Alaafin (ruler) of the famous Oyo Empire, as the founder of the town and that of its *Olúpo* dynasty. It is not clear from the traditions, how many female *Olúpo* actually reigned or for how long the matriarchal system lasted. What seems clear is the fact that the men eventually seized the initiative and excluded women from the highest political title in the state. But the women continued to be actively involved in the political process. In acknowledgement of their pre-eminence at the foundation of the kingdom, the final choice of a new *Olúpo* was made the exclusive prerogative of the senior princesses of the royal family known as *Iyamoje*, making these women, for all practical purposes, the presumptive kingmakers in the state.[25]

Similarly in Ọrà and Òrò Àgọ, women from certain non-royal lineages, for certain traditional and historical factors, had the sole prerogative for the crowning and final installation of the rulers. They alone were permitted to touch the crown or help the king to wear it on subsequent occasions. In Ọrà, this woman had the title of Iya Alase, the mother of authority. Whatever her status or domicile, once appointed by the Ifa oracle she was expected to move into the palace where she lived the rest of her life taking care of the royal paraphernalia and exercising varying influences in the palace and state affairs.[26]

Women were also involved at various other levels in the political structure of the state though the nature and degree of political influence they exercised differed from one community to the other. In some communities like Omu Aran, the female population was organized into age grade associations or *ẹgbẹ* which ran parallel to that of the male folks. Each *ẹgbẹ* performed specific functions and occupied definite positions in the socio-political structure of the community. Further, virtually all the communities had women leaders and chiefs who were known by various titles and who exercised varying degrees of influence and performed different functions. She was known in some of the communities like Ilala, Idofian, and Ọrà as *Iyalode*. In Ọrà the *Iyalode* was also known as *Iya Ọra*—mother of Ọrà and *Iya Ilu*—mother of the town. The title was not hereditary. It was usually given to any prominent woman in the town adjudged most fit by the king and his chiefs. She attended all the meetings of the council of chiefs or *Ilu* and sat in court sessions. She was also permitted to witness certain secret rituals not normally open to women. Similarly, the *Erinle* (lord or elephant of the earth) was another woman chief appointed by the *Asaoni* to represent and defend his interests in the town. As a member of all the secret cults in the town she exercised considerable influence; as the protector of the king and the secret executor of his enemies, she was regarded with fear and respect in the town. A study of the structure of power and of the processes of politics in pre-colonial Ọra would be incomplete without a proper understanding of the role and status of the three leading women chiefs of Ọra—*Iya Ilu, Erinle,* and *Iya Alase.*[27]

In other Ìgbomìnà communities there were also well estab-lished institutions of women chiefs. In Rore, Arandun, and Aran Orin, there was a class of female chiefs which ran paral-lel to that of the male in the state. In these places, like among the Ondo Yoruba, all the leading titles held by the men, apart from the kingship, were also held by woman. As chiefs they held regular meetings in the house or "palace" of their leaders where they deliberated and took decisions on town and women's affairs, though without prejudice to the power and prerogatives of the male rulers and council in the towns.[28] In Igbaja, the leading female personage was the *Iya oko*. An *elese* elect was expected to live in her house and under her custody and tutorship for three months before his final crowning and installation.[29]

In Ila, some women chiefs and royal mothers are remem-bered as having been actively involved in the game of power politics in the town. One of such was Aponbepore, a daughter of an early *Ọwa* of Ilesa and a wife to Ọràngún Igbonnibi. The term "aponbepore" (literally "red or bright as red palm oil") evokes an image of a fair complexioned woman of great beauty. Aponbe-pore is repeatedly mentioned in Ila traditions as having played a central role in the civil war that engulfed Ila early in the sixteenth century, leading to the deposition of the Ọràngún Okusu and the ascension of Okomo, the son of Aponbepore, who had fled to his maternal relations at Ilesa for political refuge. Similarly, the *Iyalode* and mother of Ọràngún Ateere, who appeared to have reigned in the late 17th century, was said to have single handedly used her great wealth and influence to bribe and completely cow the king makers into submission and the acceptance of her son as the legitimate candidate for the throne. The name by which this Ọràngún is remembered derived from the act of his mother in successfully suppressing (tẹẹrẹ) all opposition to her son's candidacy.[30]

CONCLUSION

From this study we can see that women in pre-colonial Ìgbomìnà participated actively in the process of state formation. A form of cultural asymmetry can, however, be identified in the status and functions performed by both men and women. Usually the men were associated with activities that were connected with the field (like farming and hunting) or activities considered to be highly mystical or involving a lot of ritual performances (like iron and gold smithing) or that were considered too politically significant for the community to be left to women or too onerous or too physically demanding for the woman's constitution to cope with it. Similarly, women were also dominant in functions that were associated with the home, or in activities that had domestic connotations or that were considered simple, elementary or less tasking. Even in weaving where both sexes were involved, women specialized in broadloom weaving that was done inside the house while men majored in narrow looms that required larger space to carry out and were thus usually and better done outside the home in the open. Until recent times, men were not known to engage in broadloom weaving while women were not generally involved in narrow loom weaving.[31]

The evidence shows that women were more active and more dominant in the spheres of religion and trade. They were rarely idle. From their youth until the end of their lives they remained actively engaged. Aged women were expected to spend their time taking care of their grand children, seeding cotton and spinning thread, shelling kernels from palm tree nuts, beans from locust bean pods and tending poultry, goats and sheep for domestic use and for the markets. Writing on Yoruba women in the late nineteenth century, Johnson noted:

> On the whole the women seem to be far more industrious than the men, for whereas the men always contrive to have leisure hours and off days from work, the women seem to have none. Boys and young men certainly have more idle hours than the girls.[32]

A question one might be tempted to ask then is why were Yoruba women dominant in trade and in religion? This is a question that is yet to be satisfactorily answered. Various explanations have been offered for the prevalence of female representations in Yoruba ritual context.[33] Some of the reasons offered are women's identification with fertility, their naturally cool and tempered nature considered more conducive to pacifying the deities and thus facilitating favorable consulting as well as their natural beauty and their ability to keep secrets. Some of these explanations will still need to be questioned. With few exceptions, they tend to be reductionist and deterministic in approach. There is nothing inherently natural about male dominance in Judeo-Christian religious and political traditions. Both are cultural constructs, the origin and development of which will still require further investigation.

The next question to ask is whether the female dominance in religion and trade gave political power to women. Yes, it did, but only to an extent and a very limited extent at that. Women's religious and economic weight gave them considerable influence and gained for them an acknowledgement of their importance but the gender asymmetry in the society did not permit the extension of female dominance in religion to the realm of politics in the society.[34]

Though many of the women became wealthy and influential and were given titles and formal recognition they were by and large considered secondary to and of a lower status in their dealings with men and in the social and gender structuring of the society. The myth of ideology of masculine superiority was regularly reinforced by various myths, symbolic systems and socio-structural arrangements that devalued and excluded women from active participation in realms that were believed to embody the most sacred and highest powers of the state. All over the Ìgbomìnà country there were myths and legends specifically emphasizing and legitimizing the subordination of women to men in the realm of politics. For instance, a line from the *oriki oríl̩ę* of Ẹjù states that "*Obìnrin e làkàkà oyè l'Ẹjù.*" ("A woman does not strive for political titles in Eju"). This is in line with the popular Yoruba saying: *"Ilésanmi loyè obìnrin, Obìrin to j'oyè ni da ìlu rú"* (House keeping is the status fit for women, females do not become chiefs. A female who becomes a chief will provoke chaos in the town).

In many places matters that were considered trivial or even senseless were often termed *'ǫrǫ obinrin'* (women talk' or 'matter for women). Though in most communities women had titles and were given responsibilities some of which were considered important to the well being of the state, the class of women chiefs was expected, in every case, to be subservient to the class of male chiefs. In places like Ọra, where the woman head chief was a member of the highest ruling body in the state, she was expected to defer to the opinion of the men and in any case being the only female in a male dominated council she had little room to maneuver. In addition, there were taboos specifically excluding women from titles that were considered to be of the highest order in the state. Women were not expected to witness certain aspects of the *oro* festival, while local traditions present the *Egungun Elewe* (dancing masquerades), the most important pan-Ìgbomìnà cultural festival as being both the symbol and the celebration of the triumph of positive masculine power or patriarchy over the 'negative' forces of feminine dominance or matriarchal excesses.

Throughout the seven to seventeen days the *egungun* festival lasted, women were kept away from the *Igbo Igbale,* the sacred grove from whence daily issued the masked ancestors. But during the reign of Ijimogodo, a late sixteenth century Ọràngún, an attempt was made to break this cultural interdiction against women. This struggle was led by the *Olori* or queen whose seductive entreaties made the king to hide her in the hollow base of his mobile throne which was carried to the *egungun* grove and from where she watched the sacred rites being performed by the chiefs and other ritual specialists in the *egungun* forest. When the rituals failed to consummate and instead produced an inauspicious results, it soon became clear that a major taboo had been violated. Further divinations and investigations soon exposed the culprits: the *Olori* and her complicit ruler-husband. The *Olori* was discovered and immediately put to death. Her body was cut into pieces and given to the leading male personages in the state for internment all around the edges of the *egungun* forest to ensure the impossibility of her resurrection and to ritually purify the desecrated grove. The Ọràngún, for abetting this desecration of the ancestral rite, was also killed and burnt into ashes. The ashes was stored in an *ado* or gourd and kept in the custody of the *Alapinni*, the *egungun* head priest, where it had remained for centuries as a gruesome reminder of the dire consequences that await any individual, no matter how highly placed, who dared to challenge and change the axioms of traditions or to radically alter the gender structuring of traditional society.[35] Thus in the divination, the detection, the ritual killing and internment of the Ọràngún and his *Olori,* male ascendancy and preeminence as well as female subordination were again proclaimed and effectively asserted. Among the Ìgbomìnà as in much of Yorubaland, of male cultural and political dominance did not change much till the onset of colonial rule at the end of the nineteenth century.

Notes

1. On the historiography of states formation and warfare in precolonial Yorubaland, see Saburi Biobaku, eds., *Sources of Yoruba History* (Oxford: Claredon Press, 1973); Toyin Falola, ed., *Yoruba Historiography*, (Madison: African Studies Program, University of Wisconsin-Madison, 1991); and J.D.Y. Peel, *Religious Encounter and the Making of the Yoruba* (Bloomington: Indiana University Press, 2001).

2. Among recent contributions to the study of women and gender in Yorubaland are: Niara Sudarkasa, *The Strength of Our Mothers* (Trenton, NJ: African World Press, 1996); Oyeronke Oyewumi, *The Invention of Women: Making an African Sense of Western Gender Discourses*, (Minneapolis: University of Minnesota Press, 1997) and Oyeronke Olajubu, *Women in the Yoruba Religious Spheres* (Albany: State University of New York Press, 2003).

3. Rowland Abiodun, "Hidden Power: Osun, the Seventeenth Odu," in *Osun across the Waters: A Yoruba Goddess in Africa and the Americas*, ed. Joseph Murphy and Mei-Mei Sanford (Bloominghton: Indiana University Press 2001), 16.

4. Abiodun, "Hidden Power," 17.

5. Karin Barber, *I Could Speak Until Tomorrow: Oriki, Women and the Past in a Yoruba Town* (Washington: Smithsonian Institution Press, 1991); S. O. Babayemi, *Content Analysis of Oriki Orile* (Ibadan: Institute of African Studies, 1988).

6. P. O. Ogunbowale, *Asa Ibile Yoruba* (Ibadan, Nigeria: University Press, 1966), 1.

7. Lorand J. Matory, *Sex and the Empire that is no More: Gender and the Politics of Metaphor in Oyo Yoruba Religion* (Minneapolis: University of Minnesota Press 1994), 91-125; Oyeronke Oyewumi, *The Invention of Women: Making an African Sense of Western Gender Discourses.* (Minneapolis: University of Minnesota Press, 1997); Oyeronke Olajubu, *Women in the Yoruba Religious Sphere* (New York: State University of New York Press, 2003); Elisha P. Renne, *Population and Progress in a Yoruba Town* (Ann Arbor: The University of Michigan Press, 2003).

8. S. Johnson, *The History of the Yorubas* (Lagos: C.M.S. Press, 1921), 98-103, 123-126.

9. Renne, *Population*, 89-110.

10. Johnson, *The History*, 125.

11. Ibid., 110; R. C. C. Law, *The Oyo Empire, C. 1600-1836* (Oxford: Clarendon Press, 1977), 204; W. H. Clarke, *Travels and Exploration in Yorubaland, 1854-1858* (ed. by J. A. Atanda) (Ibadan: Ibadan University Press, 1972), 152.

12. S. F. Afolayan, "Field Notes on Irese,"1987a; "Field Notes on Ila," 1987; Field Notes on Iyangba, 1987.

13. H. J. Drewal and M. T. Drewal, *Gelede: Art and Female Power Among the Yoruba* (Bloomington: Indiana University Press, 1983); A. Apter, *Black Critics and Kings: The Hermeneutics of Power in Yoruba Society* (Chicago: University of Chicago Press, 1992); Oyeronke Olajubu,

Women in the Yoruba Religious Sphere (New York: State University of New York Press, 2003).

14. J. F. Collier, "Women in Politics," in *Women, Culture and Society,* ed. Rosaldo and L. Lamphere (Stanford: Stanford University Press, 1974), 89-96; Jane F. Collier and Michelle Z. Rosaldo, "Politics and Gender in Simple Societies," in *Sexual Meanings: The Cultural Construction of Gender and Sexuality,* ed. Sherry B. Ortner and Harriet Whitehead (Cambridge: Cambridge University Press, 1981): 275-329.

15. R. Smith, "Alafin in Exile: A Study of the Igboho Period in Oyo History," *Journal of African History* 1 (1965): 57-77.

16. Abiodun Adediran, *The Frontier States of Western Yorubaland, 1600-1889* (Ibadan: French Institute for Research in Africa, 1994), 67-9; Johnson, *The History,* 7-8.

17. Pemberton III, John and Funso S. Afolayan, *Yoruba Sacred Kingship: A Power Like that of the Gods* (Washington, DC: Smithsonian Institution Press, 1996), 23-36; A. Babatunde, *Ila Orangun Traditional Rulers* (Ila: Iwaniyi Press, 1972), 9 and A. Adetoyi, *A Short History of Ila* (Ila: Iwaniyi Press, 1974), 1.

18. Johnson, *The History,* 7-8; Adediran, *The Frontier States,* 66-71.

19. Wande Abimbola, *Ifa Divination Poetry* (New York: Nok Press, 1977), 94-95; Pemberton and Afolayan, *Yoruba Sacred Kingship,* 23-34.

20. Johnson, *The History,* 161-2, 176-7; Smith, R. "Alafin in Exile: A Study of the Igboho Period in Oyo History," *Journal of African History,* 1 (1965): 57-77; *Kingdoms of the Yoruba* (London: James Currey, 1988): 32.

21. It is important to note that Samuel Johnson, the leading nineteenth century local historian of the Yoruba, did not acknowledge the female identity of either of these rulers, nor that of any other ruler of the Oyo Empire. Nevertheless, there are enough references in other extant sources on Yoruba history to give some degree of credence to the claims of these rulers being females. For an insightful critique of the general assumption of an all-male succession system for the Oyo Empire, see Oyewumi, *The Invention of Women,* most especially chapter 3, titled "Making History, Creating Gender: The Invention of Men and Kings in the Writing of Oyo Oral Traditions," 80-120.

22. Oyeronke Oyèwùmi, *The Invention of Women: Making an African Sense of Western Gender Discourses* (Minneapolis: University of Minnesota Press, 1997): 87-89.

23. Pemberton and Afolayan, *Yoruba Sacred Kingship,* 38-41 and John Pemberton III, "Festivals and Sacred Kingship among the Ìgbomìnà Yoruba," *National Geographic Research* 2 (1986): 229-30.

24. Johnson, *The History,* 147-48.

25. S. F. Afolayan, "External Relations and Socio-political Transformation in Pre-colonial Ìgbomìnà," (Ph. D. Thesis, Obafemi Awolowo University. Ile–Ife, 1991), 185.

26. Afolayan, "Field Notes on Ora," 1987.

27. Ibid.

28. Afolayan, "Field Notes on Aran," 1987; P. C. Lloyd, *Yoruba Land Law* (Oxford: Oxford University Press, 1962), 99; LaRay Denzer, *The Iyalode in Ibadan Politics and Society, c. 1850-1997* (Ibadan: Humanities Research Center, 1998).

29. Afolayan, "Field Notes on Irese," 1987.

30. Afolayan, "Field Notes on Ila."1987; Pemberton and Afolayan, *Yoruba Sacred Kingship,* 76-79.

31. On textiles among the Yoruba see: Duncan Clarke, *The Art of African Textiles,* Thunder Bay Press, 1997; John Pemberton, Ulli Beier, and Rowland O. Abiodun, *Cloth Only Wears to Shreds: Textiles and Photographs from the Ulli Beier Collection,* (Amherst: Mead Arts Museum, 2004); E. P. Renne and Babatunde Agbaje-Williams, eds., *Yoruba Religious Textiles: Essays in Honour of Cornelius Oyeleke Adepegba* (Book Builders, 2005).

32. Johnson, *The History,* 125.

33. Henry Drewal, "Art and Perception of Women in Yoruba Culture," *Cahiers d'études Africaines* 68 (1978): 545- 567; A. Apter, *Black Critics and Kings: The Hermeneutics of Power in Yoruba Society* (Chicago: University of Chicago Press, 1992).

34. Rowland Abiodun, "Women in Yoruba Religious Images," *African Languages and Cultures* 2, 1 (1989): 1-18; Oyeronke Olajubu, *Women in the Yoruba Religious Sphere* (New York: State University of New York Press, 2003).

35. Afolayan, "Field Notes on Ila," 1987; John Pemberton III and Funso S. Afolayan, *Yoruba Sacred Kingship: A Power Like That of the Gods* (Washington, DC: Smithsonian Institution Press, 1996), 122.

PART III

DISPLACEMENT, DEVELOPMENT AND EMPOWERMENT

PART III

DISPLACEMENT, DEVELOPMENT AND EMPOWERMENT

Chapter 10

MULTIPLE GENDER IDEOLOGIES AND AN ACADEMIC MEANS OF EMPOWERMENT: A YORUBA EXAMPLE

Donna K. Flynn

INTRODUCTION

Contemporary interest in cultural constructions of gender can in part be traced to Margaret Mead's research in New Guinea, where she examined extensive variability in gender meanings between culture groups. Ruth Benedict, fellow student and friend of Mead's, impressed Mead with her insistence on the diverse nature of cultures:

> The diversity of culture results not only from the ease with which societies elaborate or reject possible aspects of existence. It is due even more to a complex interweaving of cultural traits. The final form of any traditional institution, as we have just said, goes far beyond the original

human impulse. In great measure this final form depends upon the way in which the trait has merged with other traits from different fields of experience.[1]

Mead developed Benedict's notion of cultural diversity by applying it to sex roles. Her patterning of sex roles from the standpoint of temperaments revealed that cultures categorize certain temperaments as masculine or feminine, and that the categorization of temperaments is by no means universal but specific to each unique culture. She examines how as "culture creates distinctively the social fabric in which the human spirit can wrap itself safely and intelligibly, sorting, reweaving, and discarding threads in the historical tradition that it shares with many neighboring peoples, it may bend every individual born within it to one type of behavior"[2] and insists that "the cultural plot behind human relations is the way in which the roles of the two sexes are conceived, and that the growing boy is shaped to a local and special emphasis as inexorably as is the growing girl."[3] Despite challenges to the accuracy of her ethnographic descriptions,[4] Mead's theoretical premises have had substantial influence on the current trend within anthropology to construct culturally specific definitions of gender ideologies.

Discussions of the cultural construction of gender incorporate two distinct schools of thought: one which emphasizes the subordination of women as a cross-cultural and universal reality and another which emphasizes examination of gender structures in cultural contexts without presuming sexual asymmetry in favor of males. Sherry Ortner and Harriet Whitehead, as representatives of the first group,[5] focus their constructions of gender on prestige structures which accord men higher cultural value than women. They acknowledge that gender is the product of variable cultural and social processes but do not abandon Ortner's earlier ("Is Female to Male as Nature is to Culture?") assertion of universal female subordination. They do, however, recognize that "the degree and quality of social asymmetry between the sexes is also highly variable between cultures."[6] The second group of scholars (Collier & Yanagisako; Meigs; Gottlieb; Sanday; Schlegel) seeks to avoid an assumption of universal female subordination, proposing that close examination of the variability of gender structures across cultures and within cultures reveals contextual inconsistencies of relationships of power. Instead of presupposing women as the "second sex," they explore cross-sex relations within specific domains of specific cultures in an effort to better understand contextual gender conceptions. I argue here that only by suspending precultural assumptions of universal female subordination and examining gender on a contextual level, can we fully grasp the complexities of gender ideologies. By examining some multiple and contradictory gender ideologies among the Yoruba-speaking peoples of western Nigeria and eastern Benin, I hope to illustrate how contextual analysis can reveal domains of Yoruba culture in which women exert considerable power. An assumption of male dominance could effectively preclude investigation into these contexts, giving a false sense of cross-sex relations and women's opportunities for empowerment.

A CASE FOR CONTEXTUAL ANALYSIS: EXAMPLES FROM THE YORUBA

Some liberties are taken here by referring to the 'Yoruba' as if they comprised a unified ethnic group. In fact, Yoruba-speaking peoples consist of numerous diverse sub-groups which have never formed a unified political or cultural entity. The very name 'Yoruba' is a Hausa word originally used by the northern Hausa to designate the Oyo (Yoruba) subgroup.[7] Two distinct characteristics shared by all Yoruba-speaking peoples are a common language (although there are various dialects) and the claim to Ile-Ife as the cradle of their culture. For purposes of analysis, however, I use the generic term 'Yoruba' here but have tried to build my argument with examples from Yoruba culture which are largely shared by most of the sub-groups. One exception to this is my comparison of the Gelede and Egúngún rituals, which are both practised by the western-most Yoruba groups, including the Ketu and Egbado.

GENDER IDEOLOGIES IN THE
ECONOMIC DOMAIN

Yoruba men and women have historically engaged in independent economic pursuits, and a broad generalization of the rural division of labor would classify men as farmers and women as traders. However, although most rural Yoruba men engage in agricultural pursuits and virtually all women engage in some sort of trading activity, the division is not as clear-cut and simplified as it may appear. Some women participate in limited farming, some men trade, and both sexes engage in various types of craft production. As husband and wife have autonomous occupations, so they also have autonomous financial responsibilities to the household. Spouses have maintained separate incomes for several hundred years and each is expected to contribute to household expenses from their independent earnings. Traditionally, husbands are responsible for supplying the family with food while wives are supposed to provide clothing for themselves and their children and contribute to the household's basic upkeep. Both spouses are expected to contribute to ceremonies and special collections for their respective kin groups.

As stated above, men exert predominant control over agricultural production. Land is corporately controlled by descent groups, and any male member of the lineage retains the right to farm it.[8] Daughters of the lineage also inherit land with the understanding that it does not pass to her husband's lineage. Rights to land are traced to compound residence groups from original landowners in the past, and the oldest man of the descent group administers the land.[9] Farm ownership, as opposed to land ownership, passes through individuals so that after a man has cultivated a farm it is unusual for him to lose his rights to it. In general, every man is guaranteed the opportunity to build his own farm in order to support himself and his dependents; availability and affordability of land is not a hindrance to this end.[10]

Although farms are predominantly owned and controlled by men, women assist in integral farming tasks. Daily chores are generally the (male) farmer's individual responsibility; this includes the demanding work of weeding. Thus for the majority of days the farmer works alone, aided by the limited help that young male children can offer. Women's roles on farms are concentrated around intensive labor times of the year, especially planting and harvesting. During planting seasons, men are responsible for clearing the forest, burning the bush, tractor plowing, and building yam heaps while women are expected to help with hoeing and actual planting of seeds and tubers.[11] Husbands are entitled by authority to demand their wives' help during harvest-time to transport produce between farm and town;[12] this is the most important work a woman does for her husband.[13] A wife may never be asked to assist in weeding her husband's farm nor to assist in cultivation, and a wife may never ask her husband to plant specific vegetables or bring more than informal pressures to bear on his farming decisions.[14] Guyer observed that men insisted on their right to demand transport labor from their wives while simultaneously entering into additional contracts with them for other farming purposes.[15] Recruitment of women's, and wives', labor for other purposes during harvest-time is regulated by standard rewards. While assistance of a farmer's male friends is offered as exchange labor with the understanding that help will be reciprocated when it comes time for the friend's harvest, assistance of all women must be rewarded with pay, usually in the form of a portion of the crop.[16]

In short, although agricultural production is controlled by men, women perform integral functions on the men's farms and also often have small plots of their own for domestic consumption. Most of the work falls on the men for the majority of days in a year, but women make indispensable contributions at certain stages of the production process. It is significant to note, as Guyer does, that women are subordinate to men in the sense that men retain the right to demand women's labor.[17]

West African women's trade activities and control of local markets have long formed the basis of their economic independence. Yoruba ideology staunchly sanctions women's rights to independent earnings and participation in the economic sector. The notion that women and men are equally capable of performing society's integral tasks is aptly illustrated by the proverb that "Whether the man or woman kills the snake is immaterial; the essential thing is that it is gone."[18] Further, there is a definite cultural imperative for women to engage in some sort of income-earning activity; women are not just encouraged but are *expected* to be independent income earners. Sudarkasa emphasizes that "trading is regarded part and parcel of a Yoruba woman's overall role"[19] and that kin networks' demands on women in the form of financial responsibilities encourage women's participation in trade.

Whereas wives of (male) farmers are expected to contribute to their husband's business systematically during specific agricultural stages, husbands of (female) traders are obliged to aid their wives with a one-time capital contribution, either in cash or an equivalence of raw products to be sold, shortly after marriage for purposes of starting up their own trade business.[20] The amount of initial capital required varies according to the type of trade product. Although a direct comparison of these two obligations, that is, the right of a man to demand his wife's labor for transport of produce versus a man's obligation to supply his wife with capital to start her own business, seems to favor men more than women in the sense that women's obligations are annual while men's are one-time, it is difficult in this study to control for additional informal gifts of aid given to a trader by her husband. These may include donation of materials for building market stalls or donations of produce from his farm which she may then sell for personal profit. Guyer makes brief reference to the role of such informal aid: "All help given by a wife has to be directly or indirectly reciprocated by her husband, and since a woman can easily get a divorce, the reciprocity has to be maintained if the marriage is to last."[21]

Men also play more direct roles in market distributive systems. In rural markets, although the majority of *sellers* are women, certain products and services are reserved for men, such as hardware, ready-made clothing, school supplies, and lorry driving. The majority of *buyers* in the market are women as well. While women buyers travel by lorry from various surrounding towns to purchase goods for their own businesses, most male buyers who attend rural markets walk or cycle from farms or nearby towns.[22]

Men also control the marketing of the main export crops, cocoa and palm kernels. This pattern dates to the colonial economy when Europeans devalued women's traditional roles as distributors by defining cash crops and the import-export sector as male prerogatives.[23] Women were relegated to a distinct marketing disadvantage with relation to these higher-profit products. Nevertheless, women predominate over the distributive networking systems of local rural markets.

In sum, the Yoruba have two discrete ideologies of gender within the contexts of agricultural production and rural market-places. Farming is essentially a male activity and trading is essentially a female activity; men predominate in agricultural production and women predominate in rural market-place distributive systems. I prefer here to characterize the relative presence of one sex in an economic context with the term 'predominance' rather than 'dominance.' The above two ideologies are defined by control in the sense that one sex exerts greater influence in a specific jurisdiction and not in the sense that one sex commands the other sex; male predominance does not dictate female insignificance or subordination, and female predominance does not dictate male insignificance or subordination. Within each context, the predominant sex relies on the opposite sex for indispensable and integral functions. Additionally, there is not a significant hierarchical relationship between farming and trade in rural areas. Although some men have gained an upper hand since colonization by producing and trading in cash crops, the crises which the Nigerian rural economy has undergone since the discovery of oil have limited agricultural growth on a large scale.[24] Therefore, there is relative equity in import and demand between farming and rural marketing at the present time as there was when the ideologies of predominance were instituted with the division of labor in the precolonial era.

GENDER IDEOLOGIES AND RITUAL

Yoruba religion is characterized by a rich pantheon of male and female deities, ancestor worship, and numerous secret societies whose functions are often socio-political as well as religious. Here I examine two popular rituals performed in the west-ern-most areas of Yorubaland. The first, Gelede, is conducted in honor of a body of spiritually powerful women of Yoruba society, collectively called the "mothers." Gelede's complex dances, masks, and costumes are tribute to the powers of women. Egúngún festivals, our second ritual, are performed in honor of the ancestors. During this ritual, ancestor spirits are reincarnated in masquerades called Egúngún. I have chosen these particular rituals for comparison for two reasons: (1) they are both per-formed by Yoruba sub-groups of the western regions, such as the Egbado and Ketu; and (2) they exhibit numerous similarities in form, content, and function which make their contrasts with relation to gender all the more striking. It is for the latter reason that I have selected Egúngún over other arguably 'more male' cults, including the frightening bull-roaring cult of Oro. I argue here that by understanding Gelede as the 'secret of women' and Egúngún as the 'secret of men,' the two rituals can be contrasted as examples of female and male power.

GELEDE: THE SECRET OF WOMEN

Gelede rituals pay homage to the spiritually powerful women of Yoruba society; they are performed in order to please these women and encourage constructive use of their powers. Referred to as either the "mothers" of Yoruba society or *ajes*, a Yoruba term literally meaning "mother eats" which has been insufficiently translated into English as "witches." They embody a duality between constructive and destructive powers. It is their control over the processes of life and death, intricately associated with the quintessential power of childbirth in a Yoruba context, which is the root of the mothers' duality. In their constructive modes, the mothers act for the good of society by bestowing fertility on men and women and assuring bountiful harvests of crops, but they are easily angered and can turn their powers towards social destruction, in the form of barrenness, infertility, illness, or poor harvests. The type of spiritual power they are accorded is *ase*, defined by Abraham as "power, authority, command"[25] and by Drewal and Drewal as "absolute power and potential in all things"[26] Verbal utterances and visible performances are especially powerful to the Yoruba because they are "expressions of the spiritual inner self of an individual [which contain] the power to bring things into actual existence";[27] this is the power of *ase. Ase* is not characterized by an inherently good or bad morality, but is a vital force or energy which can be used in either positive or negative manners.[28] Male *ase* is portrayed as overtly aggressive while female *ase* is covert, elusive and secretive. Although all Yoruba have *ase*, some have *ase* of a more potent quality than others. Successful people and elders, those who have achieved impressive positions, have especially potent *ase*, as do the mothers and elderly Yoruba women.

Women attain their greatest power with age. The potency of *ase* in all Yoruba increases with age, and elderly women are believed to be especially powerful. Women with beards, cantankerous or odd women are strongly suspected as *ajes* and may be openly feared. Physical symptoms most often attributed to the work of the *ajes* include nightmares, sleeplessness, stomach pains, headaches, sterility, barrenness, spontaneous abortions, irregular menstruation, swollen testicles, and venereal diseases.[29] However, the mothers are vital to society and are feared because theirs is a power not only of death but of life as well. One Yoruba claimed "Yes, if there is no witch in a place, that place would be no good. We know they exist here".[30] Drewal and Drewal call the mothers the "guardians of society"[31] for their role as protectors of morality and social order and as guarantors of fair dispensation of wealth and prestige.[32] It is the role of Gelede to appease the "guardians of society" so that they may use their powers for the benefit of the people, in the form of abundant children and healthy crops, instead of bringing hardship and adversity.

Dancers of the Gelede society are all men, who join to ensure personal protection from the power of the mothers, but women are also members and, accordingly, hold the senior titles. The male dancers dress in both male and female costumes to perform for the mothers. Beier claims "The men say: Gelede is 'the secret of women.' We the men are merely their slaves. We dance to appease 'our mothers',[33] and Yoruba say that "women possess the /

Age is correlate more aged

secret of life itself, the knowledge and special power to bring human beings into the world and to remove them."[34] Gelede is an affirmation of women's secrets and an acknowledgment of the spiritual powers which constitute their secrets. By appealing to the mothers' powers, Gelede mediates relations between the mothers and the community.

Within the context of Gelede ritual, Yoruba women are accorded dominant spiritual power over men. The mothers embody the 'secret of women' which gives them the power to give life and take life; they are the "owners of the world." The continuity of humankind is dependent on their beneficence and constructive *ase*. If "prestige can be measured behaviorally by the amount of deference granted an individual, a role, or a category,"[35] then supernatural powers in the realm of Gelede are arranged into a prestige structure which forms an asymmetrical relationship conferring women a higher status than men. This is in direct contradiction to Ortner and Whitehead's assertion that gender systems are prestige systems where "men and women compose two differentially valued terms of a value set, men being as men, higher."[36] Rather, the prestige associated with spiritually powerful women of Yoruba society with relation to Gelede is explicitly systematic; it is systematically granted to one sex by the other in this specific setting.

EGÚNGÚN: THE SECRET OF MEN

Ancestor worship is a significant feature of Yoruba religion. Rooted in the belief that a human's spirit never dies but continues to actively contribute to the life of the community, ancestor worship provides the living with an important sense of lineage continuity by affirming community relationships with the dead.[37] Additionally, ancestors are believed to act as intercessors between this world and the otherworld, human beings and gods.[38] Egúngún masquerades are performed to honor the ancestors. By reincarnating ancestors in masked and costumed Egúngún dancers, descendants exhibit their "commitment to continuing the traditions of [their] predecessors and maintain-

ing the reputation of [their] lineage".[39] Egúngún masks are made
and owned by members of lineages in order to represent that lineage's ancestors, male and female, and must be worn by dancers
who belong to the lineage as well.

In its broadest interpretation, the term *egúngún* refers to any
form of masquerade or masked figure, but within the context of
the ritual, Egúngún refers to "powers concealed".[40] The supernatural powers referenced resemble the powers of the mothers in
that they may be manifested in either positive or negative modes.
Schiltz observes that "people manifest great fear in [the] presence [of certain Egúngún], for they have the power to give life
(demonstrated by the birth of children after prayers and sacrifices
have been offered to the Egúngún) and to take life (by punishing criminals and witches),"[41] and Beier comments that "the spirit
which is being worshipped is considered to be neither good nor
evil but is conceived as a power for either quality...being a power
it is potentially dangerous if wrongly treated, but if worshipped
in the correct way it will help the community."[42] Morton-Williams has argued that "there is an assertion of the superordination
of the spiritual world, particularly of the power of the ancestors,
over everyone."[43] Like the mothers, the Egúngúns possess the
supernatural power of *ase* which may be utilized either for or
against the good of society.

Despite its role in honoring male and female ancestors,
Egúngún is often identified as a 'male cult' in the sense that
women are prohibited from learning its mysteries and secrets.[44]
In pre-colonial times, if the secret that the "spirit" under the masquerade was a man was revealed to any women, those women
as well as the dancer himself would be put to death.[45] Women's
ignorance that the Egúngúns were costumed men, however, was
more a pretence to maintain the image that men kept important
secrets from women: "It will be recognized that while women
may look on freely at Egúngún performances they must be (*at
least apparently*) in complete ignorance of the deceit practised
on them. Not only must they not by sight, or touch, prove that
the vision is other than a disembodied spirit; they must not even
laugh at him, or show him any disrespect, still less say that he
is only a man in disguise."[46] The pretense that Egúngún is the

secret of men is confirmed by Babayemi, who claims "Egúngún is a secret cult . . . few women know its mysteries and such women are not to divulge the secrets of the cult... they adhere to the saying: [If a woman knows cult secrets, she must never tell]."[47] And when Pemberton asked "His Highness, the Orangun of Ila, why women were denied access to the *igbo* Egúngún and the *kaa* Egúngún, he observed that their exclusion was a way of affirming 'that men are above women, that they are the head of women.' And, he added, 'It is also because men are concerned about the power of women, their power as witches.'"[48] Barber observes that "women are not supposed to know that there is a living man under the costume. To show that she knows is for a woman an extremely grave ritual transgression ...The important thing is not women's actual ignorance, but the maintenance of a respectful silence about their knowledge. It is a matter of keeping up appearances for the sake of the ancestors' dignity. The woman collaborates to keep the *Egúngún's* 'secret'—which is no secret—so that its splendid beneficent power will remain intact for her to profit from."[49] With its essential exclusion of women from cult mysteries and the maintenance of women's pretense of ignorance of the dancers' identities, we can understand Egúngún as the 'secret of men'.

For the Yoruba, secrecy is a form of power. In an astute discussion of power and subversion in Yoruba cult ritual, Apter explains that there are two levels of interpretation for public ritual: the "public face" of symbols, songs, dances, and ritual objects and the less accessible symbolic meanings and techniques of regulating ritual power which are restricted to cult members. He asserts that "knowledge of what the symbols really signify, belongs with a body of esoteric secrets which—the Yoruba believe—provide access to ritual power itself. As far as the uninitiated public is concerned, cult festivals are largely *uninterpreted*—they are significant not in what they mean or communicate, but in what they *do* or accomplish."[50] Barber, too, points out that "it is by being made into a 'secret' that a spiritual being gets its authority."[51] Therefore, as the 'secret of women' Gelede is a tribute to women's ritual and spiritual power, and by maintaining particular aspects of Egúngún as the 'secret of men,' men are provided access to ritual and spiritual power.

CONCLUSION

I have argued here that analyses of contexts in individual domains of Yoruba culture can convey understanding of the ways in which diverse ideologies construct Yoruba gender meanings. The complexities of Yoruba gender ideologies can only be grasped by suspending precultural assumptions of universal female subordination and examining them on a contextual level. We have seen that they have multiple and contradictory ideologies,[52] which condone varying cultural conceptions of sex-linked behavior. By cultivating an awareness of contextually-specific ideologies, their ambivalences and multivalences, we can better grasp the *dynamics* of cultural meanings of gender, interactions between the sexes, relationships of hierarchy, and opportunities for agency. An assumption of female subordination veils a truer understanding of the dynamics of gender conceptions by both eliminating possibilities of female power and simplifying diverse patterns, and degrees of asymmetry. This assumption can preclude further investigation into contexts and thus give a false sense of any given culture's gender ideologies and accompanying complexities. Academic research which is committed to exploring instances of female power as well as female subordination will better inform us about women's opportunities for creativity and agency. It can also act as an effective means of empowerment for all women, especially for the women who are studied, the women researchers, and the women who read such studies.

Notes

1. Ruth Benedict, *Patterns of Culture* (Boston: Houghton Mifflin, 1934), 34.

2. Margaret Mead, *Sex and Temperament in Three Primitive Societies* (1935) (New York: Morrow Quill, 1963), vi.

3. Ibid, x.

4. Derek Freeman *Margaret Mead and Samoa: The Making and Unmaking of an Anthropological Myth* (New York: Penguin Books, 1983); F. Emngton and D. Gewertz, *Cultural Alternatives and a Feminist Anthropology* (Cambridge: Cambridge University Press, 1987).

5. See also, Michelle Zimbalist Rosaldo, "Woman, Culture, and Society: An Overview," in *Woman, Culture, and Society*, ed. M. Z. Rosaldo and L. Lamphere (Stanford: Stanford University Press, 1974); Marilyn Strathern, "Self-Interest and the Social Good: Some Implications of Hagen Gender Imagery," in *Sexual Meanings: The Cultural Construction of Gender & Sexuality*, ed. S. B. Ortner and H. Whitehead (Cambridge: Cambridge University Press, 1981).

6. Sherry Ortner, "Is Female to Male as Nature is to Culture?" in *Woman, Culture and Society*, ed. M. Z. Rosaldo and L. Lamphere (Stanford: Stanford University Press, 1974), 1.

7. Robert Smith, *Kingdoms of the Yoruba* (1969) (Madison: University of Wisconsin Press, 1988).

8. Heather Spiro, *The Ilora Farm Settlement in Nigeria* (West Hartford, CT: Kumarian Press, 1985).

9. Jane Guyer, *The Organizational Plan of Traditional Farming: Idere, Western Nigeria*, (Ph.D. Dissertation submitted to the Department of Anthropology, University of Rochester, New York, 1972).

10. Ibid.

11. Jane Guyer, "Women's Work in the Food Economy of the Cocoa Belt: A Comparison," Working Papers No. 7, (African Studies Center, Boston University, 1978); Spiro, *The Ilora Farm Settlement*.

12. N. A. Fadipe, *The Sociology of the Yoruba* (Ibadan: Ibadan University Press, 1970); Guyer, "Women's Work."

13. Guyer, *Organizational Plan*

14. Ibid.

15. Jane Guyer, "Anthropological Models of African Production: The Naturalization Problem," (Working Papers No. 78, African Studies Center, Boston University, 1983).

16. Guyer, *Organizational Plan*.

17. Guyer, "Women's Work."

18. R. C. Abraham, *Dictionary of Modern Yoruba* (London: University of London Press, 1958), 106.

19. Niara Sudarkasa, *Where Women Work: A Study of Yoruba Women in the Marketplace and in the Home*. Anthropological Papers No. 53, Museum of Anthropology, University of Michigan (Ann Arbor: University of Michigan Press, 1973), 2.

20. B. W. Hodder and U. I. Ukwu, *Markets in West Africa* (Ibadan: Ibadan University Press, 1969); Fadipe, *The Sociology*; Sudarkasa, *Where Women Work*.

21. Guyer, *Organizational Plan*, 82.

22. Ibid.

23. Sudarkasa, *Where Women Work*; Cheryl Johnson, "Class and Gender: A Consideration of Yoruba Women During the Colonial Period," in *Women and Class in Africa*, eds. C. Robertson and I. Berger (New York: Africana Publishing Company, 1986). [include page range]

24. Sara Berry, *Fathers Work for Their Sons: Accumulation, Mobility, and Class Formation in an Extended Yoruba Community* (Berkeley: University of California Press, 1985).

25. Abraham, *Dictionary of Modern*, 71.

26. H. J. Drewal and M. T. Drewal, *Gelede: Art and Female Power Among the Yoruba* (Bloomington: Indiana University Press, 1983), 5.

27. Ibid.

28. Drewal and Drewal, *Gelede*; Pierre Verger, "Grandeur et décadence du culte de Iyami Osoronga (Ma mère Ia sorcière) chez les Yoruba," *Journal de la Société des Africanistes* 35 no. 1 (1965): 141-243.

29. A. H. Leighton, et al. *Psychiatric Disorder Among the Yoruba*. A Report from the Cornell-Aro Mental Health Research Project in the Western Region, Nigeria (Ithaca: Cornell University Press, 1963); C.M.U. MacLean, "Sickness Behavior Among the Yoruba," in *Witchcraft and Healing*. Proceedings of a seminar held in the Centre of African Studies, University of Edinburgh, Feb. 14-15, 1969

30. Leighton, et al. *Psychiatric*.

31. Drewal and Drewal, *Gelede*, 8

32. Pierre Verger, "Grandeur et décadence du culte de Iyami Osoronga (Ma mère Ia sorcière) chez les Yoruba," *Journal de la Société des Africanistes* 35 no. 1 (1965): 141-243.

33. H. U. Beier, "Gelede Masks," *Odu* 6 (1958): 5-23 (5).

34. Drewal and Drewal, *Gelede*, 8.

35. Alice Schlegel, "Toward a Theory of Sexual Stratification," in *Sexual Stratification*, ed. A. Schlegel (New York: Columbia University Press, 1977), 7.

36. Sherry B. Ortner and Harriet Whitehead, "Introduction: Accounting for Sexual Meanings," in *Sexual Meanings: The Cultural Construction of Gender & Sexuality*, eds. S. B. Ortner and H. Whitehead (Cambridge: Cambridge University Press, 1981), 16.

37. Peter Morton-Williams, "The Egungun Society in South-western Yoruba Kingdoms," *Proceedings of the Third Annual Conference of the West African Institute of Social and Economic Research,* 1956.

38. Marilyn Hammersley Houlberg, "Notes on Egungun Masquerades Among the Oyo Yoruba," *African Arts* 2 no. 3 (1978): 56-61.

39. H. J. Drewal, "The Arts of Egungun Among Yoruba Peoples," *African Arts* 11 no. 3 (1978): 18-19.

40. Ibid.

41. Marc Schiltz, "Egungun Masquerades in Iganna," *African Arts* 11 no. 3 (1978): 53.

42. H.U. Beier, "The Egungun Cult," *Nigeria Magazine* 51 (1956): 392.

43. Morton-Williams, "The Egungun Society," 102.

44. Stephen S. Faith Farrow, *Fancies and Fetich, or Yoruba Paganism* (1926) (New York: Negro Universities Press, 1969); Beier, "The Egúngún Cult"; S. O. Babayemi, *Egungun Among the Oyo Yoruba* (Ibadan: Board Publications, 1980).

45. Farrow, *Fancies and Fetich.*

46. Ibid., 79 (*emphasis mine*).

47. Babayemi, *Egungun Among the Oyo,* 4.

48. John Pemberton, "Egungun Masquerades of the Igbomina Yoruba," *African Arts* 11 no. 3 (1978): 43.

49. Karim Barber, "How Man Makes God in West Africa: Yoruba Attitudes Towards the Orisa," *Africa* 51 no. 1 (1981): 739.

50. Andrew Herman Apter, *Rituals of Power: The Politics of Orisa Worship in Yoruba Society.* (Ph.D. Dissertation presented to the Faculty of the Graduate School at Yale University, 1987), 225-26.

51. Barber, "How Man Makes God," 739-40.

52. Anna Meigs, "Multiple Gender Ideologies and Statuses," *Beyond the Second Sex: New Directions in the Anthropology of Gender,* eds. P. R. Sanday and R. G. Goodenough (Philadelphia: University of Pennsylvania Press, 1990); Alma Gottlieb, "Hyenas and Heteroglossia: Myth and Ritual Among the Beng of Côte d'Ivoire," *American Ethnologist* 16 no. 3 (1989): 487–501.

Chapter 11

A WOMAN'S FERTILITY STRATEGY: THE PRACTICE AND PERCEPTION OF ABORTION BY EKITI YORUBA WOMEN[1]

Elisha P. Renne

INTRODUCTION

For many—though not all—Yoruba women in Southwestern Nigeria, abortion is considered to be one among a continuum of fertility control strategies. Women obtain abortions using traditional medicines prepared by local herbalists and "patent" medicines purchased from pharmacies, as well as by D&C (dilation and curettage) and MVA (manual vacuum aspiration) at nearby clinics and hospitals.[10] These medicines come under the general name, *oogun ti won le fi se ki oyun maa duro*—"medicine that keeps a pregnancy from staying," while D&C is locally referred to as *f'onu*—"cleaning the inside (or womb)." The latter term, *f'onu*, refers to the use of D&C to remove the detritus of miscarriage, although it may also be used to regulate menstruation and for abortion. This paper considers the persistence of abortion as a fertility strategy,[11] despite the presence of other options and the well-known dangers associated with this practice.[12] Specifically, the practice of abortion for a group of rural Ekiti Yoruba women is discussed, indicating who aborts and why.

One might simply attribute a technological explanation for the local prevalence of medicines that terminate a pregnancy over contracepting types because, as one traditional healer (*babalawo*) pointed out, "It is easier to bring down a pregnancy than to prevent one." However, there are also economic, social, and cultural factors which contribute to Ekiti women's decisions to abort pregnancies.[13] Some researchers have noted a distrust of long-term contraception use and its consequences for future fertility as well as a preference for an immediate solution to an unplanned pregnancy.[14] More specifically, I want to suggest that an analysis of beliefs about prenatal development and conception also helps to explain the continued use of abortion as a fertility strategy. For not only do such beliefs affect how abortion is perceived, they also reinforce culturally specific socio-economic relations between women and men.

KEEPING A PREGNANCY FROM STAYING IN AN EKITI YORUBA TOWN

Research for this study began in June 1991 when I moved to a small rural town in Ekiti State, in southwestern Nigeria.[15] While the town has some of the infrastructural characteristics of larger cities (e.g., electricity, a secondary school, maternity clinic, bank, police station, and post office), it is also fairly typical in terms of social and political institutions of other small Ekiti Yoruba towns (Renne 2003). In July-August 1991, two research assistants and I conducted open-ended interviews of a stratified sample of 70 women (ages 15-39) and 66 men (ages 20-44), selected by age and availability. They were asked a range of questions about their attitudes toward family size, contraceptive use, the practice of dilation and curettage, and reproductive health knowledge. This information was used to devise a survey that included a section on the use of dilation and curettage, after miscarriage as well as for abortion, and of substances used to abort or "bring down" a pregnancy. Survey interviews of 296 women aged 15-49 were conducted by four research assistants and myself in January-March 1992. The survey results suggested several areas for further questioning regarding abortion and follow-up interviews were conducted based on women's responses in this survey. Five years later, in 1997, a five-year follow-up survey of 200 women ages 15-54 was conducted in the same town, which gathered additional information about abortion and on the use of the emergency contraceptive, Postinor. The following discussion is based on the 1992 and 1997 surveys as well as on follow-ups interviews with women on menstrual regulation (Renne 2001), emergency contraception (Renne 1998), and on changing practices related to virginity (Renne 2003).

Abortion providers, including those who provided traditional and patent medicines were also interviewed. Traditional diviners (*babalawo* and *iyalawo*) and herbalists (*onisegun*) have an arsenal of medicinal and spiritual devices which, with varying degrees of success, are said to "keep a pregnancy from staying." As several of these men and women said they had learned of these medicines from their fathers, it is likely that these practices are not new (Delano 1988).

The introduction of Western "patent" medicine has also increased Ekiti Yoruba women's options for "bringing a pregnancy down." Tablets used for headache relief (Bee-Codeine, Panadol), menstrual irregularities (Dr. Bonjean, Menstrogen), and malaria (Dagaquine) taken in large doses were most commonly mentioned. It is when these medicines are ineffective that women most often go to private clinics or hospitals where abortions by D&C or MVA are performed. One clinic owner in a neighboring Ekiti town estimated that two-thirds of the ten abortions he performed monthly (on average) were a result of women using other things which had not completely worked. However because of the tendency to self-abort and the potential illegality of clinic abortions, it is difficult to get precise figures on their number and types. When I suggested to the above-mentioned clinic owner that abortion was common, he said he did not think it was; yet a woman diviner (*iyalawo*) in the same town said she had "performed uncountable abortions."

One man, a teacher described as a "social" diviner (*babalawo*) because he performed abortions to help people rather than as his primary occupation, said that abortion was very common. He attributed its prevalence to economic hardship associated with SAP (Structural Adjustment Program), a currency devaluation policy instituted by the Federal Government in 1987. The decline in the value of the naira, which has continued into the twenty-first century, when its value has stabilized somewhat, has led to continuing economic hardship for Nigerian women and men.

Regarding the extent of induced abortion in Nigeria, figures from Nigerian health sector sources vary, with estimates of 200,000 to 500,000 pregnancies aborted annually. Henshaw et al. estimated (based on health care institution records of abortions and treatments for induced abortion complications) that 610,000 abortions were carried out annually in Nigeria, with a rate of 25 abortions per 1,000 women ages 15-44 years.[16] In their community-based study of 3,743 women in Lagos and Edo States in southern Nigeria, Oye-Adeniran et al. found that 21.1 percent had had at least one abortion in their lives.[17] Furthermore, approximately 10,000 to 20,000 women die annually as a result of complications from abortions.[18] Smaller studies from the 1980s in Lagos estimated that 5 percent and 5.6 percent of the women surveyed had aborted pregnancies, although these figures may be low because of the reticence of women to admit to having abortions.[19] In the Ekiti town where I worked, 15.2 percent of women surveyed in 1992 had gone for D&C to abort pregnancies.[20] (This figure does not include women who used traditional and patent medicines.) The follow-up survey conducted in 1997 in the same town found that 20.9 percent of women had gone for a D&C to abort, similar to Oye-Adeniran et al's. (2004b) findings.

That abortion is a common practice was reinforced by another set of interviews with 70 townswomen, ages 15-39 years, conducted prior to the 1992 survey in fall 1991. Of these women, 58 knew of examples, often friends, family members, or neighbors with whom they were acquainted personally, who had aborted a pregnancy. For example:

One of my aunts used medicine [on an unwanted pregnancy] without telling her husband.

> (Q: How did you know?)
> She told me and I was the one who helped her to buy it.
> (Q: What did she use?)
> She used Bee-codeine and Andrew's Liver Salt.
> (Q: After buying these things, how did she take them?)
> She bought 7-UP and dissolved the Bee-Codeine and Andrew's Liver Salt in it and drank them.
> (Q: What happened to her then?)
> The pregnancy was aborted but it affected her so she went to the hospital where she was treated very well.

From these interviews, from in-depth abortion "histories," and surveys conducted in 1992 and in 1997, a picture emerges regarding how and why abortion serves as a fertility strategy in one Ekiti Yoruba town.

THOSE WHO ABORT

From the interviews, two groups of women were found to be the most likely candidates for abortions—unmarried school girls and married women who had outside partners. The phenomena of adolescent unmarried schoolgirls getting abortions is well documented in Nigeria.[21] In Nigeria, a recent WHO study estimated that 60 percent of the demand for abortion in Nigeria comes from these women.[22] The most common reason for aborting a pregnancy is the desire to finish school, though their unmarried status is also a factor.[23] One woman gave the following example: A lady in Lagos was already pregnant before her husband proposed marriage to her so she aborted this pregnancy before she married the man and she didn't let him know.

Women cited several examples of married women with outside affairs aborting: One woman got pregnant by a friend outside and she didn't want her husband to know about this. She couldn't go to the hospital because she had no money so she decided to use alcohol and *konun* (potash) with Menstrogen tablets and the pregnancy didn't stay.

Some married women had other reasons for aborting pregnancies which included, in order of frequency cited:

1. The desire for child spacing—pregnancy too soon after earlier childbirth;
2. The husband not caring for welfare of wife and children;
3. The desire to limit family size; and
4. The desire to remarry a wealthier man ("hypergamy strategy").

An example of a "hypergamy strategy" was given by one woman:

> Q: Can you give an example of a woman you've seen or heard of using medicine on an unwanted pregnancy without telling her husband?

A: I only heard it, I didn't see it. There was a woman who formerly had a husband whom she had left when she saw another person who was richer. But she was already pregnant for the former husband so she aborted the pregnancy and lied to the husband that she had miscarried. This caused conflict between them and she later left this man to marry the richer one. The incident happened in Ado-Ekiti.

Q: Do you know the type of medicine she used to abort the pregnancy?

A: Yes, I learned that she used Bee-codeine with alcohol.

Other village women's reasons for aborting pregnancies and the action they took may more clearly be seen in the following three abortion "histories."

ABORTION HISTORIES

Despite the secrecy surrounding abortion,[24] it is difficult to keep this knowledge from family, close friends, and neighbors, particularly when there are complications.[25] These interviews were obtained through a network of my closest women informants in the village. While not a representative sampling, there is nothing unusual about the background or experiences of these women to suggest that they are anomalous.

Woman A: 23 years old, completed secondary school, unmarried, three abortions.

Abortion 1: The first time this happened was when I was in secondary school, class 3; I was 15 years old. I didn't know I was pregnant but was thin and sick (vomiting) so that my parents took me to a nearby clinic. The doctor tested me and confirmed that I was pregnant. My parents said that since I was a student, I should abort it so the doctor charged N75 (he was talked down from N150).[26] So he did a D&C—I was two months pregnant at the time. After that he gave me some drugs to use, like ampicillin, also some other medicine. My parents didn't want me to marry my boyfriend and I didn't tell him that I was pregnant and had aborted. I spent one day at the clinic and my mother paid for the abortion.

Abortion 2: Three years later when I was completing secondary school, I was worried when I didn't see my menses. I went to a doctor who tested me and advised me to wait six days, to see if the pregnancy was strong. But as it didn't come down [on its own account] I went back after explaining to my boyfriend that I hadn't menstruated, so we went together to let the doctor know that the child was still there. My boyfriend wanted me to keep the pregnancy but I refused because I was still schooling. After the abortion I was given ampicillin and septrin. My boyfriend paid N30 for the abortion.

Abortion 3: In 1991, when awaiting entrance into university, I became pregnant by one boyfriend whom I later decided not to marry in favor of another. Since I did not want my chosen fiancé to know of the pregnancy, I decided to abort it. I first used (3) Bee-codeine tablets, Andrew's Liver Salt, and Sprite, mixing them together and then drinking them. When this did not have any effect, I went to a clinic in a neighboring town for D&C. The abortion cost N80 and was paid for by my boyfriend. There were no after effects.

Woman B: 30 years old, completed secondary school, trader, one abortion.

Abortion 1: I am married with two children, the youngest being four years old. When I realized I was pregnant (after two months), I took four Bee-codeine tablets with *agogoro* (native gin). Soon after I had stomach pain and then two days later, there was bleeding and the pregnancy came down. Except for the stomach ache, there were no other effects and I didn't go to a clinic for D&C. The reason I decided to abort the pregnancy which was by my husband was that he was unemployed and we did not have money to care for the child. He didn't know I was pregnant nor did he know that I aborted.

Woman C: 33 years old, completed secondary school, trader, one abortion.

Abortion 1. When I realized that I was pregnant after a month in early 1991, I went to a diviner (babalawo) in a nearby village. He gave me medicine which I inserted in my vagina. By the third month, when the pregnancy didn't come down, I went to a clinic in a nearby town for a D&C. My boyfriend paid N65 for the procedure. Afterwards, there was some bleeding so I returned to the clinic and was given additional medication.

I decided to abort the pregnancy because it belonged to my boyfriend, not to my husband. I did not let my husband know about it.

ANALYSIS OF ABORTION HISTORIES

These three histories display certain similarities, relating to who pays, type of abortion choice, and preferred time for abortion. In the instances involving women-students, parents, particularly mothers, get (or are forced to get) involved, both in treatment and payment. While these women as students generally attempted to abort with locally available medicines (either traditional or "patent" types), in cases where there were complications mothers supported their daughters. Also in the case of the first woman, her boyfriend paid for her abortion, even while he wanted her to keep the pregnancy. Further, while these women sometimes paid for patent and traditional abortifacients, D&C procedures were generally paid for by someone else. This fact suggests that economics and access play a large part in the types of abortifacients women choose.[27] The second woman, who aborted her pregnancy because of economic problems, preferred to use patent medicines because they easily could be obtained locally, without her husband's knowledge, and at relatively little expense. Particularly, when a boyfriend, who may or may not want the pregnancy to go to term himself, is involved and is paying, there seems to be a preference for D&C and more recently, for the emergency contraceptive, Postinor.[28] This preference is understandable considering these women's variable success with traditional and "patent" medicines used as abortifacients.

Finally, all women initially attempted to abort before the third month of pregnancy.[29] This relates to the idea that a pregnancy is fragile early on, which a combination of patent drugs, alcohol, and effervescent drink can more easily "shake down." Hence the doctor's advice in the case of woman A that she wait six days "to see if the pregnancy was strong" before performing a D&C. There is also a preference for early abortion for the sake of the woman's health. According to one woman:

> If the pregnancy was very late before the abortion was conducted (three, four, or more months), it could be complicated. It can lead to stomach pain or it can lead to bleeding. If such bleeding is excessive, it can lead to death.

Further, the preference for early abortion is related to ideas about the stages of pregnancy development itself. Whether one opts for an abortion depends, to some extent, on the definition of when the life of a child begins.[30]

ABORTION AND IDEAS ABOUT PREGNANCY DEVELOPMENT AND CONCEPTION

In Ekiti towns and villages, the reliance on abortion as a form of birth control has a basis in economic, technological, and physiological factors. Yet there are other aspects relating to traditional ideas about fertility which help to explain the acceptability of this practice, relative to other forms of birth control. In particular, indigenous ideas about when, during a pregnancy, the "real child" is formed influence attitudes about the ethics and efficacy of "keeping a pregnancy from staying."

Perceptions of Fetal Development

It is not simply the fragility of early pregnancies and the health of the pregnant woman which influence women's preference for early abortion. The local belief that the "real child" is formed sometime after the fourth month of pregnancy also affects their behavior. While some women with post-secondary education may have revised their thinking about conception, having learned about the process of fertilization of egg and sperm cells, for many, earlier ideas about prenatal development and when a pregnancy is confirmed by lack of menstruation and movement in the womb. The following three versions of prenatal development, while differing in some details, all describe a lizard-like being taking on the appearance of a child around the fifth month of pregnancy.

Version 1: Two months after conception, something like a lizard with a tail will be formed. When it is four months old, it will be something like an amoeba, shapeless. (This is why it is difficult to terminate a pregnancy in the fourth month.)

After four months, 1 week, the real child will be formed, having the head bigger than the rest of the body. The real child will grow and its size will be equally distributed when ready to be born. The child will also be kicking then. When it is about 8 months, 3 weeks, the child will just come very near the womb. During the day the mother will just see water and have a general weakness of the body. She will go to the hospital or get help to deliver. During the delivery, the child will come out first, followed by the placenta.[31]

Version 2: In the first and second months, it will be water. By the third month, it becomes solid and just looks like blood. By the fourth month, it will look like a lizard. By the fifth month, it has arms, hands, and eyes and by the sixth month, there will be certain movements in the stomach which will continue. This development continues until the child comes out.[32]

Version 3: The blood in the stomach will be in the form of a child, it will be the first month child. When it is the second month, the red color becomes whitish. The third month, it will be in the form of a lizard (during this time it has no color and the head will be in the form of a monkey and people will not like how it is formed). In the fourth month, it will be in the form of watery blood and semen. In the fifth month, the thing will be shaking the woman's body, moving up and down in the stomach and making stomach pains (but it isn't stomach pain, it is just the moving around). At this time, the tail will disappear. In the sixth and seventh months, the thing will be shaking very well. But in the eighth month, it can't shake, it doesn't have power again. It will be resting and it's not good to abort during this time. If someone aborts during this period, the person will die. It will take all her blood so she will die. When nine months, it will be strong again. It will turn the head down and shake the body very well in order to have the chance to come down.[33]

The last version is instructive as it suggests that it is not good to abort so late in a pregnancy because of excessive bleeding which will lead to the death of the woman. She may also be suggesting that it is not good in a moral sense to abort so late as the pregnancy has clearly become a child by this time.

The ambiguous morality of late abortion was also hinted at by the "social" babalawo mentioned above. He said that he could not tell me about abortions performed in the eighth month because only witches and wizards—immoral, anti-social creatures by definition—could know about such things. He intimated that supernatural intervention was involved in such cases in addition to medicines so powerful (and deadly) that he could not reveal them except to say they included part of a human body.

However, the same man and other traditional healers gave me several recipes for traditional medicines "to keep pregnancies from staying" to be taken after meeting a man or shortly after a woman discovers she is pregnant. In these cases, no overtones of immorality were evident as the pregnancy during this period was merely blood, water, or a lizard-like creature, but not the "real child." Indeed, they sometimes provide such treatments in order for women to regulate their menstruation, i.e., to establish regular monthly menstruation that will enable them to become pregnant when desired.[34]

IDEAS ABOUT CONCEPTION

Traditional ideas about conception also help to explain women's sense that early abortion is no worse ethically-speaking than other forms of birth control. Indeed, contraception as well as abortion come under a moral shadow to some extent since child-bearing represents a fundamental social ideal for women as Pearce has noted:

> The Yoruba put a premium on social relationships and the collectivity. There is an immense pressure to belong, and to identify with recognised groups within the community. . . . Attachment to appropriate groups is obtained in a variety of ways, but none is more significant, especially for women, than the birth of a child.[35]

While childbearing is critically important for women's social identity and women are often blamed for childlessness, both women and men are seen as contributing to the conception of a child.

The following two versions were given by a man and a woman, respectively, reflect a duo-genetic model of conception.

Version 1: When the male and female meet, both of them produce eggs which start eating each other as food. The last one, if it belongs to the female, then the pregnancy will result in a female child, while if it is a male egg, it will be a male child.

Version 2: When it is the time of menstruation, the child will be in the left or right hand side of the stomach, the blood will stay on the left or right also. So when it is a month, the menses blood and the semen [will mix].

These two versions agree with Buckley's findings, that, "All the herbalists I spoke to agreed that a child conceived in the womb (*ile omo*) is the union of blood (*eje*) of menstruation (*ase*) and semen (*ato*)."

It is possible that because it is generally believed that women contribute equally to the formation of a child that some women also believe that they have a certain right in deciding whether to terminate a pregnancy. There are several examples in the abortion histories of women terminating pregnancies without the agreement or knowledge of men. For example, in three instances when boyfriends wanted pregnancies to go to term, the women involved insisted on an abortion. And, in the case of the married woman who aborted because of financial difficulties, she took responsibility for this decision without telling or consulting her husband.

I am not suggesting that there is a simple one-to-one correspondence between explanations of conception and the belief in the right of women to get abortions. Nonetheless, ideas about the contribution of women and men to the creation of life are related to beliefs about gender and power which in turn may influence attitudes toward abortion as well as other aspects of women's autonomy.

CONCLUSION

In this Ekiti Yoruba town, women who terminated pregnancies expressed no particular feelings of guilt about their actions. Rather, negative attitudes about the use of abortion as a fertility strategy were expressed in terms of health, both in terms of maternal mortality and potential harm to future pregnancies. Yet while the emphasis on health may literally be the case—women who self-abort or go for D&C or MVA do sometimes die and stories about women dying from attempted abortion also contain an element of moral approbation. Abortion is associated with illicit behavior (e.g., having children before marriage, taking lovers outside marriage), emphasized by the fact that women did not speak openly about abortion in the town. Indeed, some women belonging to "gospel" churches in the town (e.g., Deeper Life Church and Redeemed Church) adamantly stated that they would never abort a pregnancy. However, for the women who relied on abortion as a fertility strategy to prevent an unwanted pregnancy, they were more concerned that their parents or husbands should not know, although as has been seen, mothers sometimes assist their daughters. For them, abortion is part of a pattern of behavior, considered sub-rosa in the first place but necessary as well. The economic and social realities of everyday life and gender relations—in which boyfriends are needed for financial support, either for school fees or caring for one's children—as well as indigenous beliefs about conception and when life begins, override conflicting ideologies about the morality of "keeping a pregnancy from staying." Abortion, often construed as women's problem—particularly young, unmarried school girls and wayward wives—may be better understood in terms of culturally specific relations between women and men.

Notes

1. The initial research (1991-1992) for this study was conducted with funding from the Andrew W. Mellon Foundation in conjunction with a joint research project organized by Ondo State University, Ado-Ekiti, and the Health Transition Centre, The Australian National University, Canberra. The 1997 study was funded by the Wenner-Gren Foundation for Anthropological Research and the Mellon Foundation through my affiliation with Princeton University. I am grateful to all these institutions and foundations as well as to I. O. Orubuloye, Jack Caldwell, and Pat Caldwell for logistical support and to Kayode Owoeye, Adenike Oso, and Iyabo Arunsoro for their research assistance. An earlier version of this paper was published in the journal, *Social Science & Medicine*, in 1996.

2. W. Koster, *Secret Strategies: Women and Abortion in Yoruba Society, Nigeria* (Amsterdam: Askant Koster 2003); O. A. Moronkola, A. Amosu, and C. Okonkwo, "Knowledge about Conception, Sexual Behavior, and Procurement of Abortion among Female Undergraduate Students in a Nigerian University," *International Quarterly of Community Health Education* 24 no. 3 (2005-2006): 241-9; B. A. Oye-Adeniran, I. F. Adewole, A. V. Umoh, N. Iwere, and A. Gbadegesin, "Induced abortion in Nigeria: Findings from Focus Group Discussions," *African Journal of Reproductive Health* 9 no. 1 (2005):133-41.

3. A. Bankole, B. A. Oye-Adeniran, S. Singh, I. F. Adewole, D. Wulf, G. Sedgh, and R. Hussain, *Unwanted Pregnancy and Unsafe Abortion in Nigeria: Causes and Consequences* (New York: Guttmacher Institute, 2006); V.O. Otoide, F. Oronsaye, and F. E. Okonofua, "Why Nigerian Adolescents Seek Abortion Rather than Contraception: Evidence from Focus-Group Discussions," *International Family Planning Perspectives* 27 no. 2 (2001): 77-81; B. A. Oye-Adeniran, I. F. Adewole, A.V. Umoh, O.R. Fapohunda, and N. Iwere, "Characteristics of Abortion Care Seekers in South-western Nigeria," *African Journal of Reproductive Health* 8 no. 3 (2004): 81-91; G. Sedgh, A. Bankole and B. Oye-Adeniran, "Unwanted Pregnancy and Associated Factors among Nigerian Women," *International Family Planning Perspectives* 32 no. 4 (2006): 175-84.

4. B. A. Oye-Adeniran, I. F. Adewole, A. V. Umoh, E. Ekanem, A. Gbadegesin, and N. Iwere, "Community-Based Survey of Unwanted Pregnancy in Southwestern Nigeria," *African Journal of Reproductive Health* 8 no. 3 (2004):

103-15; B. A. Oye-Adeniran, I. F. Adewole, A. V. Umoh, N. Iwere, and A. Gbadegesin, "Induced Abortion in Nigeria: Findings from Focus Group Discussion," *African Journal of Reproductive Health* 9 no. 1 (2005): 133-41; A. Raufu, "Unsafe Abortions Cause 20,000 Deaths a year in Nigeria," *BMJ* (Clinical Research edition) 325, no. 7371 (2002): 988; E. P. Renne, "Abortion as Illegal Conduct and its Sequelae," *Curare: Studies in Ethnomedicine* 29 no. 1 (2006): 81-95.

5.   F. Adewole, B. A. Oye-Adeniran, N. Iwere, A. Oladokun, and A. Gbadegesin, "Terminating an Unwanted Pregnancy: The Economic Implications in Nigeria, *Journal of Obstetrics and Gynecology* 22 no. 4 (2002): 436-7; E. Emuveyan, "Profile of Abortion in Nigeria," *African Journal of Fertility, Sexuality, and Reproductive Health* 1 no. 1 (1996): 8-13; G. Sedgh, A. Bankole, and B. Oye-Adeniran, "Unwanted pregnancy and associated factors among Nigerian women," *International Family Planning Perspectives* 32 no.4 (2006): 175-84.

6.   V. O. Otoide, F. Oronsaye, and F. E. Okonofua "Why Nigerian Adolescents Seek Abortion Rather than Contraception: Evidence from Focus-Group Discussions," *International Family Planning Perspectives* 27 no. 2 (2001):77-81; E. P. Renne, "Postinor Use among Young Women in Southwestern Nigeria: A Research Note," *Reproductive Health Matters* 6 no. 11 (1998): 107-14; I. A. Ujah, "Contraceptive Intentions of Women seeking Induced Abortion in the City of Jos, Nigeria," *Journal of Obstetrics and Gynaecology* 20 no. 2 (2000): 162-6.

7.   The Ekiti Yoruba comprise a sub-group of the Yoruba-speaking people of southwestern Nigeria. Traditionally men were farmers and women traders and weavers, though today many Ekiti women and men have secondary school certificates or some higher education and have taken up employment in schools and government offices. While relatively isolated in the past, nowadays Ekiti women and men attend school, visit family, and travel to major urban centers such as Lagos and Ibadan. Thus many of the women questioned in this study were exposed to trends and fashions in Nigeria more generally. The town where I lived had a permanent population of approximately 3,574 inhabitants whose occupation was primarily farming (men) and trading (women), while the population rose to approximately 11,392 during holidays. See E. P. Renne, *Population and Progress in a Yoruba Town* (Ann Arbor: University of Michigan Press, 2003). Most men and women have had some primary schooling and most are Christians.

8.   S. Henshaw, S. Singh, B. Oye-Adeniran, I. Adewole, N. Iwere, and Y. Cuca, "The Incidence of Induced Abortion in Nigeria," *International Family Planning Perspectives* 24 no. 4 (1998): 156-64. See also S. Singh, "Hospital Admissions Resulting from Unsafe Abortion: Estimates from 13 Developing Countries," *Lancet* 368 (9550) (2006): 1887-92.

9.   B. A. Oye-Adeniran, I. F. Adewole, A. V. Umoh, E. Ekanem, A. Gbadegesin, and N. Iwere, "Community-based survey of unwanted pregnancy in south-

western Nigeria," *African Journal of Reproductive Health* 8 no. 3 (2004): 103-15.

10. A. Raufu, "Unsafe Abortions Cause 20,000 Deaths a year in Nigeria," *BMJ* (Clinical research edition) 325(7371) (2002): 988; U. Uzoatu, "Terminating the Unwanted," *Times Week* 25, 30 September 1991, 18.

11. P. K. Makinwa-Adebusoye, D. J. Nichols, and S.E. Kelly, *1980 Lagos Contraception and Breast Feeding Study, Final Reports* (Benin: Center for Social, Culture, and Environmental Research, University of Benin, 1982); A. Olukoya, "Pregnancy Termination: Results of a Community-based Study in Lagos, Nigeria," *International Journal of Gynecology and Obstetrics* 25 (1987): 41-46.

12. In her 1991 survey of women in the urban center of Ado-Ekiti, Jo O'Toole, with female research assistants, found that 16.4 percent had abortions (personal communication).

13. O. Alubo, "Adolescent Reproductive Health Practices in Nigeria," *African Journal of Reproductive Health* 5 no. 3 (2001): 109-19; O. B. Fasubaa, S. T. Akindele, A. Adelekan, and H. Okwuokenye, "A Politico-Medical Perspective of Induced Abortion in a Semi-urban Community of Ile-Ife, Nigeria, *Journal of Obstetrics and Gynaecology* 22 no. 1 (2002): 51-7; J. Caldwell and P. Caldwell, "The Cultural Context of High Fertility in sub-Saharan Africa," *Population and Development Review* 13 no.3 (1987): 409-37; N. Murray, W. Winfrey, M. Chatterji, S. Moreland, L. Dougherty, and F. Okonofua, "Factors Related to Induced Abortion among Young Women in Edo State, Nigeria," *Studies in Family Planning* 37 no. 4 (2006): 251-68; D. Nichols, O. Ladipo, J. Paxman, and O. Otolorin, "Sexual Behavior, Contraceptive Practice and Reproductive Health among Nigerian Adolescents," *Studies in Family Planning* 17 no. 2 (1986): 100-6; Oye-B. A. Adeniran, I. F. Adewole, A. V. Umoh, O. R. Fapohunda, and N. Iwere, "Characteristics of Abortion Care Seekers in Southwestern Nigeria," *African Journal of Reproductive Health* 8 no. 3 (2004): 81-91.

14. Uzoatu, "Terminating the unwanted," 17-18.

15. N. Murray, W. Winfrey, M. Chatterji, S. Moreland, L. Dougherty, and F. Okonofua, "Factors Related to Induced Abortion among Young Women in Edo State, Nigeria," *Studies in Family Planning* 37 no. 4 (2006): 251-68; G. Sedgh, A. Bankole, and B. Oye-Adeniran, "Unwanted Pregnancy and Associated Factors among Nigerian Women," *International Family Planning Perspectives* 32 no. 4 (2006):175-84.

16. W. Koster, *Secret Strategies: Women and Abortion in Yoruba Society, Nigeria* (Amsterdam: Askant, 2003).

17. T. M. Mitsunaga, U. M. Larsen, and F. E. Okonofua, "Risk factors for complications of induced abortions in Nigeria," *Journal of Women's Health* 14 no. 6 (2005): 515-28; F. E. Okonofua, "Induced Abortion—A Risk factor

for Infertility in Nigerian Women," *Journal of Obstetrics and Gynaecology* 14 (1994): 272-76.

18. The exchange rate for the naira in December 1991 was $1 (US) = N14.50; in June 1997 it was $1 (US) = N86.

19. I. F. Adewole, B.A. Oye-Adeniran, N. Iwere, A. Oladokun, and A. Gbadegesin, "Terminating an Unwanted Pregnancy: The Economic Implications in Nigeria," *Journal of Obstetrics and Gynaecology* 22 no. 4 (2002): 436-7; A. Bankole, B. A. Oye-Adeniran, S. Singh, I. F. Adewole, D. Wulf, G. Sedgh, and R. Hussain, *Unwanted Pregnancy and Unsafe Abortion in Nigeria: Causes and Consequences* (New York: Guttmacher Institute, 2006).

20. In July-August 1997, a research assistant interviewed 24 college women about their use of Postinor and about whether they viewed it as a contraceptive or abortifacient (Renne 1998). The emergency contraceptive, Postinor, which is taken immediately after intercourse, cost between N150-200 for a 10-pill packet, enough to last 2 months, while monthly contraceptive tablet packets cost N25 each in 1997 (see note 5). According to women interviewed in Ado-Ekiti in 1997, they expected their boyfriends to pay for the more expensive Postinor tablets. For other discussions of emergency contraception and Postinor use by post-secondary women students, see M. E. Aziken, P. I. Okonta, and A. B. Ande, "Knowledge and Perception of Emergency Contraception among Female Nigerian Undergraduates," *International Family Planning Perspectives* 29 no. 2 (2003): 84-7; O. M. Ebuehi, E. E. Ekanem, and O. A. Ebuehi, "Knowledge and Practice of Emergency Contraception among Female Undergraduates in the University of Lagos, Nigeria," *East African Medical Journal* 83 no. 3 (2006): 90-5; A. C. Ikeme, H. U. Ezegwui, and A. C. Uzodimma, "Knowledge, Attitude and Use of Emergency Contraception among Female Undergraduates in Eastern Nigeria," *Journal of Obstetrics and Gynaecology* 25 no. 5 (2005): 491-3.

21. cf. A. O. Sule-Odu, A.O. Olatunji, and R. A. Akindele, "Complicated induced abortion in Sagamu, Nigeria," *Journal of Obstetrics and Gynaecology* 22 no. 1 (2002): 58-61.

22. E. P. Renne and E. van de Walle, "Introduction," in *Regulating Menstruation: Beliefs, Practices, Interpretations,* ed. E. Van de Walle and E. Renne (Chicago: University of Chicago Press, 2001), xvi.

23. Interview: Teacher, "social" diviner, man, about 50 years, 1992 [my emphasis].

24. Interview: Traditional diviner, man, about 75 years, 1992.

25. Interview: Traditional diviner, woman, around 40 years, 1992.

26. E. P. Renne, "Cleaning the Inside" and the Regulation of Menstruation in Southwestern Nigeria," in *Regulating Menstruation: Beliefs, Practices, Interpretations,* ed. E. Van de Walle and E. Rennee (Chicago: University of Chicago Press, 2001), 200 n12.

27. T. Pearce, "She Will Not be Listened to in Public: Perceptions among the Yoruba of Infertility and Childlessness in Women," *Reproductive Health Matters* 7 no. 13 (1999): 75.

28. Ibid.

29. Interview: Man, primary school teacher, 50 years, 1992.

30. Interview: Woman, diviner, 40 years, 1992.

31. A. Buckley, *Yoruba Medicine* (Oxford: Clarendon Press, 1985), 55-6.

32. Nancy R. Hunt, "Between Fiction and History: Modes of Writing Abortion in Africa," *Cahiers d'Etudes Africaines* 47 no. 2 (2007): 294.

33. Delaney refers to these different symbolic representations of conception as "monogenetic" or "duogenetic." In the Ekiti interviews, two non-traditional versions of conception were given by one younger woman and one younger man, reflecting ideas about conception resulting from Western education and Christian teachings. The first, a secondary school graduate, described a "monogenetic model"—perhaps because she fell "in between" both systems, knowing neither traditional nor western explanations, or perhaps because her Christian training emphasized this view. The second, a university student, gave a standard western explanation of genetics, which, like the traditional Yoruba model is duo-genetic. Version 1a: When a man and women meet, the development will start from semen (*ato*) which becomes sticky blood. I don't know what women contribute (woman, trader, 30 years). Version 2a: After intercourse, the sperm of the man fertilizes the egg of the woman. They come together to form an entirely new cell, a gamete. The sex of the child is determined by the chromosome of the man's sperm—if it is "Y" the child will be a boy, if it is "X" the child will be a girl (man, university student, 22 years). See C. Delaney, "Symbols of Procreation: Implications for Education and Population Planning," in *Turkic Culture: Continuity and Change*, ed. S. M. Akural (Bloomington: University of Indiana Press), 41-48.

34. See also O. Alubo, "Adolescent Reproductive Health Practices in Nigeria," *African Journal of Reproductive Health* 5 no. 3 (2001): 114

35. I. F. Adewole, B. A. Oye-Adeniran, N. Iwere, A. Oladokun, and A. Gbadege-sin, "Terminating an Unwanted Pregnancy: The Economic Implications in Nigeria," *Journal of Obstetrics and Gynaecology* 22 no. 4 (2002): 436-7.

Chapter 12

WOMEN'S MIGRATION, INTERCULTURAL MARRIAGE AND REGIONAL DEVELOPMENT

Joseph O. Charles

INTRODUCTION

The history of Africa is the history of series of movements of her peoples. The movements have caused the dispersion and transplantation of populations from one point to the other. Population movements, according to Guglar and Flanagan,[1] have always been a major feature in African history, because people voluntarily seek better farming, hunting, and grazing land, while others go for employment of one kind or the other. Some Africans have also been forced to move by aggressive neighbors, the slave trade and natural calamities. In pre-colonial and colonial Africa, the option of exit through migration was the most attractive decision to dissatisfied people because there was usually a significant amount of open land which could be occupied somewhere.[2] In all, much of the pre-colonial migrations were basically movements from rural to rural environments, since most of Africa was very rural and undeveloped at the time.[3]

This paper discusses one of these early rural-rural migrations involving the Ibibios of Nigeria. Their destination was Akpabuyo, in Efikland. A major objective of the paper is to explain the role played by women migrants in the promotion of inter-ethnic relations through intercultural marriage. We will also examine the role of these female migrants in the development of the host region. Women, notes Fapohunda,[4] are a distinctive human resource and also constitute Africa's human resource base, which must be mobilized for national and regional development.

WOMEN'S MIGRATION IN PERSPECTIVE

Dearth of data on women's migration is not in doubt. This problem has been addressed variously in recent gender studies. Gugler and Ludwar-Ene posit that migration research has not begun to redress what they refer to as "a severe imbalance that is the legacy of the male domination of the profession." Women, they argue, "are more urban than men" and they move to the urban centers principally as house or domestic help; some migrate with the probability of finding a companion or joining a husband, while others move to cities as widows or divorcees in order to embrace "greater opportunities, trade and economic independence."[5]

Until recently, most migration studies were on men and inferred that migration of women was primarily to join husbands.[6] However, while some women moved for family reasons, others migrated because of education and work. Such women were presumed not to have migrated on their accord but considered passive and having merely followed their husbands, uncles, brothers or fathers. Even those who migrated with or without men did so mostly to urban areas as domestics, factory workers, nurses and teachers. Some also migrated on a seasonal basis between their villages, homes and lands (areas) to produce food; others migrated for marriage.[7] Generally, women regarded "the town, as areas of expanded opportunities and resources," even if they had to migrate intermittently, shuttling between town and country.[8] Guglar and Ludwar-Ene place these women migrants in three categories: young and married women of 10-20 years with little formal education who migrated as domestics and educated young women in search of employment; those who postponed marriage "while improving their standard of living with the contribution of male friends"; and thirdly widowed, divorced or separated women who moved to the city from the countryside on their own.[9]

Adepoju argues that, until recently, female migration received relatively little attention because researchers were more concerned with economically motivated migration.[10] In addition, women's migration was seen as inconsequential because women were more of association migrants than autonomous migrants. It has also been confirmed that in recent times, women not only migrate autonomously but that they tend to dominate short-distance rural migration. It is further argued that migration has a tendency of increasing women's participation in economic and occupational activities mix at the destination.

Overall, the dearth of data on women's migration and the lopsidedness of attention to this category of migration have been blamed on government policy on women. This hackneyed attention has a history. Olurade posits that from the colonial period, women were frowned upon as independent migrants.[11] Essentially, women who migrated to the towns were branded as prostitutes. These movements were adjudged detrimental to marriage stability, family and norms and frowned upon because they encouraged the erosion or corruption of female virtues. Although it has been confirmed that motivation to migrate among women spanned social, economic and political frontiers,[12] such movements were always negatively conjectured.

Before modern voluntary migration of people to various destinations of choice, migration in pre-colonial Africa was mostly forced migration involving slave trade. The sex ratio of the slaves has not been determined. However, emerging literature has shown that all categories of human beings were sold in slave trade. An advert in *Awake* dated 24 July 1769 affirms thus:

> To be sold on Thursday the third of August next. A cargo
> to ninety-four Primes. Healthy NEGROES, consisting
> of thirty-nine men, fifteen boys, twenty-four women and
> sixteen girls just arrived in the Brigantine Dembia, Francis
> Bare, Mafter, from Sierra Leone. [13]

Millions of Africans including children were torn from their homes and families, sold, bought and shipped across the Atlantic in conditions of cruelty. They were not accorded any rights and were punished, abused, or even killed.

During the slave trade, Uya contends that Old Calabar emerged as the major slave port of the Cross River region, processing and exporting slaves from Igbo, Ibibio, Ejagham, Cameroons and the hinterland of Benue valley.[14] He further argues that the Atlantic slave trade marked a turning point in the historical development of Africa and people of African descent. Writing about the impact of women sold into slavery in Awka, Nwoji and Onyekwelu demonstrate that women along with men and children were sold as slaves. While the healthy young men and boys were used as laborers, fine young women were sold both as laborers and a source of breeding or procreation of (slave) children for their owners in the new world.[15]

The use of female slaves as wives among Nweh people of Southwest Province of Cameroon has further been confirmed by Fapohunda, when he says that slave women were a source of wealth and political power. In addition:

> Women, young and old were however, kept by buyers or
> given to their dependents, as wives .... There was no qualm
> in marrying a slave woman. And they were sometimes con-
> sidered, as better wives than the freeborn women ... slave
> wives also helped husbands to create marriage wards. [16]

THE ORIGIN OF IBIBIO WOMEN MIGRATION INTO AKPABUYO

Akpabuyo is an Efik settlement located at the southern end of Calabar municipality and stretches about 40 kilometers. Its opening as a satellite rural settlement in the early decades of the nineteenth century was not unconnected with the urge of the Efik lords to expand into the hinterland towards the end of the slave trade which formally ended in Efik land in 1842. Between 1842 and 1901 when slavery was abolished in Nigeria, the Efik community became heterogeneous. Slaves were bought by the Efiks who also acted as middlemen. They stoutly resisted any attempt by the European slave dealers to gain direct access to Ibibio and Igboland, the two principal slave suppliers in the hinterland.

It is evident that the human trade cut across sexual lines. For the Bight of Biafra (Nigeria) David Northrup records the following numbers:

Table 1: Age and Sex of Slaves from the Bight of Biafra 1659—1702 based on the Records of Five Ships

	Number			Percentage (%)		
	Male	*Female*	*Total*	*Male*	*Female*	*Total*
Adult	500	424	924	47	39	86
Child	97	49	146	9	5	14
Total	**597**	**473**	**1,070**	**56**	**44**	100

Source: David Northrup, *Trade Without Rulers Precolonial Economic Development in Southern Eastern Nigeria* (Oxford: Clarendon Press, 1978), 78.

The high number of female slaves reflected above confirms the fears that since the Ibibios constituted the second largest group of slaves, their women must have constituted a significant percentage of the figure given by the author.

In the Akpabuyo situation, the sex ratio of the slaves who were sent there by their owners to produce food has not been ascertained. But oral tradition has it that these slaves were dispatched in pairs of one-man-one-woman to various virgin locations.[18] The intention was political, demographic and economic. In the first place, these pairs of slaves were required to live and work together to increase food production in order to feed their owners and members of their households who lived in the town. In the second place, their owners regarded these slaves as members of their own maximal lineage (*Ufok*). By posting them to various locations in pairs, marriage was, by this act, consummated between the slaves. In Efik land, an "*Ufok*" is respected or feared politically by other "*Ufok*" principally because of its numerical strength and the economic quality of its members. The more slaves that could be sent out to colonize land, the greater were the chances of an "*Ufok*" in territorial acquisition.

After the slave trade, there was a lull, and a vast economic vacuum was left unfilled because these slaves were liberated from forced labor. The economy shifted from mere slave trading to palm oil trading and farming. The Efiks themselves were not used to farm work and were not prepared to arrest the situation by settling down to farming. Freed slaves, who still remained integrated into various Efik houses, were not under any obligation to give or sell their labor to their erstwhile masters. This period of economic doldrums, in which people were suffering in the midst of abundant agricultural resources, is captured by Udo[19], who writes that the loss of labor was the greatest blow to Efik chiefs because most freed slaves refused to sell their labor to the chiefs, who incidentally were in dire need of it. Efik society was already stratified before the coming of the colonialists, and this social order ultimately affected their work habit. Alderton laments how their early history of contact with cheap labor "produced in the Efik a strain of indolence, which is now inseparable from their character," and which has affected general outlook towards community development.[20]

With the invasion and subsequent opening of Ibibioland between 1902 and 1906, many Efik lords began to undertake recruitment tours of Ibibioland for farm hands. They recruited the Ibibios as laborers (*nda utom*) and house-maids (*ndito ufok*), who were instrumental to the revitalization of Efik economy. The woman constituted the bulk of the house-maids, while the men were the majority in farm laborers category. With an influx of women immigrants, many Efik men started contracting marriage with them. This intermingling through marriage further increased the heterogeneity of the population in Akpabuyo and fostered inter-ethnic unity.

WOMEN AS VEHICLE OF COMMUNICATION AND DEVELOPMENT

According to Lévi-Strauss, human communication takes one of three perspectives, namely: communication of messages, communication of goods and services, and communication of women.[21] Communication of messages demands the use of verbal and non-verbal symbols in the transmission of messages. In the communication of goods and services, man also exchanges messages through the exchange of material and non-material culture. Man is viewed at this level of communication as an "economic man" because of his motive in the maximization of profit. Communication of women through marriage is the highest type of communication. Apart from cultural elements which form integral elements in the communication package, human beings are its greatest assets. Barnes maintains that series of marriages constitute a cycle of reciprocity by which several groups are linked together.[22] A man who receives a wife from another group is given a debtor or negative sign, while the giving group is given a positive or plus sign. The creditor/debtor relationship endures. If the exchange is symmetrical, it follows that each group is free to marry from the other thus forming a complex network of affinal relationships. Offspring from the union further consolidates the relationship and establishes another level of relationship, which is higher and more sacred than marriage itself.[23]

PRIVILEGES ARISING FROM IBIBIO-EFIK MARITAL UNIONS

The benefits from the union were reciprocal and could be summarized as follows: The Ibibios were land hungry people, while the Efiks were in dire need of efficient farm-hands. The Ibibio woman, with privileges conferred on her by marriage to an Efik man, had rights to sufficient farmland. These rights were by sheer magnanimous acts also extended to her immediate patrilateral or matrilateral kin. Such changes were brighter if the Efik husband was a lineage head with access to extensive uncultivated farm land. During the deforestation era, the wife's matrilineal and patrilineal kinsmen were made to clear the virgin forest in the name of the Efikman/husband. The more farm hands he had, the more extensive his farmland would be. The working understanding was that the landlord shared the deforested land among the Ibibio farm hands. By the sharing, Ibibio immigrants were bestowed with both usufructuary and rental rights on the land.

More benefits, rights and privileges accrued to the offspring of the union. In a marriage between an Efik man and Ibibio woman, the children were Efik by birth. They stand in *"Ayeyin"* (grand child) relationship to the maternal kin in Ibibioland. The child inherited property directly from the father but only acquires privileges on the maternal side. Such privileges include liberty to pluck any fruit of interest from the mother's lineage farm and to reside with the matri-kin if he pleases. On the other hand, if it is an intercultural marriage between Ibibio man and an Efik woman, inheritance pattern is bilateral. The children inherited property from the father's side as well as mother's side. The Efik say *"Edem ete midaha Eyen, Edem eka eda"* (if the paternal side would not accept a child, the maternal side would). These children constituted an important interest group in various villages in Akpabuyo. They were free to contest for political offices in their mother's villages. As *"Ayeyin,"* they were highly regarded by the maternal kin who wield greater influence on these children because of the environment in which they grow up.

The Efik man is sure of a ready supply of farm labor with the presence of Ibibio woman as wife. The woman oversees the preparation, planting, weeding and harvesting of farmlands. In most cases, the woman would enlist the services of her immediate relatives for this purpose. To the Efiks, Ibibio immigrant women are a symbol of hard work in Akpabuyo. They have introduced Ibibio farm practices and farming technology, some of which have been adopted by their Efik counterparts. The Efik women appreciate the fact that Ibibio women are married to their farms as a second "husband" and that they "work like jackals" on the farm. They cannot see themselves competing favorably with these immigrant women who are said to have been born into farms. What seems to draw some Efik women into farming today is the sudden depletion of farm laborers in Akpabuyo with the resultant high cost of paid labor. Various crops, such as *"anem"* (sweet yam) and *"atikke idok"* (a specie of *okro* which yields only in harvesting season), and some species of cassava, such as *"obubit okpo"* and *"okot okon eyo,"* are said to be Ibibio in origin, brought of course by these immigrants.

The women immigrants also brought with them various weeding and planting hoes meant for weeds of different sizes. The smaller and shorter the weeds, the smaller and shorter the weeding hoes. The tallest of all the planting hoes is called *"san-ko."* This type of hoe was introduced in the early 1980s. The handle is made of stick and measures between 120-150 cm; the blade is about 19-22 cm in width. With this long reach, movement is reduced when making cassava holes. About six to seven cassava holes can be made on the farm while the farmer stands at one spot.

Women have also ventured into areas which were the preserves of men. They enter into reciprocal work groups to clear farmlands, make yam and cassava holes and even grate and fry cassava. All these functions were performed by men in the pre-Nigerian civil war era of surplus farmland and farm labor. By renting farmlands outside immediate village community, women immigrants have encouraged distant farming. This farming system enables unused and distant farmlands to be cultivated for increased food production. While the women migrants engage more in farm work and palm oil production, their Efik hosts make their money by renting or leasing farmlands and through share cropping agreements with the immigrants. Ibibio women have been fully integrated into Akpabuyo economy and are taking the lead in this direction *vis-à-vis* their Efik hosts. This confirms Adeyokunnu's[24] observation that integration of women into rural economy is better done if they participate in agricultural production rather than home-making.

Ibibio women encourage the accumulation of capital by organizing themselves into thrift societies (*etibe*). These monetary societies operated by women do not have a predetermined or fixed amount of money that each member must contribute at a sitting. What is fixed, however, is the amount of money which was contributed by individual members to a beneficiary. Such monies earlier contributed by each member become a fixed sum that must be given to other contributing members when it is their turn to benefit from the total contributions of the entire group.

The women immigrants make up an important source of communal work force in each village. They take active and dominant parts in the weeding, clearing and widening of village roads and paths on community sanitation days. They also pay development levies imposed for the building of some infrastructure. In fact, the immigrants complain that they paid more levies than their host counterparts who may never pay but will nevertheless be protected by their kin in the village council. They have made enormous contributions to the socio-economic climate of Akpabuyo.

In spite of these advantages, however, intercultural exchange of women in marriage and women-based development strategy tend to face some problems in Africa. We examine this assertion in the next part of this paper.

PROBLEMS AND PROSPECTS OF WOMEN-BASED COMMUNICATION AND DEVELOPMENT STRATEGY IN AFRICA

It is the view of Lévi-Strauss[25] that "from marriage to language, one passes from low to high speed communication" and that what is communicated in marriage is almost of the same nature as those who communicate. Although it occurs gradually, marriage contains and accordingly disseminates the richest, more enduring and the greatest volume of cultural elements from both the wife-giving and wife-receiving cultures.

The problem is that Africans are very selective of those they marry. It is, therefore, not fashionable again to work with the dictum: "Those whom we marry are those with whom we fight."[26] African marriages, understandably, is a pact which encourages harmonious living but not necessarily between hostile groups. In Africa, marriage is largely preferential and minimally prescriptive.

Intercultural marriage is handicapped by cultural requirements of specific African groups or sub-groups concerning the appropriate groups from where they could select their partners. These rules that prohibit marriage with certain persons or groups also designate others as appropriate partners. Although in practice there are always some deviations from the ideal, the fact remains that such marriage between hostile groups may generate more hostilities between the groups than it sought to solve. As much as possible, Africans prefer marrying into groups that have a good history of tranquility and clean moral record. Marrying into hostile and belligerent groups does not attract the co-operation of other members of the extended family. This is because marriage is a group affair. Opposition from such members marks the beginning of a frustrated union, which most often does not last.

In Africa, social stereotypes work against intercultural marriage. Where intercultural unions are contracted, they become targets of attack. Otite describes a situation where Urhobo immigrants live in isolated camps among the Yorubas. [27] They are not integrated into the host culture. The result is that marriage is not encouraged. Unlike Urhobo women, Ibibio women immigrants constitute a force in Akpabuyo development. In Akpabuyo, women immigrants are accorded the right to rent farmlands, like their male counterparts. They also control the money they make from economic ventures to a large extent. Generally, the women seem to be opposed to any joint account with their husbands. They maintain that husbands would lavish such money on other women outside the home because of the prevalent high degree of sexual freedom in the society.

It should be noted that, unlike Ibibio culture, Efik culture accords a lot of freedom and respect to women. Their women accordingly enjoy investment and financial autonomy which makes for development and self actualization. Ibibio women immigrants have over the years embraced this philosophy, as they now cultivate their own farms and manage the proceeds. Migration from a conservative and male dominated Ibibio culture to a more liberal and Efik culture that respects women's autonomy enhances investment chances of these immigrants in Akpabuyo. Such other migrations from male dominated societies in Africa could open routes of escape for oppressed African women and enhance their role in development.

It is, however, observed that the developmental efforts of these women immigrants are not organized. Their endeavors are mostly individualistic. What is needed is a group approach or women-dominated strategy for the solution of women development problems.

CONCLUSION

The study of women migration in Africa is still in its infancy. However, the developmental roles of African women have been widely documented.[28] It is unanimously accepted that women form a fairly large percentage of those who belong to the unpaid traditional sector, and that agriculture is a principal source of employment for urban and rural women in Africa. While urban women concentrate in the cultivation and production of leafy vegetables, the rural women are chief producers of root crops such as cassava and cocoyam.[29] But the role of women migrants in African regional development has not been given the attention it deserves. In some African societies, such as Akpabuyo in Efik land, it is this category of women who actually perform farming activities in contra-distinction to their host counterparts. These women immigrants built their identity around hard work and farming, which have engineered Akpabuyo as an agricultural region to become one of the food baskets to Calabar metropolis in the twenty-first century.[30]

Notes

1. J. Gugler and W. F. Flanagan, *Urbanization and Social Changes in West Africa* (Cambridge: Cambridge University Press, 1978).

2. Jeffrey Herbert, "Migration, the Politics of Protest, and State Consolidation in Africa," *African Affairs* 89, no. 355 (April 1990): 183-203.

3. O. Adegbola, "The Migrant as a Factor in Regional Development" (inaugural conference of the Population Association of Africa, Ibadan, 1974.)

4. E. R. Fapohunda, "Introduction: Women and the Industrial Development in Africa," in *Women and Industrial Development in Africa* (UNEDA: 1986), 87-147, 1-22.

5. Josef Gugler and Gudrun Ludwar-Ene, "Gender and Migration in Africa South of the Sahara," in *The Migration Experience in Africa*, ed. Jonathan Baker and Tade Akin Aina (Uppsala: Nordeska Afrika Institutet (1995), 257-268.

6. Lillian Trager, "Women Migrants and Rural-urban Linkages in South Western Nigeria," in *The Migration Experience*, 269-88.

7. Elvyne Hones-Dube, "Non-metropolitan Migration in Botswana with an Emphasis on Gender," in *The Migration Experience*, 321-38.

8. C. Obbo, "Women, Power and Political System," in *Women and Social Change in Nigeria,* ed. Lai Olurode (Lagos: Unity Publishing and Research Co., 1990).

9. Gugler and Ludnar-Ene, "Gender and Migration."

10. A. Adepoju, "Migration in Africa – An Overview," in *The Migration Experience,* 87-108.

11. Lai Olurade, "Women in Rural-urban Migration in Two of two in Nigeria" in *The Migration Experience*, 289-302.

12. Jean-Bernard Ouedrago, "The Girls of Nyoruuru-Dagara Female Labour Migration to Bobo-Dioulasso," in *The Migration Experience*, 303-20.

13. *Awake*, The Chains and Tears of Slavery," June 8, 1995, 3-8.

14. Okon E. Uya, "Slave Routes of the Lower Cross River Region" (seminar paper presented at the International Museum Day, Old Residency Museum, Calabar, May 18, 2001.)

15. Q. J. Nwoji and N. Onyekwelu, "The Impact of Umuada (women) Sold into Slavery in Awka, South-Eastern Nigeria: The Lingering Impression," (paper presented at International Conference on the Atlantic Slave Trade and its aftermath, Nike Lake Hotel Enugu, July 10-14, 2000.)

16. E. R. Fapohunda, "Introduction: Women and the Industrial Development in Africa," in *Women and Industrial Development in Africa* (UNEDA, 1996), 1-22.

17. David Northrup, *Trade Without Rulers: Pre-colonial Economic Development in South Eastern Nigeria* (Oxford: Clarendon Press, 1978), 78.

18. J. O. Charles, "The Frontier Perspective and Rural-Rural Migration: The Case of Ibibio Migration to Akpabuyo in Efikland, Nigeria," *Ibom Journal of Social Issues* 6, no. 2 (2001): 161-184.

19. E. A. Udo, *Who Are the Ibibio?* (Onitsha: Africa Fed. Publishers, 1983).

20. National Archive of Nigeria Enugu (NANE) CALPROF 7/1/148, 11/2/48 E. C. Alderton, Intelligence Report 1948.

21. Claude Lévi-Strauss, "Claude Lévi-Strauss 1908," in *High Point in Anthropology*, ed Bohannan Paul and Mark Glazer (New York: Alfred A. Knopf, 1973), 371-409.

22. J. A. Barnes, *Three Styles in the Study of Kinship* (Berkeley: University of California Press, 1971).

23. J. O. Charles, "Marriage and Lineage Segmentation in Ibibioland," Anthropologia 47 (1996): 81-92.

24. T. O. Adeyokunnu, *Women and Agriculture in Nigeria* (Ethiopia: UNECA, 1980).

25. Lévi-Strauss, "Claude Lévi-Strauss 1908," 387.

26. Lucy Mair, *An Introduction to Social Anthropology*, 2nd ed. (Oxford: Clarendon Press, 1975).

27. Onigu Otite, "Rural Immigrants as Catalysts in Rural Development: The Urhobo in Ondo State of Nigeria," *Africa* 49, no. 3 (1979): 226-236.

28. Mere Kisseka, "The Role of Women in Socio-economic Development: Indicators as Instrument of Social Analysis," in DESI/UNU (op. cit. 1985), 33-47; (see also INSTRAW, 1985 and UNECA, 1988).

29. J. O. Charles and C. Bassey, "Nation Building through Food Security by Immigrant Farmers: An Alternative Agricultural Development Strategy," *Nigerian Journal of Economic and Development Matters* 2 (2003): 101-21.

30. J. O. Charles, "Women Migration, Intercultural-Marriages and Agricultural Development: The Case of Ibibio Women of Eastern Nigeria," *Development Studies Roundtable* (A Journal of Development) 1, no. 1 & 2 (2004): 102-23.

Chapter 13

WOMEN IN THE AFTERMATH OF ETHNIC CONFLICTS IN NIGERIA: THE CONSEQUENCES OF EGBIRRA-BASSA CRISIS, 1986—2000

Ibrahim Umaru and Theophilus D. Lagi

INTRODUCTION

The ethnic crisis between the Bassa and the Egbirra communities... has inevitably retarded their own individual and collective social, economic and political development. It has also affected other tribes in the area both directly and indirectly because they have been sucked into the crisis itself. Similarly, it has adversely affected the overall development of the state. The poison of hatred has corroded the bonds of mutual trust among them. Years of peaceful co-existence between them have been sacrificed on the altar of personal ambition. Mindless violence has brutalized the psyche of the people and thus created the unfortunate impression that might is right. The task of re-orientating the psyche of the people is not going to be easy.—*Abdullahi Adamu, "The Fruits of the Tree of Peace," 3 July 2000.*

Communal relations in Nigeria in the last two decades have been largely characterized by frequent protracted violent conflicts.[1] In almost all cases, they leave heavy casualties and anguish in their wake; they leave their victims and the state apparatus with limited opportunities to rebuild their homes and patch together their societies from the ruins of war and despair. Incidentally, women bear the brunt of war and burden of difficult transition from armed conflict to reconciliation and reconstruction. From the beginning of conflict or war, women and girls are subjected to exploitation not only by armed elements and combatants but also by new societal pressures and expectations. In fact, they are exposed to great risk of sexual violence and physical harassment in flight,[2] in refugee and internally displaced persons (IDPs) camp situations; and during post-conflict transition, they are often excluded from access to power structures and active representation in decision-making process.[3] It is true that those who instigate and perpetrate conflict in Africa are primarily men; however, it would be erroneous to view women merely as innocent bystanders. It is quite true that some women fight alongside men as soldiers during conflicts or wars; they often support conflict indirectly by providing food and shelter for soldiers; they also act as nurses and educators. There is evidence pointing to the fact that women are sometimes cruel to their own kind during times of conflict.[4]

The literature on violent conflict is rich with documented evidence on the toll of such conflict on local communities, and how it takes generations to overcome the anger, hatred, and distrust and make the communities whole again, though in most cases, victimization of non-combatant civilians, women and children as a deliberate strategy of armed groups is underestimated. However, little effort has been made by violent conflict studies to analyze or document the resilience of women in conflict and post conflict situations, or the ingenious strategies they adopt in coping with the consequences of conflict in the aftermath of war, especially in Africa, but particularly in Nigeria. An appreciation and understanding of this is important, because no approach to peace and prosperity can succeed if it does not factor in women as equally important components of the solution; for a successful post-conflict community, or post-conflict democracy, cannot exist without active participation from all its members, especially women.

This study is therefore an attempt to understand the dynamic role of women in an African community and how they have coped with socio-economic and environmental effects of a fifteen-year old conflict against the framework of a typical patriarchal system and the challenges posed by existing traditional-cum pseudo-modern economic reality of Nigeria. The remainder of this chapter is divided into three parts. The next section gives a brief background to the conflict; the second section outlines a time-path model of women in conflict; while the next section discusses the findings of the survey conducted in the study area. The last section forms the recommendations and concluding part of the discourse.

BACKGROUND

Nasarawa State is located in central Nigeria. It lies between latitudes 7 and 9 degrees north, and longitudes 7 and 10 degrees east, and shares boundaries with five states (Benue, Kogi, Kaduna, Plateau and Taraba), and the Federal Capital Territory (FCT). It is made up of thirteen local governments (LGAs) namely, Akwanga, Lafia, Nasarawa, Nasarawa-Eggon, Keffi, Keana, Karu, Obi, Wamba, Doma, Awe, Kokona, and Toto. The state has a projected human population of slightly over 2 million.[5]

The conflict took place in Toto, a rural community located in the southwest and western parts of the state (Figure 1). It is made up of three districts, Toto, Umaisha, and Gadabuke. There are two paramount traditional institutions namely, the *Ohimege Opanda,* based at Umaisha, and the chief of Toto, based

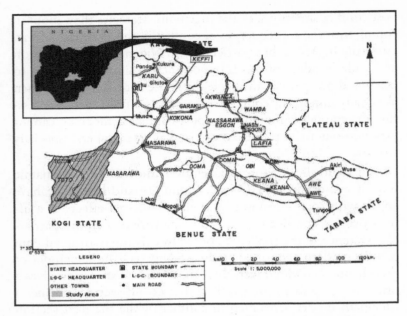

Figure 1: Nigeria: Nasarawa State showing the Study Area

at Toto.[6] Ethnic or communal conflict is a recurrent theme in
Nasarawa State. Conflict in varying degrees has become pervasive to the extent that virtually every local government area has
an unresolved ethnic or communal conflict at various stages of
escalation/de-escalation over power, privileges, status, and land.
However, the most protracted and bloodiest of them is the one
that took place in Toto local government area between Egbirra
and Bassa ethnic groups over chiefdom and land.[7] The Gbagyi
ethnic group was a neutral party in the earlier phase of the conflict but became entangled gradually, especially after the events
of May 3, 2003.

Studies have shown that the conflict has a long history. It
seems to owe its origin to the age-long perceived notion of marginalization and injustice lorded over relatively larger Bassa and
Gbagyi ethnic groups by the Egbirra chiefdom.[8] In the early 1980s,
the Chief Solomon Lar Administration of former Plateau State
(1979-1983) created two chiefdoms within the Toto area, with
the Egbirra insisting that they should come under the jurisdiction

of the *Ohinoyi* of Toto. This, by implication, excluded the Bassa and the Gbagyi, thereby fueling the embers of hostilities between them and the Egbirra. It was not until 1986 that the bubble of tension burst into a full scale encounter between the Bassa and the Egbirra. In the ensuring skirmishes, the Bassa had the upper hand. The Egbirra had more of its villages raised, and sacked, and its people displaced.[9] For the next ten years, the Bassa remained the most assertive and consistent in the 'protest' against injustice.[10] The conflict later metamorphosed into an unconventional warfare, especially from November 1997 to December 1998. Small firearms and light weapons were widely used in this encounter, resulting in destruction of lives and property, and internal displacement of Bassa men, women, and children from Toto (Figure 2).[11]

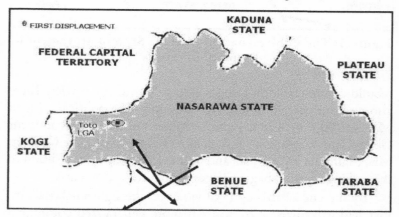

Figure 2: The Egbirra-Bassa Conflict: First Movement of Displaced Persons

With tremendous support from the Federal Government of Nigeria, and the international humanitarian community, commendable efforts were made by the Nasarawa State Government to return the Bassa refugees to their homes from June 2000. Initially, it was quite successful; however, the exercise was to be aborted by a fresh armed attack on the Bassa refugee camps in June 2001, dispersing the people to distant locations outside the state (Figure 3).

The Bassa remained displaced until 2003, and no serious intervention was made, either by the government or individuals, to

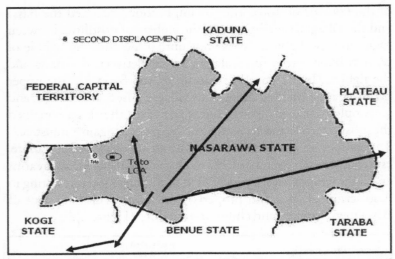

Figure 3: The Egbirra-Bassa Conflict: Second Movement of
Displaced Persons

rebuild communication bridges across the warring parties. There
also were no peace-building activities up to the political crisis of
May 3, 2003, in which Egbirra militia murdered a prominent
Gbagyi female politician and member of Nasarawa State Cabinet,
Mrs. Maimuna Joyce Katai, and over thirty Gbagyi, in addition to
the sacking of two Gbagyi villages—Zokutu, and Yewuye.[12]

By the end of this cycle of violence, the Egbirra-Bassa conflict had galvanized into an even more generalized communal
conflict. This is how Shedrack G. Best sums up the significance
of the events of May 3, 2003:

> The ... [events] ... led to the deployment of soldiers and
> Mobile Policemen to Toto. The effect of the deployment
> was the gradual return of law and order to the local gov-
> ernment. This helped to reopen the issues in the conflict.
> The return of the Bassa since their second displacement in
> 2001, also became possible from June 2003. The issues in
> the conflict are many and complex.[13]

A MODEL OF WOMEN IN CONFLICT

Let us define civil conflict, or war, as the negative physical confrontation that occurs mainly between two or more social groups.[14] Also, let us conceptualize 'gender' as the network of socially defined functions and attributes of being a woman, or man in a given society, or community, at a particular time. Gender is an English word that might not be translated well into other languages. What is common, however, is its use in describing power relations between men and women as well as the roles they are culturally oriented to play in the family, community, and national life of a people. Gender roles can dramatically shift in times of conflict, either under authoritarian or democratic regimes. These changes often challenge power structures, especially patriarchal power structures, and have the potential to destabilize interpersonal relations between women and men and between generations.

Thus, women typically do not remain mere onlookers or innocent victims of conflicts. They often take on roles and responsibilities, partake in combat and political struggle, and build new networks in order to obtain needed resources for their families. While civil wars impose tremendous burdens on women, they often contribute to the redefinition of traditional roles and the reconfiguration of existing gender relations in the society. Women in conflict situations pass through three phases namely, pre-conflict peacetime; armed conflict phase; and post-war phase.

Under each phase, women are ascribed specific social roles and responsibilities as well as face cultural and religious inhibitions.[18] In the pre-conflict situations, women's social role is taken to be complementary to those of men. However, this does not mean equality in any way, as the extent of inequality between sexes depends on ethnic group, geographical setting, social class, and historical epochs. It would seem more apt to say that in most societies, the male sphere of activity is traditionally accorded more value and prestige. A woman therefore derives her social status from her two roles—that of wife and mother. As mothers, women are the custodians of cherished values of their societies or communities: life-preserving activities, procreation, nursing, and domestic chores. A major feature of most societies and especially traditional communities is patriarchy—a system of social stratification and differentiation on the basis of gender, which provides material advantages to males while simultaneously placing severe constraints on the roles, and activities of women. In most patriarchal societies, women are socialized into a culture of female subordination, not only to their husbands and men in their own extended family of orientation, but to the entire members of her community.[19] This kinship structure, residence patterns, marital practices, and attitudes across different ethnic groups put men in an advantaged position in most war ravaged or conflict-prone communities, especially in Africa.

Indeed, in most African societies, the family institution cushions other social relations namely, economic, political, religious, and other social institutions. The basic division of labor is often based on age and gender. In this arrangement, marital relations dictate familial ties, lineage membership, and property relations (access to property, social status, and political offices, basically).[20] The access of women to important resources like land, labor, and capital in the patriarchal system depends on their position in the family, lineage, and communities. Men automatically have access to land, essentially as lineage members, while in most cases, women gain access to it as wives, and sometimes as daughters; and such access is often times limited.[21]

Once the stage for the escalation of hostilities and conflict is set in a community, some gender roles shift (for example, women become heads of households) and new responsibilities are added to women. In fact, under the second phase, women bear the additional burden of armed conflict. There is evidence to believe that women experience armed conflict in different ways than men. Although these depend on cultures and roles of women in particular societies, one fact remains that armed conflict, more often than not, worsens inequalities based on gender in communities in conflict. That makes women particularly vulnerable when armed conflict erupts.

Needless to say, it is often too presumptuous to state that armed conflict impacts negatively on women; indeed, for some women it can be a time of empowerment as they take over roles traditionally performed by men.[22] However, upon stoppage of hostilities, many of these advantages are lost.[23] In assessing the experience of women in armed conflict, it is therefore imperative to consider a wide variety of factors, the relevance and impact of which is dependent on peculiarities of the culture and the individual. This notwithstanding, it is possible to identify some common features regarding the experiences of women in conflict across communities or societies.

Women can experience armed conflict either as civilians or combatants. In fact, three scenarios under which women experience armed conflict can be hypothesized. The first is, 'women as escapees or in flight victims'; the second is, 'women as resident

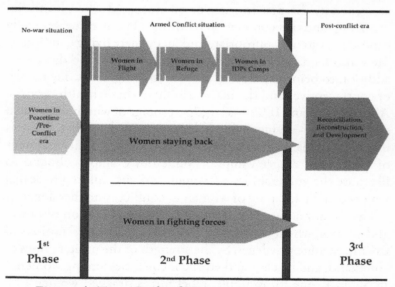

Figure 4: Time Path of Women in Armed Conflict

or domiciled victims'; and the third is, 'women as combatants in fighting forces' (Figure 4).

In periods of hostilities, and armed confrontation, the majority of women would most probably experience conflict as civilians. As members of the civilian population therefore, women experience unique economic problems. They are often separated from their men who traditionally may be the bread earners. As a matter of fact, lack of education, their role in caring for others, and general community attitudes make it extremely difficult for women to support themselves financially.[24] Indeed, in most cultures, especially African cultures, it is the women who have to gain from economic development, and are therefore especially at the losing end when these resources are diverted into war preparation and execution during armed conflict.

In addition, cultural factors help to worsen the economic problems suffered by women in armed conflict, for armed conflict often forces women out of their homes. Women civilians are generally the first to leave or be evacuated when hostilities break out, and this comes with hardships. Evacuees are generally exposed to often inappropriate and inadequate living conditions. They also tend to be at risk of accidents, injuries, and disease, in addition to being exposed to death from pregnancy, due to lack of contraceptives and the inaccessibility to basic health services. Also, refugees and IDPs—a large percentage of whom are women and children—are inevitable fallouts of armed conflict. There is incontrovertible evidence pointing to widespread mistreatment of women in refugee camps.[25] Numerous examples abound to illustrate the vulnerability of women and girl children to sexual violence. In fact, raping of women in conflict is neither a matter of chance nor a question of sex; it is rather a question of power and control, which is structured by male combatants' notions of their masculine privileges, by the strength of the military lines of command, and by class and ethnic inequalities among women.[26] In Sierra Leone for example, rebel forces dragged women into sexual slavery, rapping them repeatedly and compelling them to cook and clean for their abusers. In fact, the United Nations High Commissioner for Human Rights once reported evidence of well-planned attacks, including rape, on civilians in East Timor.[27] In various other armed conflicts, women are raped and then killed.[28] Others face permanent injuries and long-term health risks.

In the heat of hostilities in an armed conflict, women are sometimes compelled to play an enormous part in the 'family' and 'home' life of soldiers. If not drafted as combatants in the war front, they are either used as spies for their side or captives, or forced to stay in military camps to provide sexual services to their abductors. Sexual violence in Nepal's conflict presents evidence of the horrific cases of women and girl children of all ages forced to carry guns, and whet sexual appetites of the insurgents.[29]

From findings of studies conducted in Rwanda, Cambodia, Guatemala, El Salvador, Georgia, and Bosnia-Herzegovina, as well as experiences from other African conflicts, five major impacts of armed conflicts on women and gender relations can be identified:

1. Physical and sexual violence against civilians, of which 95 percent are women;
2. Internally displaced persons, of which 90 percent are women and children;
3. Redefinition of female identities in the society, both as victims and as perpetrators;
4. Increased poverty and starvation, as a result of systematic destruction of civilian property;
5. Frictional and ethnic violence leading to bitterness and hatred.[30]

Perhaps the most harrowing experience of women in the post-conflict period is lack of physical security. It often forces women to stay at home. Rape in particular is sometimes used as a systematic tool of warfare and torture. Also, many women see themselves compelled to engage in prostitution in the post-conflict era as the only available means of income. Family structures are damaged through death and trauma, leading to women becoming heads of households and an increased incidence of domestic violence.[31]

Further, women encounter economic restrictions which often lead to a decline in their social status. Lack of property rights for women in many conflict societies make female-headed households lose their land in addition to not having access to critical bank loans. Also, the number of women entering the labor market often increases after the conflict, as many of them lose their jobs in the formal sector once the ex-soldiers returned for reintegration into civilian community. Another possible impact of the conflict in the aftermath is increased poverty among women, more than their male counterparts; and they are most malnourished and often deprived of basic education and health services.

One of the positive effects of conflict on women could be the increasing awareness and determination to expand their public role by running local political institutions after the conflict. However, in the more traditional setting, the post-conflict era could disenfranchise them due to the non-inclusion of women in peace negotiation and design of reconstruction program arising from existing cultural and religious inhibitions.

In addition, as most conflict prevention and reconciliation work is executed in post-conflict societies, little attention is paid to the impact of political violence, even though it has the potential of affecting many more women and children than other forms of violence. Incidentally, political violence could be more damaging to the children than other forms of violence, as it is often concealed, cumulative and unresolved. Its prolonged state and unpredictability makes it even more damaging, psychologically.[32] Elizabeth Scheper summarizes the long-term implication of political violence of armed conflict on children, and society at large, as follows:

> The malleability of children's physical and psychological development makes them more apt to changes and adaptations to violent situations. But living in constant fear, without possibility of planning ahead, makes that a child's body, mind and thinking will adapt permanently and restructure accordingly, which seriously affects their ability to function in the society in future. Research into political violence and impunity in Cambodia indicates that the impact after twenty years is clearly visible in the lack of a long term vision, mutual trust, accountability

and respect for the judiciary. This makes political leaders act mainly in the interest of short-term profits for themselves, and their supporters. Perpetrators learn that there is nothing to fear for committing crimes because prosecutions and trials rarely take place—especially not with connections in high places. The impact on the society and the insecurity of civilians is devastating.[33]

THE AFTERMATH:
THE CONSEQUENCES OF EGBIRRA-BASSA CONFLICT

This section is an analysis of findings of a survey conducted by the authors in the study area between January and July 2006. A random sample of 128 women (67 Bassa and 61 Egbirra) and 57 men (29 Bassa and 28 Egbirra) were identified and interviewed, in addition to about 100 copies of a structured questionnaire administered among Bassa and Egbirra women.

The immediate political fallouts of the Egbirra-Bassa post-conflict period are the prevalence of physical insecurity and political violence in the community. Unfortunately, women happen to be majority victims of physical and political violence. There are even reported cases of gang rape of Bassa women by Egbirra youth. In fact, about 20 percent of respondents indicated having knowledge of rape being perpetuated against women at one occasion or another.

Another security-related problem is reprisal killings of perceived murderers of close relations during the conflict period. Reprisal killing are even alleged to have been masterminded at home but perpetuated at far-away refuge settlements like Jos, Bauchi, Ilorin, and the Federal Capital Territory. Another political impact of the conflict is the destruction of popular democratic institutions and participation. In fact, the Toto area has remained without elected representatives since the return to democratic rule in 1999, simply because elections could not be conducted due to deep-rooted animosity between the major groups in the conflict.[34] The repercussions of this are not only that people of the area are disenfranchised, but women are seriously discriminated against, politically. The findings of our study seem to support this assertion; when asked if women were allowed to participate in political activities in their community, 87 percent answered in the affirmative. However, when further asked to indicate the community's approval of women assuming top ranking positions like senior ranking public office or elected representative, only 43 percent of respondents (both female and male) were in favor. This goes to show that religious and cultural barriers conspire to debase the social status of women in this community. Indeed, just like most local communities in the state, the Egbirra-Bassa community is an essentially typical African patriarchal society, in which women play an essential and dynamic role, yet are disadvantaged by religious and cultural barriers.[35] It could be argued that the events leading to the political crisis of 2003, where a female politician was killed at Toto, lend credence to this assertion.

A major economic impact of violent conflict on the affected African communities in general is often the loss of livelihood for both the ex-combatants and non-combatant, especially women, who assumed additional roles of producers of wealth and war materials and as breadwinners. In the case of post-conflict Egbirra-Bassa, women who took over the places of men in some traditional pre-conflict occupations as the conflict raged on, found themselves losing their jobs to the decommissioned ex-combatants. What is more, even those economic activities that were the 'exclusive preserves' of women in the pre-conflict periods have been taken over by men in the post-conflict period. This is due to the fact that available jobs and sources of livelihood are limited by the massive destruction of economic infrastructure and institutions and loss of private sector confidence. Furthermore, the loss of husbands, guardians and relatives who were the bread winners of the families force women and young girls to resort to petty and sometimes odd jobs (or even prostitution) to provide for their families. Table 6 shows the change in percentage distribution of economic activities of respondents in the pre- and post- conflict periods.

Women respondents were further asked to indicate whether the shift in observed structure of economic activities occasioned by the conflict has adversely affected their overall monthly profit margin. About 67 percent of them answered in the affirmative. Further effort was made to find out how they have been coping with their meager earnings, in spite of added responsibilities, in the aftermath of the conflict. Another 25.7 percent of the women interviewed admitted receiving income supplements from close or distant relations.

Table 6: Change in Percentage Distribution of Economic Activities of Respondents by Gender

Activity	Men		Women	
	Pre-conflict	*Post-conflict*	*Pre-conflict*	*Post-conflict*
Farming	50.7	52.2	25.5	26.4
Fishing	4.8	3.3	5.0	-
Labor (eg farm, construction)	4.8	4.4	2.5	3.8
Animal husbandry	2.6	0.7	10.7	11.0
Fuelwood/firewood or fruit gathering	-	-	25.6	26.0
Wood/tree planting	1.2	-	1.2	0.3
Trading	12.1	16.8	10.8	15.0
Hunting	0.7	3.0	-	-
Cottage industry (eg furniture, mechanic repairs, etc)	8.6	4.0	2.4	1.8
Traditional/modern medicine	2.6	4.7	0.5	0.2
Construction and building aggregates (eg sand/gravel collection)	4.7	3.3	12.7	13.3
Civil service	6.0	5.0	3.1	2.2
Transport and allied business	3.2	2.6	-	-
Total	100	100	100	100

The overall effect of all this is: the loss of property rights, lack of capital and other necessary inputs for production, shortages of commodities due to low levels of production, and low supplies by itinerant merchants due to fear of physical, and personal insecurity of self and property, acute unemployment and poverty.[36]

On the social consequences, the Egbirra-Bassa conflict has inflicted damage on the traditional African family structure, which provides social and economic security to women and children by extended family members upon the demise of their spouses. Our survey revealed a 15 percent increase in the number of families headed by women in the community during the period of the conflict.

Yet another fallout of the Egbirra-Bassa conflict is internal displacement. Using figures 2 and 3 we have demonstrated in the preceding section that there were at least two massive internal displacements from the conflict area, the first involving movement of about 50,000 persons to neighboring towns and villages including Kogi, Benue, and the FCT. The second displacement was more massive, in terms of number and pervasive in nature, involving over 100,000 persons.[37] Incidentally, the majority of these IDPs are women and children. What is more, even though peace has been brokered by the state government, a sizeable number of IDPs are still reluctant to return from their places of refuge such as Ibadan, Kaduna, Jalingo, Kano, Bauchi, Jos and Lafia,[38] due to low density hostilities between the main warring parties, stories of gruesome but silent reprisal killings by highly embittered members of the community, severe destruction, and costs of rebuilding deserted human settlements. Indeed, the conflict has done a deep and lasting damage to the community, and it will take generations to overcome the anger, hatred, and distrust to put the community back on its feet again.

Perhaps a more serious social impact of the conflict on women is the subtle redefinition of their status in the affected community. Limited economic and political opportunities, lawlessness, and opportunism coupled with brigandage brought about by sudden cessation of hostilities, and the collapse of civil society and traditional legal institutions, have created a serious social and physical insecurity in the area. As a direct consequence, unemployed youth and de-commissioned combatants (who were used to looting, rape and other physical violence against civilians during the conflict) are alleged to have been used by organized crime syndicates to rob members of the community of their property and by politicians to settle scores with their opponents in the state. Women, especially those in hapless female-headed families, are the preferred victims of such crimes. Our survey findings seem to buttress this point. Out of 128 women interviewed, 62 percent of them admitted being victims or witnesses to such violent assaults or crimes.

The Egbirra-Bassa conflict has environmental implications. The immediate environmental effect of the conflict is the systematic destruction of farms and woodland as a deliberate policy to discourage the return and resettlement of IDPs. Related to this is the disruption of the normal practice of protecting natural habitats for plant and animal species considered in traditional belief systems in the area as essential for healing and invoking ancestral spirits. Also, traditional planting and other forms of investment in the natural environment, which are basic elements in this semi-forest farming system of the people of the area, have been adversely affected by the conflict.

Another effect of the conflict on the environment is the destruction of former human settlements through the activities of 'illegal' mining of solid minerals in the post-conflict period at places like Ugya. In addition, the temporary state of lawlessness gave illegal loggers the opportunity to harvest timber forests unscrupulously, thereby destroying further natural habitats for rare tropical flora and fauna.

The reproductive role of women in the community made them vulnerable to shortages in medicine, treatment and maternity care and birth control during the conflict. Medical services and availability of sanitary towels and other essential commodities, which were scarce or not available during the conflict, are still either in short supply or just not affordable. This situation is perhaps responsible for the outbreak and spread of diseases that ordinarily could have been contained in the past in the area. Our survey findings show that common ailments such as diarrhea, malaria, fever, typhoid, meningitis, respiratory, and maternity-related problems are rampant in the area. Also a comparison was made between the average distance women had to travel to the nearest health facility for medical attention in the pre- and post-conflict periods. The result is shown in Table 8 below.

Table 8: Women Accessibility to Health Facility in the Pre- and Post- Conflict Periods

Distance in Kilometer	Respondents			
	Pre-Conflict Period		*Post-Conflict Period*	
	Number	Percentage	Number	Percentage
Less than ½	77	60.2	14	10.9
½ - 1	25	19.5	19	14.8
2—5	10	7.8	20	15.6
6- 10	9	7.0	25	19.5
Over 10	7	5.5	50	39.2
Total	128	100	128	100

RECOMMENDATIONS

Because women are often the largest beneficiaries of development in peacetime and losers during conflict, improvements in the physical, economic and social protection should be based on the peculiar nature of the effects of armed conflict experienced by them. It is widely acknowledged that conflict and development, or lack of it, are closely related. The Egbirra-Bassa conflict, like other conflicts of its nature, has its origin in deep-rooted social and economic injustices, which were related to identity politics and prolonged periods of targeted deprivation. In order to cushion the impact of the conflict on women in the area therefore, the following should be considered: First, long-term development programs, in addition to structural political and social changes, are urgently needed to eradicate the causes of poverty and related factors that aggravate it namely, social fragmentation or the widening of income disparities, lack of job/income creation, insecurity, financial volatility, organized crime and brigandage, diseases, and environmental degradation.

Second, equal opportunity and social justice for all with a dose of gender sensibility is needed. This will require constant consultations across the gender divide and holistic approach to all matters relating to civil and corporate decision-making in the community. Third, the need for the state government to review its concept of security in the conflict area in view of the alleged cases of silent reprisal killings by aggrieved members of community, as well as the alleged involvement in brigandage and crime in the state by elements in the community. Since the early 1990s, a new concept of human security has been developed and advocated. According to this concept, the prime human security objective is to provide to all members of society or community basic food, economic, health, and environmental, cultural and political security. It also advocates a new moral obligation for local authorities and community leaders and instituting policies of equity and distribution of resources to all the groups in the conflict area.[39] Lastly, a fundamental change in the traditional approach to conflict management in the area is required. Emphasis should not only be placed on early warning, preventive diplomacy, and shows of force, but on the use of the so-called 'foundational prevention approaches,' which emphasize resolving horizontal inequalities based on social, religious, cultural, and ethnic identities, as suggested by Hans van Ginkel and Edward Newman.[40]

Notes

1. Social conflict is defined in this study to mean prolonged and often violent struggle by communal groups for such basic needs as security, recognition and acceptance, fair access to political institutions, and economic participation. This definition of conflict borrows from O. Ramsbotham and N. Lewer, *"Something Must be Done": Towards an Ethical Framework for Humanitarian Intervention in International Social Conflict* (Bradford: Department of Peace Studies, 1993); Edward Azar, *The Management of Protracted Social Conflict: Theory and Cases* (Darmouth, NH: Aldershot: 1990); and Shedrack Gaya Best, *Protracted Communal Conflict and Conflict Management: The Bassa-Egbura Conflict in Toto Local Government Area, Nasarawa State, Nigeria* (Ibadan: John Archers, 2004).

2. The sad reality of the situation is that women and children are increasingly becoming targets of deliberate aggression and hostility around the world. See Elizabeth E. Scheper, "Role of Women in Violent Conflict Prevention and Negotiation"(paper prepared for the Women, Peace

Building and Constitution Making Conference, organized by the International Center of Ethnic Studies, May 3– 5, 2002).

3. See Amnesty International, *Women in Peru: Rights in Jeopardy* (London: Amnesty International, 1995), 21; Amnesty International, *Women in the Middle East: Human Rights Under Attack* (London: Amnesty International, 1995); and Araine Brunet and Stéphanie Rousseau, "Acknowledging Violations, Struggling against Impunity: Women's Right, Human Rights," (International Conference on Violence against Women in War and Armed Conflicts, Tokyo, October 31– November 3, 1997).

4. Sally Matthews, "Women in Conflict," *Conflict Trends* 4 (2000). For theoretical and empirical discussions of the plight of women in conflict situations, see Penny Summerfield, "Gender and War in the Twentieth Century," *International History Review* 19, no. 1 (1997): 3–15; Sima Wali, "Women in Condition of War and Peace," in *From Basic Needs to Basic Rights: Women's Claim to Human Rights*, ed. Margaret Schuler (Washington D.C.: Women, Law, and Development International, 1995); Su Zhiliang, "The Nanking Massacre and the Comfort System of the Japanese Military" (paper presented at the International Conference against Women and Armed Conflicts, [venue] October 31–November 3, 1997); Caroline Nordstrom, ed., "Women and War," *Cultural Survival* 19, no. 1 (1994); and H. O'Connell, ed., *Women and Conflict* (Oxford: Oxfam, 1993).

5. NASEEDS, *Nasarawa State Economic Empowerment and Development Strategy*, report of the Drafting Committee (Zero Draft), Nasarawa State Government, 2004, 36.

6. There is disagreement over the use of the title of *Chief of Toto* among the three ethnic groups in the area. The Egbirra prefer to call it *Ehinoyi* of Toto, to give it an Egbirra identity in order to deny other ethnic groups from laying claim to the stool; the Bassa and Gbagyi, while still advocating for a separate traditional institutions, refer to it as the Chief of Toto, which also makes it a common institution for the entire three ethnic groups. However, the official gazette gives the three groups eligibility to the stool. See Best, *Protracted Communal*, 12.

7. In fact, the conflict represents an example of ethnic cleansing of one ethnic group by another of some sort in Nigeria; it is estimated that over 100,000 people have been affected. The conflict also appears to have generated probably one of the most significant cases of internally displaced persons (IDPs) to be found in any one LGA in Nigeria in the last two decades. See Best, *Protracted Communal*, 10.

8. For full accounts of the events and issues leading to first encounter, see for example Jibo Mvendaga, Anthonia T. Simbine, and H. S. Galadima, *The Northcentral Zone of Nigeria*, Vol. 4, *Ethnic Groups and Conflicts in Nigeria* (Ibadan: Program on Ethnic and Federal Studies, Department

of Political Science, University of Ibadan, 2001), 141–167; Ibrahim Umaru "Exploring the Economic Underpinnings of the Toto Ethnic Conflicts in Nasarawa State of Nigeria: A Primer," in *Conflicts in the Benue Valley,* ed. Timothy Gyuse and Oga Godwin Ajene (Makurdi: Selfers Educational Books, 2006); and Ibrahim Umaru. "The Economic Cost of Government Policy on Displaced People in Central Nigeria" (paper presented at African Conference 2006 on Movements, Migrations, and Displacements in Africa, The University of Texas at Austin, March 25– 27, 2006).

9.   Statistics on the ethnic cleansing of Egbirra by the Bassa after 1986 are not available due to the turmoil in Toto. Best, 11.

10. In February 11, 1995, the Bassa attacked and sacked the Egbirra in Ugya village and destroyed their property. The village was then taken over by the Bassa. It is instructive to mention that Ugya village has large deposits of solid minerals that are already being exploited in large commercial quantity. Mvendaga, Simbine and Galadima, 158.

11. At the end of this cycle of violence, Toto had been ethnically cleansed of the Bassa. Mvendaga, Simbine and Galadima, 155–158 and Best, *Protracted Communal,* 11.

12. Late Mrs. Maimuna Joyce Katai was the then Honorable Commissioner for Women Affairs in the Abdullahi Adamu administration of Nasarawa State (1999 – 2007), Best, 11.

13. For further discussion of these issues and more, we recommend Best, *Protracted Communal.*

14. The academic definition of civil conflict or war is not acceptable to all. This is because it excludes small conflicts, and most conflicts among indigenous communities, as well as their numbers, are too small. Three important elements of the definition are: one, there should be at least 1,000 battle deaths a year; two, the two parties should be organized and purposefully equipped to engage in warfare; three, the constituency of an ethnic group should be at least 50,000 persons.

15. "Gender" has been defined as "the term used to convey the processes of social construction which mediate the relations between men and women. Gender relations are not primarily biological or sexual relations although they may include elements of either. They are social as well as ideological and cultural relations, suffused with power differentials, that map the range of processes, behavior activities, forms of organization considered appropriate for women and men, for a given collectivity over a particular period of time." Charmaine Pereira, "Introduction" *Gender Studies: An Overview of Concepts,* (Abuja: Social Science Academy of Nigeria, May, 2001), 1.

16. Meredeth Turshen, "Africa: Women in Post-War Reconstruction," *Africa Policy E-Journal* (September 30, 1999), http://www.africaaction. org/docs99/aft9909.htm (accessed May 10, 2008).

17. Krishna Kumar, ed., *Women and Civil War: Impact, Organization, and Action* (Boulder: Lynne Rienner, 2001).

18. Guarantees of equal rights and protection under the law often do not prevent discrimination against women in the family; this is in spite of the governments' promises to guarantee women's equality and full rights as enshrined in the constitutions of their countries. In many countries, statutory restrictions curtailed, among other things, women's ability to inherit property, contract marriage, and seek divorce. For example, in South Africa, women marry under customary law are still considered as minors, and can not enter into any legal contract without the consent of their husbands or guardians. In India, Syria, and Pakistan, women are discriminated against in divorce and inheritance laws. Human Rights Watch, "Women's Human Rights," *World Report 1999*, http://www. hrw.org/wr2k/Wrd.htm (accessed May 12, 2008).

19. Dora O. Chizea and Juliet Njoku, *Nigerian Women and the Challenges of Our Time* (Ikeja: Malthouse Press, 1991).

20. Ibrahim Umaru, *Women: Phases of Deprivation in Nigeria*, GADA's Constitutional Debate Series Mongraph (Lagos: Gender, and Development Action, 2004).

21. Olabisi I. Aina, "Women, Culture and Society," in *Nigeria Women in Society and Development*, ed. Amadu Sessay and Adetanwa Odebiyi (Ibadan: Dokun Publishing House, 2001), 3–32.

22. In some instances, armed conflict even removes abusive partners from the home and allows women the opportunity to develop new skills in the management of household resources.

23. Judith Gardam and Hillary Charlesworth, "Protection of Women in Armed Conflict," paper prepared for *Wookbook/Readings/5 Protection of Women in Armed Conflict*, 1999.

24. Ibid. Also see Radhika Coomaraswamy, "Report of the Special Rapporteur on Violence against Women, Its Causes and Consequences," submitted in accordance with Commission on Human Rights Resolution 1995/85, Economic and Social Consequence, U.N. ESCOR, Commission on Human Rights., 52nd Session, U.N. Doc. E/CN.4/1996/53/ Add.2, 1996. See also Beijing Platform for Action, supra note 1, qq 72-81, 152 – 66.

25. Women also face distinctive problems that are largely unacknowledged as they attempt to rebuild their lives as refugees in a new community or land. See Matthews, "Women in Conflict"; S. Swiss et al., "Violence

against Women during the Liberian Civil Conflict," *JAMA* 279, no. 8 (1998): 625-29.

26. C. Peters, ed., Collateral Damage: *The 'New World Order' at Home and Abroad* (Boston: South End Press, 1992), 93, and 97. Also Coomaraswamy has identified a number of reasons for sexual violence against women, especially rape in armed conflict: one: complex, combined emotions of hatred, superiority, vengeance for real or imagined past wrongs, and national pride are promoted, and deliberately manipulated in armed conflict which finds expression in rape. Two: studies have established the connection between militarization of the nation state and sexual violence against women.

27. Human Rights Watch, "Women's Human Rights."

28. It has been reported in the news media recently that the US Army has been detaining Iraqi women to help track down, and obtain information about husbands or fathers who were suspected to be terrorists. "Conflict in Iraq: U.S. has Detained Women in Iraq as Leverage," *Keep Media*, June 28, 2006, http://www.keemedia.com/pubs/MiamiHerald/2006/01/28/1173123?extID=10032&oliID=(accessed May 10, 2008).

29. Kamala Sarup, "Women in Conflict Exploited Sexually," *World Security Network*, May 20, 2005, http://www.worldsecuritynetwork.com/show-Article3.cfm?article_id+11441. Also, reports from Algeria, East Timor, and Bosnia indicate that where fighting raged, women were raped; and where conflicts subsided, women looked fruitlessly for protection, help, and justice. Human Rights Watch, "Women's Human Rights."

30. US Agency for International Development, *Women and Women Organizations in Post-conflict Societies: the Role of International Assistance*, Program and Operations Assessment Report No. 28 (Washington DC: USAID, 2000).

31. Trauma in women manifests itself in depression, chronic fatigue, stress, anguish and listlessness.

32. For an in-depth treatment of this issue, see Ed Cairns, ed., *Children and Political Violence* (Oxford: Oxford University Press, 1996); and E. Scheper, "On the Brink: the Prevention of Violent Conflict and the Protecting Children in Deeply Dividend Divided Societies," paper prepared for the World Conference on Religion and Peace Conference, Women, Children and Conflict, Cordoba, March 2002.

33. Scheper, "Role of Women."

34. Best, *Protracted Communal.*

35. Ibrahim Umaru and Sam Tende, "Impact of Poverty on the Environment in Nasarawa State," *Nigerian Journal of Tropical Geography* 1, no. 2 (2006).

36. An interesting exposition of these issues can be found in Dagusa J. Samuel, "Harvesting the Potentials of N.E.E.D.S for the Benefits of the Vulnerables: Fine-tuning the Poverty Alleviation Program of Toto Local Government Council, Nasarawa State," (B.Sc. project, Nasarawa State University, 2005).

37. http://www.n-today.ndtilda.co.uk/mnew170.htm (accessed April 5, 2008).

38. Serious research is required to determine the specific psychological consequences of the Egbirra-Bassa conflict on women and children.

39. Scheper, "Role of Women," 9–10.

40. Hans Van Ginkel and Edward Newman, "In Quest of Human Security," *Japan Review of International Affairs* 14 (Spring 2000): 1.

Selected Bibliography

Abiodun, Rowland. "Women in Yoruba Religious Images," *African Languages and Cultures* 2, 1 (1989): 1-18.

Achebe, Chinua. *Things Fall Apart*. London: Heinemann, 1958.

Achebe, Nwando. "And She Became a Man: King Ahebi Ugbabe in the History of Enugu-Ezike, Northern Igboland, 1880-1948," In *Men and Masculinities in Modern African* History, edited by Stephan F. Miescher and Lisa A. Lindsay, 52-68. Portsmouth, NH: Heinemann, 2003.

_____. *Farmers, Traders, Warriors, and Kings: Female Power and Authority in Northern Igboland, 1900–1960*. Portsmouth, NH: Heinemann, 2005.

Ade Ajayi, J. F. *Tradition and Change in Africa: The Essays of J. F. Ade Ajayi*, edited by Toyin Falola. Trenton, NJ: African World Press, 2000.

Adewole, F. Oye-Adeniran, B. A., Iwere, N., Oladokun, A. and A. Gbadegesin. "Terminating an Unwanted Pregnancy: The Economic Implications in Nigeria. *Journal of Obstetrics and Gynecology* 22 no. 4 (2002): 436-7.

Adeyokunnu, T. O. *Women and Agriculture in Nigeria*. Ethiopia: UNECA, 1980.

Afigbo Adiele E. "Revolution and Reaction in Research Nigeria: 1900 – 1929." *Journal of the Historical Society of Nigeria* 3, 2. (1966): 539-557.

_____. *The Warrant Chiefs: Indirect Rule in South-Eastern Nigeria, 1891-1929*. London: Longman, 1972.

_____. *Igbo History and Society: The Essays of Adiele Afigbo,* edited by Toyin Falola Trenton, NJ: Africa World Press, 2005.

_____. "Textile Art and Culture in Southern Nigeria." *Nigerian Heritage: Journal of the National Commission for Museum and Monuments* 7 (1998): 11-20.

_____. and C. S. Okeke. *Weaving Tradition in Igboland.* Lagos: Nigerian Magazine, 1985.

Afonja Simi and Bisi Aina. *Nigerian Women in Social Change.* Ile-Ife, Nigeria: Obafemi Awolowo University Press, 1995.

Ahanotu, Austin M. "Social Institutions: Kinship Systems." In *African Culture and Societies Before 1885,* edited by Toyin Falola, 35-58. Durham, North Carolina: Carolina Academic Press, 2000.

Aina, Olabisi I. "Women, Culture and Society." In *Nigeria Women in Society and Development,* edited by Amadu Sessay and Adetanwa Odebiy, 3–32. Ibadan: Dokun Publishing House, 2001.

Akpabio, A. *Ibibio Language and Customs.* Uyo: Marshall Press, 1980.

Akpan, E. O. and V. I. Ekpo. *The Women's War of 1929: A Popular Uprising in South Eastern Nigeria (Preliminary Study).* Calabar: Government Press, 1988.

Alubo, O. "Adolescent Reproductive Health Practices in Nigeria." *African Journal of Reproductive Health* 5, no. 3 (2001): 109-19.

Amadiume, Ifi. *Male Daughters, Female Husbands: Gender and Sex in an African Society.* London: Zed Books, 1987.

Amnesty International. *Women in Peru: Rights in Jeopardy.* London: Amnesty International, 1995.

Apter, A. *Black Critics and Kings: The Hermeneutics of Power in Yoruba Society.* Chicago: University of Chicago Press, 1992.

Arifalo, S. O. "The Evolution of Women in Nigerian Politics." In *Essays in Contemporary Nigerian History,* edited by S. O. Arifalo and Gboyega Ajayi, 99-121. Lagos: First Academic Publishers, 2003.

Awe, Bolanle, ed. *Nigerian Women: A Historical Perspective.* Lagos: Bookcraft, 2001.

_____. "The Iyalode in the Traditional Yoruba Political System." In *Sexual Stratification: A Cross-cultural View,* edited by A. Schlagel, 144-60. New York: Columbia University Press, 1977.

Awolowo, Obafemi. *The People's Republic.* Ibadan: Ibadan University Press, 1968.

Azar, Edward. *The Management of Protracted Social Conflict: Theory and Cases.* Dartmouth, NH: Aldershot, 1990.

Aziken, M. E., P. I. Okonta, and A. B. Ande. "Knowledge and Perception of Emergency Contraception among Female Nigerian Undergraduates." *International Family Planning Perspectives* 29 no. 2 (2003): 84-7.

Babayemi, S. O. *Content Analysis of Oriki Orile.* Ibadan: Institute of African Studies, 1988.

Bankole, A., B. A. Oye-Adeniran, S. Singh, I. F. Adewole, D. Wulf, G. Sedgh, and R. Hussain. *Unwanted Pregnancy and Unsafe Abortion in Nigeria: Causes and Consequences.* New York: Guttmacher Institute, 2006.

Barber, Karin. *I Could Speak Until Tomorrow: Oriki, Women and the Past in a Yoruba Town.* Washington: Smithsonian Institution Press, 1991.

Basden, G.T. *Niger Ibos: A Description of the Primitive Life, Customs, and Animistic Beliefs and Customs of the Igbo People of Nigeria.* London: Frank Cass, 1966.

_____. *Among the Ibos of Nigeria.* London: Frank Cass, 1966.

Bastian, Misty L. "Dancing Women and Colonial Men: The Nwaobiala of 1925." In *"Wicked" Women and the Reconfiguration of Gender in Africa,* edited by Dorothy L. Hodgson and Sherry A. McCurdy, 109-129. Portsmouth, NH: Heinemann, 2001.

Bender, Donald. "Agnatic or Cognatic: A Re-Evaluation of Ondo Descent." *MAN* 5 (1970): 71-87.

Biobaku, S. "Madame Tinubu." In *Eminent Nigerians of the Nineteenth Century,* edited by K. O. Dike, 3– 41. Cambridge: Cambridge University Press, 1960.

Birke, Lynda. *Women, Feminism, and Biology: The Feminist Challenge.* Sussex: The Harvester, 1986.

Caldwell, John and Pat Caldwell. "The Cultural Context of High Fertility in sub-Saharan Africa." *Population and Development Review* 13 no. 3 (1987): 409-37.

Charles, J. O. and C. Bassey. "Nation Building through Food Security by Immigrant Farmers: An Alternative Agricultural Development Strategy." *Nigerian Journal of Economic and Development Matters* 2 (2003): 101-21.

Chizea, Dora O. and Juliet Njoku. *Nigerian Women and the Challenges of Our Time.* Lagos, Nigeria: Malthouse Press, 1991.

Chuku, Gloria. "Women in the Economy of Igboland from 1900-1970: A Survey." *African Economic History* 23 (1995): 37-50.

_____. *Igbo Women and Economic Transformation in Southeastern Nigeria, 1900–1960.* New York: Routledge, 2005.

Coleman, James S. *Nigeria: Background to Nationalism.* Berkeley, CA: University of California Press, 1960.

Collier, Jane F. "Women in Politics." In *Women, Culture and Society,* edited by Rosaldo and L. Lamphere, 89-96. Stanford: Stanford University Press, 1974.

_____. and Michelle Z. Rosaldo. "Politics and Gender in Simple Societies." In *Sexual Meanings: The Cultural Construction of Gender and Sexuality,* edited by Sherry B. Ortner and Harriet Whitehead, 275-329. Cambridge: Cambridge University Press, 1981.

Comaroff, Jean and John Comaroff, eds. *Modernity and its Malcontent: Ritual and Power in Postcolonial Africa.* Chicago, IL: University of Chicago Press, 1993.

Dangarembga, Tsitsi. *Nervous Conditions.* Seattle: Seal Press, 1988.

Dei, George J. S. "Sustainable Development in the African Context: Revisiting Some Theoretical and Methodological Issues." *African Development* 15, no. 2, (1993): 97-110.

Delaney, C. "Symbols of Procreation: Implications for Education and Population Planning." In *Turkic Culture: Continuity and Change,* edited by S. M. Akural, 41-48. Bloomington: University of Indiana Press.

Denzer, LaRay. "Yoruba Women: A Historiographical Study." *International Journal of African Historical Studies* 27, no. 1 (1994): 1-39.

_____. and Bolanle Awe. *The Iyalode in Ibadan Politics and Society, C. 1850-1997.* Ibadan: Sam Bookman Publishers, 1998.

Drewal, Henry. "Art and Perception of Women in Yoruba Culture." *Cahiers d'études Africaines* 68 (1978): 545-567.

_____. and Margaret T. Drewal. *Gelede: Art and Female Power Among the Yoruba.* Bloomington: Indiana University Press, 1983.

Ebuehi, O. M., E. E. Ekanem, and O. A. Ebuehi. "Knowledge and Practice of Emergency Contraception among Female Undergraduates in the University of Lagos, Nigeria." *East African Medical Journal* 83 no. 3 (2006): 90-5.

Echeruo, Michael, J. C. *A Matter of Identity, Ahiajoku Lecture 1979.* Owerri, Nigeria: Ministry of Information, Culture, Youth and Sports, 1979.

Egharebva, Jacob. *A Short History of Benin.* Ibadan: Ibadan University Press, 1968.

Ekejiuba, F. I. "Omu Okwei: The Merchant Queen of Ossomari." *Nigeria Magazine* 90 (1966): 213-20.

Emuveyan, E. "Profile of Abortion in Nigeria." *African Journal of Fertility, Sexuality, and Reproductive Health* 1, no. 1 (1996): 8-13.

Fadipe, N. A. *The Sociology of the Yoruba.* Ibadan: Ibadan University Press, 1970.

Falola, Toyin, ed. *Yoruba Historiography.* Madison: University of Wisconsin Press, 1991.

Faseke, M. "The Role of Women in Traditional Yoruba Society: A Review." In *Culture and Society in Yorubaland,* edited by Deji Ogunremi and Biodun Adediran, 149-156. Ibadan: Rex Charles, 1998.

Fasubaa, O. B., S. T. Akindele, A. Adelekan, and H. Okwuokenye. "A Politico Medical Perspective of Induced Abortion in a Semi-urban Community of Ile-Ife, Nigeria. *Journal of Obstetrics and Gynaecology* 22 no. 1 (2002): 51-7.

Feierman, Steven. *Peasant Intellectuals: Anthropology and History in Tanzania.* Madison: University of Wisconsin Press, 1990.

Flax, Jane. "Postmodernism and Gender Relations in Feminist Theory." *Signs: Journal of Women and Culture* 12, no. 14 (1987): 621-43.

Foucault, Michel. *The History of Sexuality: A Reader,* R, Hurley, trans. New York: Pantheon Books, 1978.

Freund, Bill. *The Making of Contemporary Africa: The Development of African Society Since 1800.* Boulder, CO: Lynne Rienner Publishers, 1998.

Gailey, H. A. *The Road to Aba: A Study of British Administrative Policy in Eastern Nigeria.* New York: New York University Press, 1970.

Gramsci, Antonio. *Selection from the Prison Notebooks*, edited and Trans, Quintin Hoare and Geoffrey Nowell Smith. New York: International Publishers, 1971.

Green, M. M. *Ibo Village Affairs: Chiefly with Reference to the village of Umueke Agbaja*. London: Frank Cass, 1947.

Gugler, Josef and Gudrun Ludwar-Ene. "Gender and Migration in Africa South of the Sahara." In *The Migration Experience in Africa*, edited by Jonathan Baker and Tade Akin Aina, 257-268. Uppsala: Nordeska Afrika Institutet, 1995.

Hafkin, Nancy J. and Edna G. Bay, eds. *Women in Africa: Studies in Social and Economic Change*. Stanford: Stanford University Press, 1976.

Hay, Margaret Jean. "Queens, Prostitutes and Peasants: Historical Perspectives on African Women, 1971 – 1986." *Canadian Journal of African Studies* 22 no. 3 (1988): 431-47.

Henderson, Richard. *The King in Everyman: Evolutionary Trends in Onitsha Ibo Society and Culture*. New Haven: Yale University Press, 1972.

Henshaw, S., S. Singh, B. Oye-Adeniran, I. Adewole, N. Iwere, and Y. Cuca. "The Incidence of Induced Abortion in Nigeria." *International Family Planning Perspectives* 24, no. 4 (1998): 156-64.

Horton, J. A. *West African Countries and Peoples* (New edition with introduction by George Shepperson). Edinburgh: The University Press, 1969.

Hyden, Goran. *No Shortcut to Progress: African Development Management in Perspective*. London: University of London Press, 1983.

Ifeka-Moller, Caroline. "Female Militancy and Colonial Revolt: The Women's War of 1929, Eastern Nigeria." In *Perceiving Women*, edited by Shirley Ardener, 128-132. New York: John Wiley & Sons, 1975.

Ikeme, A. C., H. U. Ezegwui, and A. C. Uzodimma. "Knowledge, Attitude and Use of Emergency Contraception among Female Undergraduates in Eastern Nigeria." *Journal of Obstetrics and Gynaecology* 25, no. 5 (2005): 491-3.

Imam, A. M., "The Presentation of African Women in Historical Writing." In *Retrieving Women's History*, edited by Jay S. Kleinberg, 30-40. Berg: UNESCO, 1988.

Jean Allman, Susan Geiger, and Nakanyike Musisi, eds. *Women in African Colonial Histories.* Bloomington: Indiana University Press, 2002.

Johnson, Samuel. *The History of the Yorubas.* Lagos: CMS Bookshops, 1921.

Kopytoff, Jean Herskovits. *A Preface to Modern Nigeria: The "Sierra Leonians" in Yoruba, 1830-1890.* Madison: University of Wisconsin Press, 1965.

Korieh, Chima J. "The Invisible Farmer? Women, Gender, and Colonial Agricultural Policy in the Igbo Region of Nigeria, c. 1913–1954." *African Economic History* 29 (2001): 117–62.

Koster, W. *Secret Strategies: Women and Abortion in Yoruba Society, Nigeria.* Amsterdam: Askant Koster, 2003.

Kumar, Krishna, ed. *Women and Civil War: Impact, Organization, and Action.* Boulder: Lynne Rienner, 2001.

Lamb, Venice and Judy Holms. *Nigerian Weaving.* Lagos: The Shell Development Company of Nigeria, 1980.

Law, Robin. "The Evolution of the Brazilian Community in Ouidah." In *Rethinking the African Diaspora: The Making of a Black Atlantic World in the Bight of Benin and Brazil,* edited by Kristin Mann and Edna G. Bay, 22-42. New York: Frank Cass, 2001.

Leith-Ross, Sylvia. *African Women.* London: Routledge & Kegan Paul, 1965.

LeVine, Robert A. "Sex Roles and Economic Change in Africa." In *Black Africa: Its Peoples and their Cultures Today,* edited by J. Middleton, 174-80. London: Macmillan, 1970.

Lynne, Hanna Judith. "Dance, Protest, and Women's Wars: Cases from Nigeria and the United States." In *Women and Social Protest,* edited by Guida West and Rhoda Lois Blumberg, 333-45. New York: Oxford University Press, 1990.

Mann, Kristin. "The Dangers of Dependence: Christian Marriage among Elite Women in Lagos Colony, 1880-1915." *Journal of African History* 24 (1983): 17-56.

_____. "Women's Rights in Law and Practice: Marriage and Dispute Settlement in Colonial Lagos." In *African Women and the Law: Historical Perspectives,* edited by Margaret Jean Hay and Marcia Wright, 151-71. Boston: Boston University, 1982.

_____. *Marrying Well: Marriage, Status and Social Change among the Educated Elite in Colonial Lagos*. Cambridge: Cambridge University Press, 1985.

_____. *Slavery and the Birth of an African City: Lagos, 1760-1900*. Bloomington: Indiana University Press, 2007.

Martin, Susan. "Slaves, Igbo Women and Palm Oil in the Nineteenth Century." In *From Slave Trade to 'Legitimate' Commerce: The Commercial Transition in the Nineteenth century West Africa*, edited by Robin Law, 172-194. Cambridge: Cambridge University Press, 1995.

Matory, J. Lorand. *Sex and the Empire that is No More: Gender and the Politics of the Metaphor in Oyo Yoruba Religion*. New York: Berghahn Books, 2006.

_____. "The English Professors of Brazil: On the Diasporic Roots of the Yoruba Nation." *Comparative Studies in Society and History* (1999): 72-103.

Mba, Nina. *Nigerian Women Mobilized: Women's Political Activity in Southern Nigeria, 1900-1965*. Berkeley: Institute of International Studies, University of California, 1982.

_____. "Heroines of the Women's War." In *Nigerian Women in Historical Perspective*, edited by Bolanle Awe, 75-88. Ibadan: Sankore/Bookcrat 1992.

Mead, Margaret. *Sex and Temperament in Three Primitive Societies*. New York: Morrow Quill, 1963,

Meek, C. K. *Ethnographical Report on the Peoples of Nsukka Division Onitsha Province*. Lagos, 1930.

Misty, Bastian L. "'Vultures of the Market Place': Southeastern Nigerian Women and Discourses of the *Ogu Umunwanyi* (Women's War) of 1929)." In *Women in African Colonial Histories*, edited by Jean Allman, Susan Geiger, Nakanyike Musisi, 206-81. Bloomington, IN: Indiana University Press, 2002.

Mitsunaga, T. M., U. M. Larsen, and F. E. Okonofua. "Risk Factors for Complications of Induced Abortions in Nigeria." *Journal of Women's Health* 14, no. 6 (2005): 515-28.

Moronkola, O. A., A. Amosu, and C. Okonkwo. "Knowledge About Conception, Sexual Behavior, and Procurement of Abortion among Female Undergraduate Students in a Nigerian University."

International Quarterly of Community Health Education 24 no. 3 (2005-2006): 241-49.

Murray, N. W. Winfrey, M. Chatterji, S. Moreland, L. Dougherty, and F. Okonofua. "Factors Related to Induced Abortion among Young Women in Edo State, Nigeria." *Studies in Family Planning* 37 no. 4 (2006): 251-68.

Nichols, D., O. Ladipo, J. Paxman, and O. Otolorin. "Sexual Behavior, Contraceptive Practice and Reproductive Health among Nigerian Adolescents." *Studies in Family Planning* 17 no. 2 (1986): 100-6.

Nicklin, K. "The Ibibio Musical Pot." *African Arts* 7, 1 (1973): 50-55.

Njoku, Raphael Chijioke. *African Cultural Values: Igbo Political Leadership in Colonial Nigeria, 1900-1966.* New York: Routledge, 2006.

Nnaemeka, Obioma. "Fighting on All Fronts: Gendered Spaces, Ethnic Boundaries, and the Nigerian Civil War," *Dialectical Anthropology* 22, nos. 3-4, (1997): 235-263.

_____. ed. *Female Circumcision and the Politics of Knowledge: African Women in Imperialist Discourses.* Westport, Conn.: Praeger, 2005.

Noah, M. E. *Ibibio Pioneers in Modern Nigerian History.* Uyo: Scholars Press, 1980.

Nzegwu, Nkiru. "Confronting Racism: Toward the Formation of a Female- Identified Consciousness." *Canadian Journal for Women and the Law* 7, no. 1 (1994): 15-33.

O'Connell, H. ed., *Women and Conflict.* Oxford: Oxfam, 1993.

Ojo, J. R. O. "The Symbolism and Significance of Epa-type Masquerade Headpieces." *MAN* 13 (1978): 455-470.

Okere, L. C. *The Anthropology of Food in Rural Igboland: Socioeconomic and Cultural Aspects of Food and Food Habit in Rural Igboland.* Lanham: University Press of America, 1983.

Olajubu, Oyeronke. *Women in Yoruba Religious Spheres.* Albany: State University of New York Press, 2003.

Olupona, J. K. *Kingship, Religion and Rituals in a Nigerian Community.* Stockholm: Almqvist & Wilksell International, 1991.

Omole, B. I. "The Oyo Palace: An Historical Analysis of Its Organisation." *The African Historian* 8 (1976): 31-57.

Onwuteaka, U. C. "The Aba Riot of 1929 and Its Relation to the System of 'Indirect Rule.'" *Nigerian Journal of Economic and Social Studies* 7 (1965): 273-82.

Otoide, V. O., F. Oronsaye, and F. E. Okonofua. "Why Nigerian Adolescents Seek Abortion Rather than Contraception: Evidence from Focus-Group Discussions." *International Family Planning Perspectives* 27 no. 2 (2001):77- 81.

Ottenberg, Phoebe V. "The Changing Economic Position of Women among the Afikpo Ibo." In *Continuity and Change in African Cultures*, edited by Bascon Russell William and Melvin J. Herskovits, 205–23. Chicago: University of Chicago Press, 1958.

Ottenberg, Simon. *Igbo Religion, Social Life and Other Essays by Simon Ottenberg* edited by Toyin Falola. Trenton, NJ: Africa World Press, 2006.

Oye, B. A., Adeniran, I. F. Adewole, A. V. Umoh, O. R. Fapohunda, and N. Iwere. "Characteristics of Abortion Care Seekers in Southwestern Nigeria." *African Journal of Reproductive Health* 8 no. 3 (2004): 81-91.

Oye-Adeniran, B. A., I. F. Adewole, A. V. Umoh, E. Ekanem, A. Gbadegesin, and N. Iwere. "Community-Based Survey of Unwanted Pregnancy in Southwestern Nigeria." *African Journal of Reproductive Health* 8 no. 3 (2004): 103-15.

Oye-Adeniran, B. A., I. F. Adewole, A. V. Umoh, N. Iwere, and A. Gbadegesin. "Induced abortion in Nigeria: Findings from Focus Group Discussions." *African Journal of Reproductive Health* 9 no. 1 (2005):133-41.

Oyewumi, Oyeronke. *The Invention of Women: Making an African Sense of Western Gender Discourses*. Minneapolis, University of Minnesota Press, 1997.

Peel, J.D.Y. "Gender in Yoruba Religious Change." *Journal of Religion in Africa* 32, no. 2 (2002): 136-61.

_____. *Religious Encounter and the Making of the Yoruba*. Bloomington: Indiana University Press, 2001.

Perham, M. *Native Administration in Nigeria*. London: Oxford University Press, 1937.

Pritchard, Evan. *The Position of Women in Primitive Societies and other Essays in Social Anthropology*. London, 1965.

Ramsbotham, O. and N. Lewer. *"Something Must be Done": Towards an Ethical Framework for Humanitarian Intervention in International Social Conflict.* Braford: Department of Peace Studies, 1993.

Ranger, Terence. "Growing from the Roots: Reflections on Peasants Research in Central and Southern Africa." *Journal of Southern African Studies* 5, no. 1 (1978): 99-133.

_____. *Dance and Society in Eastern Africa, 1890-1970.* Berkeley, CA: University of California Press, 1975.

Renne, Elisha P. "Abortion as Illegal Conduct and its Sequelae." *Curare: Studies in Ethnomedicine* 29, no. 1 (2006): 81-95.

_____. "Postinor Use among Young Women in Southwestern Nigeria: A Research Note." *Reproductive Health Matters* 6 no. 11 (1998): 107-14

_____. *Population and Progress in a Yoruba Town.* Ann Arbor: University of Michigan Press, 2003.

Rosalyn Terborg-Penn and Andrea Benton Rushing, eds. *Women in Africa and the African Diaspora: A Reader.* Howard University Press, 1996.

Schatzberg, Michael G. *Political Legitimacy in Middle Africa: Father, Family Food.* Bloomington: Indiana University Press, 2001.

Scott, James. *Weapons of the Weak: Everyday Forms of Peasant Resistance.* New Haven: Yale University Press, 1985.

Sedgh, G., A. Bankole and B. Oye-Adeniran. "Unwanted Pregnancy and Associated Factors among Nigerian Women." *International Family Planning Perspectives* 32 no. 4 (2006): 175-84.

Sheba, Eben. "Aale: A Deterrent Symbol and Communication Device among the Ikale Yoruba of Nigeria." *Journal of the Institute of Cultural Studies* 7: (1999): 10-16.

Shirley Ardener. "Sexual Insult and Female Militancy." *Man* 8 (1973): 422-40.

Singh, S. "Hospital Admissions Resulting from Unsafe Abortion: Estimates from 13 Developing Countries." *Lancet* 368 (9550) (2006): 1887-92.

Sklar, R. L. *Nigerian Political Parties.* Princeton: Princeton University Press, 1963.

Smith, M. G. "The Beginnings of Hausa Society, A.D. 100-1500." In *The Historian in Tropical Africa*, edited by Jan Vansina, R. Mauny, and L. V. Thomas. London, 339-57. Oxford University Press, 1964.

Snow, David A. et al., "Frame Alignment Process, Micromobilization, and Movement Participation." *American Sociological Review*, 51 (1986): 464-81.

Snyder Margaret C. and Mary Tadesse. *African Women and Development: A History*. London: Zed Books, 1995, 1-15.

Summerfield, Penny. "Gender and War in the Twentieth Century." *International History Review* 19, no. 1 (1997): 3–15.

Swiss S., Jennings P. J., Aryee G. V., Brown G. H., Jappah-Samukai R. M., Kamara M. S., Schaack R. D., Turay-Kanneh R. S., "Violence against Women during the Liberian Civil Conflict." *JAMA* 279, no. 8 (1998): 625-29.

Talbot, D. Amaury. *Women's Mysteries of a Primitive People* (1915). London: Frank Cass, repr. 1968.

Talbot, P. "Land of the Ibibios, Southern Nigeria." *Geographical Journal* 44 no. 3 (1914): 286-306.

Tamale, Sylvia. "Taking the Beast by its Horns: Formal Resistance to Women's Oppression in Africa." *African Development* 21, 4 (1996): 5-21.

Uchendu, Egodi. "Women, Power, and Political Institutions in Igbo-land." In *Precolonial Nigeria: Essays in Honor of Toyin Falola*, edited by Akinwumi Ogundiran. Trenton, NJ: Africa World Press, 2005.

Uchendu, Victor C. "Concubinage Among the Ngwa Igbo of Southern Nigeria." In *The Igbo As Seen by Others*, edited by F. C. Ogbalu. Nsukka, Nigeria: University of Nigeria Publishing Company, 1988.

_____. *The Igbo of Southeastern Nigeria*. New York: Holt, Rinehart & Winston, 1965.

Udo, E. A. *Who Are the Ibibio?* Onitsha: Africa Fed. Publishers, 1983.

Ujah, I. A. "Contraceptive Intentions of Women seeking Induced Abortion in the City of Jos, Nigeria." *Journal of Obstetrics and Gynaecology* 20 no. 2 (2000): 162-6.

Umaru, Ibrahim. "Exploring the Economic Underpinnings of the Toto Ethnic Conflicts in Nasarawa State of Nigeria: A Primer." In *Conflict in the Benue Valley*, edited by Gyuse, Timothy (Makurdi: Selfers Educational Books, 2006).

_____. *Women: Phases of Deprivation in Nigeria,* GADA's Constitutional Debate Series Monograph. Lagos: Gender, and Development Action, 2004.

Van Allen, Judith. "Sitting on a Man: Colonialism and the Lost Political Institutions of the Igbo." *Canadian Journal of African Studies*, 6, 11 (1972): 165-81.

_____. "'Aba Riots' or Igbo `Women's War'? Ideology, Stratification, and Invisibility of Women." In *The Black Woman Cross-Culturally*, ed., F. C. Steady. Cambridge, Mass: Schenkman Publication, 1981.

Whyte, Martin K. *The Status of Women in Preindustrial Societies*. Princeton, NJ: Princeton University Press, 1978.

Wipper, Audrey. "Riot and Rebellion among African Women: Three Examples of Women's Political Clout." In *Perspectives on Power: Women in Africa, Asia and Latin America*, edited by Jean O'Barr, 50-72. Durham, NC: Duke University Press, 1982.

Zeitlin, Irving M. with Robert J. Brym. *The Social Condition of Humanity*. Toronto: Oxford University Press, 1991.

Notes on Contributors

Ihuoma F. Abaraonye received her PhD in History from the University of Lagos in 1997. Her dissertation is titled *Gender and Politics in Ibibioland, 1900-1903: The Role of Ibibio Women*. She has been involved in the cataloging and identification of objects in the Ethnographic Store of the Lagos Museum, as well as various research projects and exhibitions, including "Women in Traditional Societies in Akwa Ibom State," and "Dynamics of Change: Women in Development." Her publications include "The Women's War of 1929 in South-Eastern Nigeria," in *Women and Revolution: Global Expressions* edited by M. J. Diamond (Kluwer, 1998).

Nwando Achebe, Professor of History, Michigan State University, received her PhD from the University of California, Los Angeles in 2000. She served as a Ford Foundation and Fulbright-Hays Scholar-in-Residence at The Hansberry African Studies Institute and History Department of the University of Nigeria, Nsukka in 1996 and 1998. Her research interests involve the use of oral history in the study of women, gender and power in Eastern Nigeria. Her first book, *Farmers, Traders, Warriors and Kings: Female Power and Authority in Northern Igboland, 1900-1960* was published by Heinemann. Dr. Achebe's second book, *The Female King of Colonial Nigeria* (Indiana University Press, 2010) is a full length critical biography on the only *female* warrant chief and king in all of colonial Nigeria, and arguably British Africa. The writing was funded by a generous grant from the Wenner-Gren Foundation.

Biodun Adediran is a Professor of African History. He was formerly the Deputy Vice Chancellor (Academic) at Obafemi Awolowo University, Ile Ife, Nigeria. He is currently the Director of the University's Division of Linkages and Sponsored Research. He was a member of Nigeria's National Commission for UNESCO and at various times Visiting Professor at the University of Wisconsin-Parkside, USA, and the African Studies Center of the University of Bayreuth, Germany.

Adiele Afigbo (1937-2009) was an authority on the history and historiography of Africa, particularly Igbo history. He spent many years of teaching and research at the University of Nigeria, where he rose to become the Head of the Department of History and Archaeology and the Dean of the Faculty of Arts. He was a professor in the Department of History and International Relations at Ebonyi State University, Nigeria until his death in 2009. Afigbo authored numerous books and scholarly articles on Igbo, Nigerian, and African history. His most recent book is *The Abolition of the Slave Trade in Southeastern Nigeria, 1885-1950* (Rochester, NY: The University of Rochester Press, 2006).

Joseph Okokon Charles is a Professor of Social Anthroplogy and former chair of the Department of Sociology, University of Calabar, Nigeria. He has published five books and more than 40 articles in learned journals and books and attended 65 conferences and workshops. His research interests include: farming systems, food security, migration, health, population and family life studies, poverty and child abuse. Professor Charles is a consultant to many local and international bodies and organizations and has traveled widely in Africa, Europe, United States and Asia.

Violeta Ivanova Ekpo is a historian and museologist. As a Bulgarian born Nigerian wife, she has lived and worked in Nigeria for the past 38 years. She is the founding Curator of National Museums at Calabar and Uyo in Southeastern Nigeria, where she has done extensive research on the history and culture of the Cross River groups, including the Efik and Ibibio people.

She has over 25 published works on Cross River and Akwa Ibom archaeology, history and culture, including the position of women in traditional society and women's resistance in the colonial period. Ekpo has recently retired as Director of Museums in the National Commission for Museums and Monuments, Abuja, Nigeria. She is currently an independent cultural consultant.

Donna K. Flynn received her PhD in Anthropology from Northwestern University in 1997. As a Fulbright scholar, she investigated the impacts of cross-border trade movements and smuggling on West African border communities. She then went on to work in applied research on economic development and microfinance, leading projects at the International Center for Research on Women, the U.S. Agency for International Development and the World Bank. Prior to joining Microsoft, Donna was a Senior Manager of User Experience for Sapient Corporation in San Francisco, where she worked with technology and telecommunications clients, including Cisco Systems, Sun Microsystems, and Sprint. Donna Flynn uses her training in anthropology to analyze how ordinary folks make daily use of their cell phones.

Chima J. Korieh teaches African History at Marquette University, Milwaukee, Wisconsin. He holds a PhD in African History from the University of Toronto, Canada. He recently completed a prestigious fellowship as a British Academy Visiting Fellow at Oxford University, Oxford, UK (2007/2008). He has authored many articles and essays in journals, books, and encyclopedia. His publications include *The Land Has Changed: Studies in Agrarian Change, Gender, and Society in Eastern Nigeria, c.1880-c.1980* (The University of Calgary Press, 2010) and the following edited volumes: *The Aftermath of Slavery: Transition and Transformation in Southeastern Nigeria* (Trenton, NJ: Africa World Press, 2007); *Missions, States and European Expansion in Africa* (New York: Routledge, 2007); *Gendering Global Transformations: Gender, Culture, Race, and Identity* (New York: Routledge, 2008). He is associate editor (Africa) of *Encyclopedia of Western*

Imperialism and Colonialism since 1450 (New York: Macmillan Reference USA, 2006). He is the founder and editor of *Mbari: The International Journal of Igbo Studies*.

Tomarra A. Adams has a PhD in Social Work from the University of Louisville, and is a Licensed Clinical Social Worker. She is currently an Assistant Professor at the Department of Pan-African Studies, the University of Louisville, Kentucky. Her research areas are Black student retention, Black identity development, and Black women's issues.

Theophilus D. Lagi, an industrial sociologist, teaches Sociology at Nasarawa State University, Keffi, Nigeria. He attended Kliment Oxridfki University, Sophia-Bulgaria, between 1986 and 1991 and is currently a doctoral student at the University of Jos, Nigeria. His main areas of research interest are social psychology and leadership studies.

Lisa A. Lindsay is an Associate Professor of African History at the University of North Carolina-Chapel Hill. Her research focuses on the social history of Nigeria, gender and colonialism, the Atlantic slave trade, and the African diaspora. She is the author of *Working With Gender: Wage Labor and Social Change in Southwestern Nigeria* (Heinemann, 2003) and the co-editor, with Stephan Miescher, of *Men and Masculinities in Modern Africa* (Heinemann, 2003). She has also published a textbook called *Captives as Commodities: The Transatlantic Slave Trade* (Prentice Hall, 2008).

Raphael Chijioke Njoku, a first class honors graduate of University of Nigeria Nsukka, is an Associate Professor of African History. He received a PhD in African History from Dalhousie University, Canada, 2003, and another PhD in African Politics from Free University, Brussels, 2001. Before his current appointment in the Department of History, and Department of Pan African Studies at the University of Louisville in 2003, Njoku taught at the Department of History, Alvan Ikoku College of

Education, Owerri, Nigeria. He is the author of *Culture and Customs of Morocco* (Greenwood, 2005), and *African Cultural Values: Igbo Political Leadership in Colonial Nigeria 1900-1966* (Routledge, 2006), and co-editor of *Missions, States, and European Expansion in Africa* (Routledge, 2007). Njoku has also published 20 articles in scholarly journals, edited volumes, and encyclopedias. His most recent awards include Victor Olurunsola Endowed Research Award (2007) and a research fellowship from the Schomburg Center for Research in Black Culture, New York (2006-07). Njoku is currently working on a book manuscript entitled *African Masks and Masquerades and Carnival of the Diaspora.*

Obioma Nnaemeka is Chancellor's Distinguished Professor at Indiana University, Indianapolis, where she teaches French, African and African Diaspora studies, and women's/gender studies. Professor Nnaemeka—a former Rockefeller Humanist-in-Residence (University of Minnesota), Edith Kreeger-Wolf Distinguished Visiting Professor (Northwestern University) and Verne Wagner Distinguished Visiting Professor (University of Kansas)—is the President of the Association of African Women Scholars (AAWS) and the President/CEO of the Jessie Obidiegwu Education Fund. Her numerous books include *The Politics of (M)Othering; Female Circumcision and the Politics of Knowledge; Paratext and Author(ity): Agrippa d' Aubigné and the Poetics of Power and Change;* and *Engendering Human Rights.*

Olukoya Ogen teaches in the Department of History, Obafemi Awolowo University, Ile-Ife, Nigeria. He holds a PhD in History from the University of Lagos, and a certificate in Trade, Growth and Poverty from the World Bank Institute, Washington D.C. Dr. Ogen was a British Academy Visiting Postdoctoral Fellow at the Centre of West African Studies, University of Birmingham, during the spring term of 2009. He is also the current African Regional Editor of *Nebula*, the international quarterly affiliated to the University of Western Sydney.

Elisha P. Renne is an associate professor in the Department of Anthropology and the Center for Afroamerican and African Studies at the University of Michigan, Ann Arbor. She received a PhD in sociocultural anthropology from New York University. Her research focuses on fertility and reproductive health, medical anthropology, religious textiles, and social change, specifically in Nigeria. Recent publications include *Regulating Menstruation: Beliefs, Practices, Interpretations* (co-edited with E. van de Walle), University of Chicago Press, 2001; *Population and Development Issues: Ideas and Debates* (co-edited with J.A. Ebigbola), Ibadan, African Book Builders, 2000; *Population and Progress in a Yoruba Town*, University of Edinburgh Press/ University of Michigan Press, 2003 as well as articles in *Africa, Anthropology & Medicine, Curare, Economic Development & Cultural Change, Population & Development Review, Reproductive Health Matters, Social Science & Medicine*, and *Studies in Family Planning*. She is presently revising a manuscript on the Polio Eradication Initiative in Northern Nigeria for publication.

Ibrahim Umaru received his PhD from the Ahmadu Bello University, Zaria, Nigeria. Umaru is currently teaching economics and environmental management at Nasarawa State University, Keffi, Nigeria. He has published books and several articles in professional journals and edited volumes and has also presented papers at academic conferences. His main area of specialization is environmental and health economics with special interest in arid economics, economic valuation, social conflicts and gender dynamics.

Index